THE CRIERS OF THE SHOPS

THE CRIERS OF THE SHOPS

BY

SHERLOCK BRONSON GASS

Essay Index Reprint Series

BOOKS FOR LIBRARIES PRESS

FREEPORT, NEW YORK

First Published 1925
Reprinted 1971

INTERNATIONAL STANDARD BOOK NUMBER:
0-8369-2049-X

LIBRARY OF CONGRESS CATALOG CARD NUMBER:
74-142633

PRINTED IN THE UNITED STATES OF AMERICA

To

HARTLEY BURR ALEXANDER

CONTENTS

THE CRIERS OF THE SHOPS

I

THE BAZAAR

The Criers of the Shops

I

THE BAZAAR

SOMEWHERE in his book on Dickens Mr. Chesterton has thrown out a lively defense of dupes and dupery to the effect that those who are never taken in are likely never to get in. It is a comforting reflection. I don't know how much it will bear looking into, but certainly to have gone to the fair, to have listened to the criers, and never to have been lured into the booths behind the gilt gingerbread, though it argues wisdom, perhaps, does leave you a little less gay at the end of the round, and a little graveled for matter at the fireside after dinner. If you have not been wise, however, your being at the fireside at all argues your having got out after being taken in; and the quality of your gayety there will depend upon the air with which, in the morning, you had worn the mantle of your illusions.

I

The particular fairing that I am about to speak of occurred at the intellectual bazaar in the typical adventures of those of us who have wandered into it within the present century. The term is not quite inappropriate, for it is a kind of bazaar, lively, noisy, and a little disorderly, and our goings about in it were altogether casual and errant, a series of adventures, unforeseen and a little amazing. For we were very young, and very unsophisticated, and going without guides we enjoyed a freedom, once we were there, that was almost without precedent.

I remember an early vision of the kind of freedom I, for one, had anticipated in coming up. It must have come from a chance reading in someone's crib of Plato — an Aegean sky, the sunlit porch of a temple, boys at knucklebones on the marble floor, young men shining from the sacrifice, and the glance of one of them looking with eager modesty for the chance of a beckoning nod and a vacant place on the bench near the great questioner. The picture had seized my imagination and quickened my expectations. But our own freedom was altogether ampler. There was for us no great questioner. The bazaar was simply turned over to us.

What the particular feel of this freedom was to those of us who enjoyed it I despair of expressing. Freedom is elusive in the nature of things. Restraints chafe in particular places and lend themselves to sharp outcry. And we had none, and no recollection of any to measure our freedom by. It may even be that we lost a little of the zest that comes from listening to forbidden criers or wandering into forbidden shops. Nothing was forbidden. Still we flaunted our freedom and were gaily defiant about it. Imagination served us with foils —

though, to change the figure, the foils were buttoned and perhaps did not prick very deep.

At all events we were human, and if our traditions did not provide us with no-thoroughfares we soon began to lay them out for ourselves. I am speaking in all this about those of us who did not know as yet what to make of ourselves in the future. We were there to find out. Those who did know found it all simple enough from the start — found channels to flow into so narrow and straight that the rest of us shuddered. We held them a little in contempt, I think, at least outwardly, and inwardly at times a little in envy. They baffled us. They were not as unhappy as by our single canon of freedom they should have been. They were not as unhappy as we.

"Nuns fret not," Wordsworth had said, indeed; and he was one of our early idols. But the Wordsworth who had said this was the old sonneteer, a little subdued to the world he worked in. So we scorned our plodding fellows as we should have scorned the nuns. They lacked spirit. Perhaps they did; they were willing at least to forego a good many curiosities that we were not. And in our most blessed moments our restless melancholy over the cosmos consoled us with its obvious superiority to their enthusiasm over the microscope.

As for us, it was the cosmos or nothing. And when we saw those others, with their home-keeping wits, following down their prescribed paths, we blessed our own freedom, created a defiant convention against conventions, and erected a prescription against prescription. We saw no humor of inconsistency in this, and perhaps there was none. We were acting under necessity, for we had to have some foothold for our push at the universe. And I mention it, vague as it is, to indicate our bent.

It was consistent, at least, with the breadth of our curiosity, and with the absence of any official recognition that that curiosity was a legitimate one. As for the curiosity itself, it was looked at askance. Perhaps it was not understood. Certainly there was no provision for taking care of it. Consequently we were outlaws, or as much outlaws as gypsies are, and we set up our tents on the common, mistrusted by the solid householders, and suspected by the authorities, but tolerated.

II

Most of us, I dare say, had come by our bent and our curiosity through our reading before coming up to the bazaar. I call it a bent and a curiosity, though only much charity, a little sentiment, and a little irony will guess aright at the nebular state I refer to — three fourths adolescence, the vivid expectancy of something just around the corner, just beyond the next curve, just over the horizon; part reluctance to take any road for good and forego the rest; and only a very little part, no doubt, a real curiosity to understand, with any austerity, either ourselves or that spectacle about us that seemed to justify itself so completely by simply being there with its bright colors and its infinite and changing pattern. It was the state of mind that drifts into cosmic speculation if, as is more likely, it does not remain in cosmic vagrancy. Perhaps these are not so different as the phrases imply.

The long generations had closed whose theory of youth was that its reading should be orthopaedic. Ours had never been so. And certainly we were never like to waste time later inventing curses for the schoolmaster who had made us loathe Horace. We didn't loathe Horace. We didn't know him. We had never felt the birch, and we were never forced and never forced ourselves through anything that had no thrill for us. We had no hatreds, therefore, but only degrees of appreciation. Within we lived in a state of maiden expectancy. And our reading had caught us where we lived. It gave release to our expectant emotions; it touched off our taut imaginations with a bright imagery, about which hung the endearing chromatic tints of our irresponsible youth. Imagery and emotion were the very stuff of our expanding spirits, and here in the things we had read so freely they were copiously to be found, of a kind to which we were akin by every native affection and every headlong ardor, and in a degree so far above our own unaided pitch that naturally we supposed that this was what we had come up to secure in still greater plenty.

Our reading had been romantic, lyric, and it fed the romantic and lyric veins in us. It had not only fed, it had stimulated. Perhaps it had intoxicated. Certainly some of us were never afterwards wholly out of our cups. But for the moment it did us the service of keeping our wings rebellious at any sort of confinement. And those of us who matured in spirit beyond the lyric moment of adolescence, and with an awakening dim curiosity of intellect came formally up to the bazaar for further and other adventures, never wholly lost the impulse of that rebellion. Whether under the lure of other curiosities we subjected ourselves to discipline, or whether we kept our wings unclipped, we blithely refused to forego our cosmic melancholy or console ourselves with the snugness of a single cell.

III

When we did strike out into the bazaar in earnest, we went about with minds avid, in spite of us, to seize and rationalize our experience. We couldn't help it. It was the penalty of growing up, though we should have rebelled if we had known what it was likely to lead us to. As it was, those of us who were most jealous of our freedom turned at once to the criers that promised to reveal to us the clear significance of those moments when we seemed, in the intensity of our lyric responses, to come nearest to grasping — I still cannot say what, but it was no less real to us for our utter ignorance of what it was.

We turned, that is, to the literary shop. And there,

appropriately, we came into the first definite installment of our intellectual heritage. For literature had at least this advantage over our minds from the start, that it lay on every hand, and insinuated itself at more moments and in more varied moments than anything else that we found there. It seemed to look out on life after the native manner of the mind itself. It required no displacement, no special attitude. It looked out from the whole mind, and saw life in the round, and brought it home as it felt when experience itself brought it home.

It was natural, therefore that what we were led to read or were confirmed in reading by those criers that we listened to so eagerly and with so thrilling an acquiescence, should have done much to color existence for us from then on. They spoke with all the authority of the bazaar we had been so ardent to come to. If they had clashed among themselves, dinning conflicting rigmaroles into our ears from rival booths, we might have been disturbed and thrown back on the necessity of choice. But they cried out in lively harmony. There were, indeed, among them creatures who cared nothing for what a book said, but delved grub-like into the circumstances that surrounded the creation of it, good or bad, but these were so far from seeming to speak of literature at all that we were never disturbed by them. We were not even aware that in certain back alleys of the bazaar there still lingered on a few who clung to an older cult, and who read books for what they said, indeed, but for what they said to the judgment and the intelligence. If we had known of them we should probably have reflected the pitying smiles of our own criers. As for these latter, they cried in harmony not only with each other but with our own instincts, and confirmed us in the sense that on the tide of our responsive emotions we should find an ineffable significance in the color and variety of the pageantry that marched, as we read, before our entranced imaginations.

In all these preoccupations our intellects as intellects tended not only to be neglected but to be rather snubbed. We acquired for them a degree of contempt. At the same time they must of their own native impulse have been a little wearied at the neglect they were falling into, for they drove us restlessly into long reasonings to prove their unimportance. All this was before the modern anti-intellectuals had come into vogue; but we were post-rousellians and were not without our prophets. We pounced with glee, for instance, upon another phrase of Wordsworth's that seemed to put the reason once for all upon its proper footing —

> *— that false secondary power*
> *That multiplies distinctions.*

There it was, the intellect, of course, but it was an intruder, sordid and impertinent. And certainly the reason as we knew it in ourselves was altogether a painful and pedestrian affair. The evidence was conclusive.

IV

Before this rational impulse had gathered enough audacity to be disturbing we came into our second installment. It was but a step from the literary shop to the adjacent one of the fine arts. I do not think that the social reputability of the fine arts attracted us. We were trying hard to be Bohemian. But certainly the tacit acceptance of them into the body of modern culture, the echoes of them in book and talk, the place they were winning in the bazaar, and the touch they gave us with a world that was not sordid, all led us to incorporate them into the body of our own vague philosophy. At their worthiest they were disinterested, and they appealed to whatever was young and generous and improvident in us.

And here, maliciously and secretly egged on to it by our reason, we came into the further philosophy that justified our devotion. Beauty itself, indeed, was enough. But we must rationalize it and fortify ourselves in our allegiance to it. And thus we came upon aesthetics. Aesthetics helped us again to snub the reason, by several logical demonstrations. Under its tutelage we saw the reason as a means to very near and intermediate ends. For learning and science, in which intellect took a major part, ended in the possession and organization of knowledge, useful in the pursuit of mere existence, and useful for moral wisdom. And moral wisdom, in which it played a further part, was, as we saw with ease, only a calculation of conduct to make life free for the pursuit of ends that *were* ends — but ends which morals did not define. None of these were ends for the spirit itself.

The effect upon our minds was at once stimulating and simplifying. We felt at greater ease once we were in possession of a philosophy that rationalized our dearest moments. For until now we had suffered periodic qualms. We were often uncomfortable in the contrast we made with others who were on the treadmill of knowledge. We despised their restrictions, but we suffered from the sense of something passive in the part we were playing. From outside we were looked upon, we knew, as idlers loafing through the elegancies, on the prowl for the soft titillation of our sensibilities. And our activities had so much the look, even the feel, of sheer self-indulgence, that if we had not been saved by something gritty for our minds to ruminate on we might, in some moment of reaction, one by one have furled our wings, drawn in our quivering antennae, and reverted to the grubs.

Our difficulty with aesthetics as a sop to the restlessness of our minds was that it was so promptly disposed of. Once we had settled the doctrine there was nothing more to do about it. If we had been practitioners in any of the arts we might have gone each his own way, each producing objects that he tried at least to bring up to his own vision of beauty, succeeding or failing in his own esteem, and succeeding or failing in the esteem of the world. But we were not. We were young men coming into our inheritance, with an itch to understand the world, not indifferent to our own careers but not indifferent either to the larger significance of what we were facing, and youthfully eager to give it the largest significance it was capable of. And we took what guidance we found.

Our guides did something real for us — or to us. At all events they were the only ones who took us in just as we were, with our senses keen, our imaginations lively, our emotions fresh and intense, our minds empty and unformed. And they gave us a point of view. In behalf of our native itch to understand, and despite our colossal ignorance, they took care in their own way, what with romantic literature, with wild nature, and with the fine arts, of one whole aspect of life — of the immediate impingement upon us of *things* — things real and things imagined. In view of the state we came to them in perhaps they were the only ones who could have tried, there was so little else impinging on our minds to be taken care of.

V

Many of us lingered here for good — enough of us to keep up the tradition, to take care of the newcomers, to fill the coteries in Bohemia, to gossip in the weeklies about books, the theater, and the arts, and, broadly, to represent what everyone by now had come to call culture. In one sense all of us lingered here for good. For even those of us who grew restless and moved on to another quarter of the bazaar found nothing there to disturb us radically. It was in fact by a kind of permission gained in the aesthetic quarter that we moved on at all. We had discovered with logical ease that the disinterested love of knowledge was like the disinterested love of beauty, an aesthetic delight. Only in the case of knowledge one had to toil for it, and that toil was the toil of the intellect. Where the adventure was worth the toil, even the intellect acquired a fine aesthetic sanction.

We were all for adventure, and now that we had attained a point of view we saw that there were high adventures to be had on every hand. Inevitably we fell in with the natural sciences. The world was ringing with them, and their gorgeous shops in the bazaar were thronged. There was no need of motley criers there. Long queues serpentined away from every ticket window.

At first glance few things could seem more antipodal than aesthetic delights and natural science. On the contrary they existed in fine harmony. They could live in the two halves of the same dwelling without encroachment on either side. As for us, we found that they dealt with the same stuff — the material universe, or as much as came home through the senses — though they dealt with it in different ways. With Sprat-like amenity one cherished what the other eschewed.

For those of us who were not going on for a life

of scientific study, the specific knowledge that we got from the natural sciences was a matter of large indifference. What we were after, true to our aesthetic bent, was the scientific point of view. And to acquire that we had to have enough of its methods to give it edge. We acquired something more, indeed — a wholesome respect for fact, for the measurable, and the ponderable, for the values of definiteness and constancy in the premises of thought, and for the meticulous patience needed to establish those qualities. The experience led us, as probably nothing else could have done, to a sense of the sharp demarcation between the fact, on the one hand — as it was in itself, out there, discrete, objective, indifferent to the observer in us — and on the other hand the observer, with all the accidents of his particular case — a cast in his eye, a sorrow on a particular day, a liking for certain sights and sounds, an aversion to a certain odor. For what, indeed, had these to do with the facts as they really were!

Through daily contact with such objective data and the habit of such reflections we came, little by little, to the larger outlook of natural science — first to the sense of a detached, impersonal view of the facts we dealt with, and then, as we saw those facts falling into orderly array in larger and larger organic units, to a sense of the cosmos itself as seen from that same impersonal point of view — a view in which man himself was but an objective item among the rest, making a great to-do on his little pill of a planet, perhaps, but a matter of indifference to it, his likes and dislikes themselves but mechanical reactions to be explained at last in a minor chapter of the great text-book of the universe.

This was the one jest of science, and making the most of it we could laugh for moments at a time over the great fuss men had always made of their own selves, their hopes and fears, their affections, their ambitions, their little destinies. We could understand, now, the deepest of all the influences of the scientific revolution — the attitude struck out by the new philosophy toward the anxious, pleasing agitations of men in the interest of their own aspirations and desires. Their art, their letters, their governments, their humane philosophies, their moral wisdom — all were trivialities, some playful, some solemn, all a little ludicrous.

For as we now saw, if the personal impulses, the little individual preferences, of the swarming genus *homo* were a mere by-play of their chemical organism, the organized efforts to gratify them were play also. Play was a natural human instinct and met our approval, for we were human, but as play it was to be taken in a holiday mood. Heroically thus we saved our aesthetic predilections, a little diminished from their old romantic glamour, but safe in the sanction of science, as science had once been saved for us by the sanction of aesthetics.

It was amusing to us now to remember that but a little half-century ago a man of learning was one steeped in the details of merely human lore, and the educated mind a mind perfected in the brief traditions of one little part of one species of animate beings inhabiting one little planet of a solar system almost negligible in a universe itself perhaps but a molecule of some upturned clod in the vasty fields of infinity. The men of science had earned the right to smile!

Surely no change that had ever come over the human outlook could have been more complete. Instead of the center of it all we were a mere detail. Darwin had lent the new conception a dramatic, or at least an hilariously picturesque, symbolism in his *Descent of Man,* and this had got the attention, not to say the breath, of the unsophisticated. To the sophisticated, however, the significance of the change lay in the new perspectives opening up before them, and a wholly new scale of values. And as for us, over and above these perspectives and these values we came to understand certain sincerities in the new attitude that at first were shocking.

We had drifted into the scientific shop a little idly, after a stay among the elegancies, and we had noticed, a little superciliously, a lack in the men of science of what we called culture. Some of them, it was true, were all that we could ask, but in general we were repelled by what we thought of as a degree of crudity in their intellectual manners. They had little literature; they wrote in what we called a barren style, or with no style; they displayed a kind of tolerant contempt for art and poetry; their taste was unformed; their knowledge of the past was frequently sophomoric and their attitude toward it a little patronizing. For we had come upon the second or third generation after the great change. Darwin charmed us, and Huxley and Clifford commanded our intellectual admiration without affronting our susceptibilities, but they had been brought up in the atmosphere of our own culture if not on its special diet. These successors, however, had been bred from childhood to the new point of view; the patterns of their minds had been etched without many of the colors that we had come to think of as necessary to the highest cultivation. So that our first impression was that their misprisal of much that was very dear to us was a kind of insincerity, made up of ignorance and chagrin and self-defense.

It was only after a fuller initiation, therefore, that we saw how sincere these misprisals were, and how insignificant to the new culture were the chief ingredients of the old — manners, taste, moral tradition, and an intellect formed and disciplined to the point of wisdom in human lore. To be sure, there they were, these ingredients, to be scrutinized and their evolution traced from primitive beginnings. But this was a different view of them — an outside view. The inner feel of them of the older culture, their direct returns, so to speak — right conduct as the response to a warm sense of duty, the play of taste as the delightful obligation of a delicately cultivated consciousness, the exercise of the intellect in sympathetic comprehension of the human spirit — all this was beside the point, relic of a day when men spun their sense of the universe out of their own minds, and put themselves at its center.

I have wondered since why we didn't pause then to ask in whose minds this new sense of the universe *had* been spun. But we didn't, and the question would have shocked us unspeakably. Already in our stay in the shop we had begun to lose our gayety. The universe was a serious matter. In a mechanism without flaw or accident there were no incongruities to be laughed at. We had started out, as I have said, to make a drive at the cosmos. We had got it at last, and perhaps it weighed a little heavily on our minds. But we took this change of tone as inevitable, and asked no disconcerting questions. The truth was true, no matter what we felt about it. If it did not touch our affections deeply, so much the worse for us. There we were.

With this, I think, we had come into the full principle of our inheritance. We went on spending the interest of it, so to speak, here and there, in various diversions, reading, wrangling, readjusting our spirits, pricking ancient bubbles. Even men of science couldn't seem to themselves but chemical reactions, *in propria persona.* And we were not even men of science. None the less we seemed to have arrived. We were abreast of our age. Our bearings were the bearings of our times. There was unmistakable comfort in the realization, and an assuring sense of intellectual majority. We were in touch. We belonged.

VI

I have dwelt at length upon our stay in the scientific shop partly because it was the commonplace of the times we grew up in, and records the way the situation came home to us, and partly because of a dilemma it created for those of us who did not linger there and become men of science. Many of us, indeed, who had come so far, did stay. They remained, and picking out some unexplored or unperfected corner of the cosmos set themselves at it for a lifetime. There was plenty to be done still. And I dare say that to them the dilemma which troubled the rest of us looked then and will always look a little sickly, so frank, open, objective, and healthy is the scientific vision, so relatively simple for all its complexity, so free from gratuitous subjective considerations that after all the universe is blithely indifferent to.

None the less there were some of us who were not destined to be men of science, and who could not, as a consequence, satisfy our curiosities in some one corner of the cosmos. We could understand that devotion now, and even feel as of old a kind of envy of those who had it. But when we had drifted away from the bazaar, and had begun to take on responsibilities that ought to have seemed ludicrous in view of men's insignificance, we were unable to keep ourselves, as human beings, properly snubbed. Something of the old concern to make the best of the human situation began, traitorously, to edge back into the center again.

Our case was once more what it had been with aesthetics. Once in possession of the point of view there was nothing more for us to do about it. We were not practitioners in either affair. In both we had got what we were after, and there we were. Science was more far-reaching than aesthetics, but just on that account it exposed itself to more jostling. Its point of view affected, or ought to have affected, our way of taking everything, even to the things that science itself took no specific care of at all. For while science did not even purport to take care of the quality of life once we had it, it tended to nullify that problem altogether; men were so pitiably unimportant in a universe 200,000,000,000,000,000 miles across. And now that we were in a position to smile at a concern for the character of so unimportant a thing, we found ourselves with just that one concern on our hands and no other — the character of life once we had it.

That we had it, in fact, wasn't our responsibility at all. There even came moments when it occurred to us that a universe 200,000,000,000,000,000 miles across might be counted on to take care of itself without our help. And if it could be trusted to do that, our looking into it must be simply for our own sake — a thing to do or not to do as we chose. This was a heresy. It made the pursuit of science simply one response to the problem of what to do with life once we had it — a purely subordinate affair.

VII

I have followed through this typical experience to the end, or nearly to the end. We had been taken in; and now we were out. The day was spent, our pockets empty, and we in a state of mind appropriate to such a moment — divided between anger and laughter. We had gone into the bazaar to get our bearings, and we could not honestly say that we had failed; we had seen it through, and now we saw through it. What more could we have asked? We could laugh at the comedy of it; but secretly I dare say that we all felt that in comedy there is more fun for the spectator than for the comic character. We were both, of course.

Meantime, however, something had happened to us ourselves, and because we were, in a way, typical products of the bazaar I linger for a moment over our after state. And I don't know how better to put it than to say that the milk of our minds had turned; we were all curds and whey. We had had in the bazaar two enthusiasms, and in pursuit of them we had got what knowledge and what habits of thought we were to go on with. In one of these pursuits the immediate personal feel had been everything and the ineluctable fact and the reason nothing. In the other the immediate personal feel was nothing, and the ineluctable fact and the reason everything. But when we came out of the bazaar we found that what had chiefly to be thought about were matters where we ourselves in all our complexity, and our human responses, and the ineluctable fact, and the reason were all inextricably involved, and where intellect had to take feeling into account, and feeling was cognizant of the intellect. In this kind of thinking we had had no discipline at all. We were men in the street.

Other men in the street would come to us, say, for subscriptions to scientific foundations, to galleries of art. We could feel the humor of their coming to us, acknowledging that science itself, or art — those human pursuits — were dependent on our human judgment as to whether, all things considered, the one or the other was a good thing, or which was the better. We might out of hand follow someone else's judgment, it is true, and fall in with the drift of the times, respond to the current slogans as the slogans were calculated to suggest our response. But the problem was still there. And as for us, we could give only sophomoric answers to it.

We were not artists, and we were not men of science. We had hoped, in our young presumption, to gain a philosophy. "The cosmos or nothing," we had cried. Neither art nor science had given us one. And now that we were out we discovered that the cosmos was by definition only what men knew about it in their orderly minds, that thought was conduct, and that the pursuit of this knowledge was subject to judgment as to whether it was a good thing. The cosmic problem was at bottom humbly moral. The bathos was shocking. The very term *moral* was in a kind of muddled disrepute.

When we went our ways we parted in two directions, according to our various tempers. All of us fronted the same problem; none of us had the knowledge we needed. It was not — this knowledge — like the facts of nature, always there, automatically preserved, waiting all about us with an infinite and indifferent patience. It could be lost — was lost in our case. It was only to be recreated by an imaginative acquaintance with the experiences and reflections it had been accumulated by. And we had been fed on a different diet. We had vigorous opinions on all manner of subjects, as was natural. But even the amoeba has its instinctive leanings, and ours were not very different in kind. For those of us whose tempers were constructive our opinions were ideals and not ideas, Utopias and not states, products of desire and fancy and not of knowledge and imagination. And those of us whose tempers were skeptical and rebellious — as the sporadic growth of satire reveals — stayed arrant guerillas to the end of the chapter, Betsy Trotwoods forever seizing our umbrellas and chasing donkeys off the green.

The happiest of us were those who never, in spirit, emerged from the bazaar at all, but lingered on, taking up, one by one, the activity of some shop that caught and held our fancies. As for the others who did emerge, and foregathered around the fire at evening to talk over the experiences of the day, there was observable in us then, and always afterwards, a curious unrest. Our spontaneous feelings and our clear knowledge were at sixes and sevens.

We were "turned about," like one for whom on first coming to a strange city east seems west and west east. We could later face about and true our calculations, but could never in our heart of hearts bring to these calculations an instinctive feel of orient rightness.

II

ET TU IN ARCADIA

II

ET TU IN ARCADIA

IT had been a summer to renew our youth, as the two relics who were left behind to look back upon it agreed — a little ruefully now in the cloudless October afternoon, with the still radiance of autumn on the hills and the sudden quiet that had fallen around us since the last good-byes of the morning.

And we were disturbed. The summer had sloped into the past while our eyes were full upon it duped and charmed by its lively current of gesture, and had eluded us before we had put to it our detaining questions. In so far it *had* renewed our youth. But the grimmer truth of the moment was that our beards were growing gray, and that after a summer of willful deafness we were once more hearing time's winged chariot at our backs.

I glanced at Philip. His eyes were on the sundial that had been Hugh's preoccupation during much of the summer.

"For our forgetfulness," he nodded.

We laughed. Day after day in the long month just gone the dial had told off the hours under our eyes without a hint that it had this irony in store for us.

The shadow of the gnomon lay upon the slender radial of four. On the canvas overhead the sun was blotting the shadows of the pines in intricate patterns. The sky was level blue, indigo where we saw it through the branches overhead; the trees by the stream were still; the yellow road with its green border of meadow loitered on to the village two miles away without vehicle or pedestrian. The moment itself was perfect enough, if we could have been content with it. At twenty, no doubt, we should have been content — and even now we should have been content to be twenty. But at forty!

"Now for the tea-bell," I added, willing to make my own contribution to the twinges of our plight.

A moment more and we heard the slow strokes, faint with distance, from the church tower that was all we could see of the village. Philip smiled. The tea-bell had been a fancy of Hugh's. He had discovered, he told us one day, that there was no service at the church at that hour. With his frank eyes on Philip, and in the serious way he had when something lay in his thoughts behind his raillery, he went on to describe the prodigious exchange of tea-drinking in the late afternoon among the summer cottages, the going to and fro at the sound of the bell, the chatter from the porches a few minutes later, and his inference as to the meaning of the four-o'clock peal.

Philip's brusque nod over his own teacup had rewarded the boy, whose open laugh rang out for a moment, and then, before the rest of us had taken up the thread, had subsided into the musing, distant look that suggested what was so inexplicable in him to his own people.

Now, as we looked down at the dial, with which Hugh had captured for us so ironic a reminder of time, and heard the footsteps of the faithful Martha as she came along the path from the house with our own tea tray, Philip pointed out the fitness of the moment and we laughed again. We laughed a little grimly, it is true, for the summer was gone, and we knew well enough that if it were to have any point now that it *was* gone we should have to make it ourselves. Perhaps there was none. Its incidents had been undramatic from first to last, placidly uninsistent. It had laid a duty upon us, but the duty had remained undone at the end. We could at any time have gone through the form of doing it. But we had not been able to bring ourselves to that. And now, there we were.

I

Hugh had been sent out to us ostensibly for his health. Neither of us had seen him since he was a child, and our recollections of him were vague. Even our acquaintance with his father and mother had lapsed, cordially, and with a proper pride on our part appropriate to poor relations. We were amused, therefore, and a little touched, at the conflict of command and entreaty with which we had been asked to give Hugh a home during the summer, and at something in the tone of the letter that seemed less like solicitude than chagrin. The plea of health had evaporated before a warning that perhaps firmness would be the surest note in our treatment of him.

The effect was to make us anticipate rather the tarnish of gilded youth than any signs of recent or threatened sickness. Otherwise we were glad to have him come. If we hesitated it was because we did not see how a boy could be content between two oldsters who were approaching their first climacteric, and who took their walks over the hills in the spirit of a constitutional. We fortified ourselves, however, with the thought of the village and the summer cottages there, picturing him as a kind of lodger at our inn, with his days spent in the bright business of youth beyond our ken.

What we saw, when he arrived, was a tall slender boy on the edge of manhood, or perhaps not yet on the edge, obviously robust, a little too boyish to be handsome, but boyishly fresh, and, in view of our anticipations, disconcertingly quiet and open and direct in the frank inquiry of his eyes.

Indeed, he took us so naturally and simply that instead of a hope that he would promptly find himself at home in the village, we found ourselves from the first a little abused at the thought of the village welcome we had gratuitously forecast for him, and goaded ourselves with a sudden sense of being thrust a little further back on the shelf. We took to him from the first moment of his coming, and the old place seemed a little the lonelier that he was to find his attractions elsewhere.

During his first week or two he was content to

stay about a good deal, sometimes going off for a day's tramp across the country and coming back with a boy's fierce appetite, but for the most part lingering through the old house, reading a little, but more often finding something in its odd corners to occupy him. There were the accumulations there of the idler moments of a score of years — outing utensils, old guns and tackle, and the residue of old discarded tastes and the groping experiments of our own youth. And there was a library, thumbed to homeliness, that might have been called learned by an amateur, but certainly amateurish by a scholar.

He seemed even happy to be with us. He joined us whenever we were disposed to sit and talk, and left us on impulses of his own that kept us from ever seeming to have him on our hands. Once, however, after he had quitted us thus with some apparent purpose, Philip came upon him lying idle and alone on a steamer chair in an angle of the porch. Touched with the intolerable sense that the boy was lonely he suggested the village. With the quick, natural way he had of entering into a suggestion, Hugh surprised him with the news that he had found acquaintances there already, and soon went off with an expectant air. Philip came back with a rueful face.

"Can he be thinking that we are tired of him?" he asked as he settled down in his own chair and opened his book. He did not read, however, but sat looking up the road after Hugh's dwindling figure.

For the next few days Hugh spent much of his

time away from home, and enlivened us at dinner with touches of village life, at first a little hesitantly, and then with a pleasure and wonder at our interest that heightened his color. We gathered that he had not confined himself to the summer colony but had gone about among the villagers as well. When he spoke of the latter it was with a quickened curiosity, but most of his references were to the summer people, among whom, no doubt, he was more at home. We noticed, however, that an air of latent amusement hung about his accounts of the vacationists. He made no explanation of it, perhaps himself not conscious of the difference. But to us who listened, piecing out our theories of him, it added to the things that we were still at a loss to reconcile.

How long he would have kept himself amused at the village we never knew. We were uncertain then whether he was really amused there at all. If he did feel himself dismissed from the house, however, he took his dismissal apparently without chagrin, even with a kind of sympathy for us, and kept himself away lest we think him lonely, or — so we complicated the matter — lest we be chagrined at seeming to have dismissed him.

II

Our tangled speculations on this score were brought to an end one day when the prospect of other guests led Philip to bemoan the lack of a retreat from the cramped sociability of the house.

Hugh suggested that an old tent which he had found in the attic might be pitched on the hillside a hundred yards away on the path that wavered off to meet the bend in the road below. He put the suggestion with the quiet eagerness that we found so attractive in him. And for our part, though we had little faith in the tent as a retreat, we were glad enough to have him by us again, and glad enough to quiet the uncomfortable sense that perhaps he might have felt himself got rid of.

From Hugh's own eagerness we expected to see the tent set up at once. And one of us, at least, was a little troubled, not perhaps at the thought of the old battered canvas marring what was in itself a graceful curve of the hill, but with the thought that Hugh should have been so taken with a prospect that might, it seemed, have jarred on him as well. Instead of climbing at once to the attic, however, he lingered with us over our after-breakfast coffee, and then wandered out along the overgrown path to the foot of the two pines which he had had his eyes upon from Philip's first mention of a retreat.

"I foresee how it will go," Philip commented as we settled down in our chairs on the porch. "We are cowed. We'll be afraid of hurting his feelings, and we'll banish ourselves to the intolerable stuffiness and dreariness of that mildewed canvas."

We looked off toward the trees. Hugh had thrown himself on the ground and was lying in the shadow with his hands under his head. An hour later he was still there, propped on his elbow gazing at the sky through the filter of pine boughs. A high-crested jay, indigo as the sky, floated up from the ground at his feet to a low bough overhead, and scolded there unheeded.

Had Hugh forgotten the tent? For me, I was at once forgiving him for so elaborate a forethought over so trivial an affair, or if he had forgotten it already, forgiving him his inconstancy. And when a little later he came back to the house and said that he was going to the village for the day, searching our faces for some share in the latent amusement that always played about his own when he spoke of the summer colony, he left us chagrined at having worked up a gratuitous pathos in ourselves over his interpretation of his dismissal. He preferred the village then, after all.

"A pair of old fools," Philip muttered, watching him down the road.

Two passers-by that day, one in a car and one smartly on horseback, left notes for Hugh — invitations no doubt. And for two or three days we saw little of him except at breakfast. He spoke lightly then of his village adventures, and lapsed easily into other topics, or sat listening with his intent eyes on Philip's face. We concluded that he had forgotten the tent, that after all he was a boy, soon tired of two sedentary recluses, and that naturally he found his account in the gayer leisure of the village. That was what we had hoped for him when we had first consented to his coming. And I dare say that neither of us had ever felt so old as we did then, when we realized that in relaxing the affection we had begun to feel for him, with its voluntary responsibility and its brooding hopes, there was a touch of relief.

We were lingering as usual over our coffee on the breakfast porch one morning not long after, but in unwonted silence. Some subtle zest had gone out of the occasion, and we were impatient to get away to other absorptions. We stayed on, however, unwilling to signalize too sharply the sense that we had of the moment. Hugh, preoccupied on his own part, had apparently noticed nothing, or at least when he looked up and spoke he did so with no obvious effort.

" After all, you see," he said tentatively, " it isn't much to look at."

We glanced at him across the table, and then followed his gaze out over the hillside to where the two pines stood beside the path.

" I don't quite see it there," he added.

Philip's own gaze was too abstracted to suggest that he too didn't quite see it there. It returned in a moment, however, with a whimsical, resigned puzzlement to Hugh's face.

" You may when you do see it there," he said gruffly.

Hugh laughed, catching an overtone in Philip's voice. He got up then, and wandered off once more along the path to the trees. We had him back again, it was clear, but whether from his own preference or from a perception of our disappointment at his desertion we did not know. An hour later Philip burst out in a gale of Homeric laughter, and confessed that he had detected himself mulling over this dilemma.

Hugh had apparently taken Philip's suggestion to let his idea grow as he proceeded. We saw him during the day back and forth along the path, sometimes audible in long conferences with Martha who ruled us from the kitchen, and sometimes among the tools and lumber of the store room. For our own part we anticipated for him already the chagrin of final failure, foreseeing nothing at the last but the gray canvas askew on the slope, shamed beneath the stately pines. And our concern was heightened by the sense that he too had been sensitive to failure. We kept away from the spot, therefore, and when he saw that we kept away from the topic as well he said nothing further about it.

Sometimes I saw him looking at Philip in the quiet way he had of being sociable without speech, not looking away when Philip looked up, but with a kindling readiness to respond that had at once no hint that he had been waiting. For the most part, however, he was active about his task, or stretched out before the fireplace with a book, or merely idling.

Sometimes we heard the drone of his saw in the warm afternoon, and the blow of his hammer, and the fall of boards. Now and then, above the odor of the pines, we caught the whiff of new-cut lumber. Looking out, as we did oftener than we would have admitted to ourselves, we could see him bending over his work in the flecked shadow of the trees, or erect and staring at it in thought, or, not infrequently, abandoning it altogether to lie on his back and look up at the sky.

The days had come off fair after a week of unsettled weather, with a breeze that had recollections of the sea in it and brought up a white low scud across the blue. From time to time a car slipped by on the road, or a horse and rider, or a slow team creeping on to the village, but otherwise there was a serenity of quiet in which we could hear the articulate flow of the stream, and now and then the grating fall of a pine cone. Once we heard voices on the hillside. It was evident that if Hugh did not go to the village the village was threatening to come to him. They were welcome. And at that distance the group on the green slope, half in shade and half in sun, in their bright summer tints and with the wind adding movement to their momentary poise, rewarded the glimpse we allowed ourselves.

We turned back to books that were dulled for the moment, wondering what Hugh would do with his visitors or they with him. There were three of them, two girls and a slender youth in flannels, augmented after a time by another couple from a car on the road. For an hour or more we heard their voices, and then saw them disappearing, two and two over the path, with Hugh the last to dip below the curve of the slope. Once on the following day as we looked out we saw a group of five or six, with much give and take of shout and laughter, working together at the unwieldy canvas.

Whatever impression we had anticipated, we had not anticipated quite the one that came to us as we stood at the porch rail some time later looking out at our " retreat." Hugh had gone off with his visitors, and we felt that our present survey was all that was legitimate without his sanction. It was rather an absence of impression that struck us — as though, after the first moment, the tent had always stood there. It seemed at home, inconspicuous beneath the two pines, and faced us without a challenge. The canvas was old and gray, the lumber was old and gray. Above the bulk of the tent the taut planes of a broad fly swept up a little from the slope above, and swept down again on the other side, with the grace of wings percepubly lifted.

Philip's laconic nod, as he stood contemplating it, was his only comment.

Hugh said nothing of the tent when he joined us on the porch before dinner. After a glance at each of us he drew up a chair and told us, with his latent amusement, of the silent antagonism in the village between the natives and the summer colony, marked in the large by the social line between church and mission. At dinner he fell silent, however, looking at us with the frank inquiry that always filled Philip with gruff compunction.

" Well," the latter asked abruptly, " when are we to see the tent? "

Hugh's face brightened.

" You haven't been out, then? " he asked.

It occurred to us that he had gone away to give us the chance to take it casually, and to disapprove, if we did, without the sense that he himself set much store by it. And when he gathered that we had waited with nice scruples for his permission he had his laugh and begged, in that case, for another day.

I think in the end, when we took formal possession, we said nothing of approval or disapproval. He had built a floor or platform fitted to the tent on three sides, and on the fourth facing the house had extended it in some seven or eight feet of balcony, railed in with a balustrade of aspen stems, and both tent and balcony canopied with the fly. Two steamer chairs lay stretched out on the balcony itself and within the tent were a table and a couple of camp stools and cots. We sank with a sigh of comfort into the two chairs, and Hugh sat on the edge of the floor in the opening of the rail.

" A snug corner of the deck," Philip said, touching the impression that was inevitable to both of us.

The smooth canvas, the lounging chairs, the rail, the taut guys sweeping downward, the breeze lifting and depressing the canopy and straining at the ropes, the intimacy of the sky, all lent their suggestions. None of us spoke further. After a while Hugh looked up and Philip nodded. Hugh looked at both of us for a moment, and then turned away, got up, and went slowly toward the house.

We did not wait for the arrival of guests to take up our occupancy. Whether it was the association of the sea and the memory of old voyages, or the prompt agreement that the spot was more cheerful than the old house, at all events we had no desire to postpone our own pleasure in it, or blur Hugh's evident pleasure at our own. Once established there, too, as it proved, we came into closer touch with Hugh. We were, in a sense, his guests there, though he never assumed the rôle of host. But we found him with us more often, loitering in the shade, or, when reading had lapsed into talk, seated on his favorite perch at the edge of the balcony.

III

He began to ignore the village, content, to all appearances, to be alone; and the village, with a greater show of reluctance, began to give him up. Sometimes he sat apart in apparent abstraction, though he never, when we spoke to him, seemed to come back to the present from any great distance. When he was not by we grumbled over these reveries, finding in them and in his assumption of our aloofness from them a kind of pathos. To Martha he was altogether a puzzle and an exasperation.

" Sometimes," she confided to us one day, " he is that young you'd say he was a child, with that smile of his, and asking you questions, and taking your word for gospel. And then — "

She threw up her hands for the rest. She had tried, it seemed, to persuade him to go to the mission, seeing that he did not go to the church. And the reason he had given her for not going to either had seemed to her the best of all reasons for going to one — that there were two with a sharp antagonism between them.

The point was enlightening for us as we speculated over the boy's inner life, and touched his reveries with a suggestion of thoughts that dissipated our fears for their dreamy futility.

It was still a few days before the arrival of the expected guests — the widow and the niece of an old friend of ours — that Hugh's idleness germinated anew. He had unconsciously, and to our own amusement, been occasion for the postponement of this visit. Margaret had heard of him in our desultory letters, and had been filled with alarm. It had developed then that her plan to bring Katherine with her had been the response to a kind of panic at the girl's sudden maturity and attractiveness. She wanted an interim, she said, to catch her breath, to grow up to the idea that Katherine was a woman. And some glitter of wealth that had fallen to Katherine's lot had made her panic the more precipitate.

"You are the only utterly safe people I know," she had written in her downright way. We accepted the praise as we could, but in return produced Hugh, an obstacle that made her pause for the exchange of a letter or two. We must have satisfied her, though the course of her reasoning was never clear to us. The date of her coming was set at last, and the house was made ready.

It was in the interim that Hugh put his new idea

to us, one afternoon on the tent balcony, where Martha, grumbling at our desertion, had set out tea, and where we sat unreluctantly idling.

" If it doesn't do it won't be much to clear it off," he ventured. " You know I'm not sure it will do. Besides if I'm going to be too distracting working here — "

" You're distracting whether you're working here or not," Philip said abruptly.

Hugh looked up quickly, and then responded with a frank laugh that was yet no disclaimer of the seriousness in Philip's voice. But he had no self-consciousness on the alert — none at all of the self-consciousness that flushes. He had never had to learn the drift of Philip's gruffness. It had been a part of his quality from the first that he had fallen in understandingly with our bluntness, and it had been a delicate heightening of that quality that he had never attempted to answer in kind. He kept to his own instincts.

" The shadow there on the crack," he mused. " You see — just here — yesterday it fell five minutes earlier than to-day. Funny! How long ago, do you suppose, did they invent sundials? Funny for us, I mean, not to know what those old boys knew! "

This curiosity set him off. The " old boys " absorbed him. There was an ancient *Ninth Edition* in the house yielding a fine pollen of crumbling sheepskin to everyone who came for honey to that old flower. Hugh pursued his quest in it with a bloom on his clothes and an eager light in his eyes. A scramble of disorderly notes were stuffed into his pockets, and a neglected air hung about his garments. It was an odd association of Philip's that linked him with the extinct race of scholars, rappee sprinkled and disorderly, who, unlike their successors, took a naïve joy in the adventure of reading and an absurd love of what they read for its own sake. As for Hugh, however, he came back into the world of things with a keen enough relish, and spent another day roving the hills. Some exigent picture in his mind sent him far afield. And from time to time we saw him labor down from over the ridge with a single stone in his arms, drop it by the path, and climb back again.

On the day before Margaret and Katherine arrived he completed the table of his dial — a mushroom of rounded boulders two or three feet high rising out of the grass a few paces from the tent balcony, and capped by a shallow, overhanging basin of a single rock. The weathered stones were green and gray with lichen and without a trace of workmanship. Even more than the tent it had an air of always having been there.

Hugh sat resting after his labors.

"The real thing is still to do," he explained, pleased none the less at Philip's evident approval.

We were sitting as usual on the balcony, and feeling idly that we ought to be making the most of the time that was left before the noon stage should bring the arrivals and break the charm that now seemed to have fallen on the earlier weeks of the summer. Hugh sat in his old place in the break of the rail, the great volume dusting his knees and the sun sifting down upon him, flecking the open pages. Once he looked up, and seeing that we were not reading started to speak, and then checked himself with a heightened color. After a moment he did speak.

" Do you think you have ever read of this? " he asked.

I said that I, for one, hadn't.

" Not in the sun," Philip admonished.

Hugh smiled and looked up.

" It isn't bright coming through the tree," he said. " And it ought somehow to be read in the sun. I think that is nonsense, but still — "

" Let's have it, then, read in the sun."

" You see it was in Arabia," Hugh explained, and then he began reading, a little diffidently at first, and then with eager forgetfulness.

IV

We had expected the coming of Margaret and Katherine to change the routine of our summer. And perhaps for a fortnight there was a change, though not so much for us as for Hugh. Hugh had made our retreat for us, and now made the link that saved it from seeming a rout.

With the downrightness that was her charm, however, Margaret had seen through our fraud at once.

" You men," she said, " have made yourselves an asylum. Don't tell me, Philip! But I know we're welcome or we wouldn't have come; and now you've cleared away my only compunction. You're not to change your wretched ways in the least. They are wretched ways but they're men's ways and I respect them. Now tell me about Hugh."

If it had not been for Hugh we could hardly have followed Margaret's injunction and gone on in our wretched ways. He took our place by some natural impulse, getting the newcomers settled, breaking the bleak edge of their first days in a new place, taking them to the village, introducing them there, and altogether doing what we never could have done to make their initiation pleasant and their welcome actively hospitable. He and Katherine developed a bantering comradeship that filled the house with laughter when they were about. Frequently they were not about, but off on long tramps over the hills or at informal gayeties in the village. Margaret watched them with frank interest. The village itself began to frequent the house, freed from the old fogies that had darkened it before. Hugh's earlier desertion of the village had now in their eyes a forgivable color.

By what means he managed, or whether he managed at all in any specific sense, was not apparent, but little by little he drifted back to the tent and took up again the progress of his dial. We watched him for evidence of some late eruption, but we saw nothing. He had his old gayety, his old latent amusement, his old readiness. Even his moments of indolence and revery never had the quality of moods. He came out of them with his quick smile, armed with some clear intention. When Katherine was by there was the same rallying give and take and the same open laughter. But unless she had some open request for him he let her go off with the others, took up his crumbling *Britannica* and his scraps of calculation, and sat on the edge of the balcony or in the "wabe"—the allusion was Katherine's—absorbed in his self-imposed task.

What took place in Katherine's thoughts we only guessed one afternoon much later when she flung back at him a "Good-bye, Sir Percival!" as she went off to join a party of young folks waiting for her on the road below. Hugh's answering laugh sobered as he looked after her. He sat so long staring after the retreating party that Philip, stirred as was his impatient wont at anything that might have stung Hugh, called him to the tent with an irrelevant question as to his future.

Hugh laughed.

"You didn't know, then," he asked, "that that was the great thing I was sent out to decide. I supposed they'd told you. You two were to help."

Philip shook his head.

"I didn't want to bother you with it," Hugh went on. "It seems to be a desperate affair altogether, and nobody's been very happy about it when it's come up."

"You've settled it for yourself, then?" I asked.

"Oh no. That's just it, you see. I can't."

He laughed again, and glancing at his watch went back to the dial. Some time before, he had filled the shallow basin of his cap-stone with cement and made it a smooth and level table. And now he had rigged up a slender gallows over it, and suspended a plumb to a point near the center of the southern edge. There was an arc drawn on the level surface from the point of the plumb as a center. A foot or so up the plumb line was a tiny jet bead — Katherine's contribution, for they had worked there much together before Katherine's desertion. At some nice moment that morning they had nicked the point at which the shadow of the bead had crossed the arc, and now he was waiting for the moment and the point at which the afternoon shadow should cross it again. But the wind had come up since morning, and now sent the plumbline swaying and the shadow of the bead dancing back and forth across the arc in minute circles. Hugh came back to the tent amused by his failure.

"All for to-day," he said. "The thing for me is to be a maker of dials. To-morrow the sun will be off true noon and won't be back till September. Four work-days a year. I shall be a maker of dials." He sat for a moment looking back at his apparatus. "It's curious," he added after a moment. "We take our time from the sun, and then find the sun wrong."

Next day he was back again watching his shadows. Toward evening he showed us a line joining the two nicks in the arc and another at right angles to it drawn through the point beneath the plumb — his north and south.

"Perhaps it's near enough," he commented. "Of course it isn't true north, but perhaps we can wink at that. It's my great fault, you know, that I have no sense of the value of time."

From then on he was occupied with other details of his task. The gnomon was still to be mounted — true north and pitched to the angle of the latitude, he said — and the hours to be marked as its shadow crept along the arc. He worked with a zest that never hurried him, as though, now that he had captured time, he had all time at his command. Sometimes a drifting cloud slipped under the sun at a crucial moment and postponed the record of that hour for another day; sometimes his own abstraction let the shadow slip by unrecorded, and brought from him the hearty laugh that he always had for his own defeats. It was the afternoon hour of four that thus proved most elusive, till it became the standing jest of his enterprise, capped in the end by his finding it one day already marked for him, and Katherine sitting by in his customary spot.

We had wondered what his relations with Katherine would be after the occasion of her parthian fling, but they seemed unaltered. Sometimes she sat with him beside the dial — they had come to marking the halves and the quarters as well as the hours — and their talk or their laughter or their silence, drifting to us on the tent balcony, seemed untouched by restraint. Usually, however, Hugh was alone.

Once or twice as he kept his exigent vigil there we caught glimpses of Katherine sitting silent near Margaret, her hands idle. Little by little she too had begun to neglect the village, spending her time with Margaret or talking to Martha in the kitchen, or sometimes climbing to the ridge and sitting on a rock there overlooking the valley. There was no brooding traceable upon her face when we came upon her so, but she was clearly quieter than she had been in the earlier weeks of her stay.

As for Margaret, she looked on from her own angle until that became too acute, and then, one day near the close of the summer, she came to us to rail at herself over the comedy of her errors.

"I've been a fool once more, Philip," she said. "It's no use your telling me. I know it. At first I was afraid to bring her lest he make love to her, and now I'm in tears because he won't. If I'd followed my instincts I'd have stayed away. Oh, I know, that if he hadn't been here at all she might have formed some wild attachment in the village, and as it is she's safe. I know. I know. And there are young men there who are ready — unexceptionable young men, as they go. I've seen them. But my dears, I'm like Katherine. I want Hugh. He's so simple — so — No he isn't simple; he's unbelievably complex, but there he is — all that you dream of. How did he grow up so, and what will become of him? Meantime what have you two — you bachelors — done to him?"

The comedy played itself out on these terms.

It was possible to feel a sharp pity for the girl, for it was clear that her fancy had been touched by something more than the charm that we all of us found in him, and piqued by the impersonal note that held out, for her at least, through the friendliness of his evident liking. There were moments when a relaxing emotion seized us, made us impatient with him — with anyone — who could see her thus and not fling all colder visions to the winds. Her girlhood and her beauty, her quick spirit and wholesome nature were rich in promise and fulfillment.

At such times we tried to see in him the elements of the eternal prig in men, nursing some cold virtue at the expense of youthful and generous abandon. But he was not a prig. And we watched the silent conflict, that seemed so much more conscious in her than in him, with divided sympathy, seeing in her the endearing eternal impulse of life, and in him another impulse, hardly yet articulate to his own listening spirit, that carried him so unreluctantly past the ordinary ports of youth.

Their last good-byes, when the summer was gone and we stood on the road by the stage which was to carry Margaret and Katherine away, marked no change in their relationship. They came down the hill together with their old bantering laughter, and stood by, a little apart, while the driver stowed away the last pieces of luggage. Margaret's eyes rested broodingly upon them from inside. The driver climbed to his seat.

" Good-bye, good-bye, Hugh."

"Good-bye, good-bye."

Their hands and their eyes met for a moment, and then he helped her in, and the coach moved off.

We stood, all three, looking after it till it disappeared around the curve of the road, and then went slowly up the hill, Philip and I to the tent, and Hugh on toward the ridge.

V

Whatever it was that had set him so apart, it had troubled his friends at home — good ordinary folk of ample means and the bewildered life of the American well-to-do. It was clear from Hugh's talk and their own evasive letters that they had found themselves embarrassed with an unintelligible son, and easy to imagine their incomprehension of his aloofness, his frank directness, his voyaging fancy, his easy ignorance of all their cherished values. And feeling our own responsibility we set ourselves from then on to probing him a little further.

He responded readily, even gratefully, and with the amused smile that he always had for his own concerns. But he had already given himself up.

"You see I have no idea, myself," he laughed.

"No ambition?" I asked.

"That is it. I don't think I have."

"You will have a living to make?"

He hung upon that for a time, nodding a slow assent, and then looked up at us with a kind of appeal not to be misunderstood.

" You yourselves haven't minded being poor? "

He said it half questioningly, half musingly, and was a little tardy in joining the laugh with which we answered it. He did join, however, heartily enough, though he probably failed to see all that amused us in it. Our poverty was not very onerous, as poverty, though no doubt he had heard it discussed at home as somewhat desperate. And no doubt, too, his taste of it this summer was mingled with other tastes that had endeared its flavor for him. Philip was evidently a hero to him. He had come, it was safe to conjecture, from an atmosphere at home that was not one of understanding. And here he had suddenly found himself more at home than at home, the vague groping of his spirit free to grope in an atmosphere of tolerance and sympathy.

The occasion was not one to be lost, and we pushed him further.

" Lawyer, doctor, merchant, thief? "

He shook his head. " A thief, perhaps," he added.

Philip caught at the note of soberness in his voice.

" Freedom, you mean," he nodded.

" Something like that. Before he's caught, of course." He laughed out. " I seem to have thought of everything. I dare say I haven't. I don't quite see myself in anything."

A procession of himself in various rôles apparently passed before his imagination, for he laughed out again after a moment.

" Perhaps you would after you were there," I suggested a little lamely. " Remember the tent."

"But that's it," he said simply. "I'm afraid I should."

We stared at him for a space, joining his laugh, startled a little, and then aware that a window had been thrown open, and a fresher air and serener light were about us. Clearly he had lived in a region of higher skies than we had till now glimpsed above him.

We saw him under it then, and when after a long silence he rose and went off through the grass toward the ridge, we looked after him with new eyes. We were under the handicap of our affection and the play of our own imaginations, but as we watched him now climbing the hill with his easy buoyancy, and thought back over the earlier impressions of the summer, we seemed to be seeing him for the first time.

We had thought of his charm as lying in his simplicity. And he was simple, so far as the quick candor, the almost ardent openness and modesty of his mind could simplify him. But Margaret's arrow had flown straight to the mark long before we learned to take him for what he was. He was not simple. The latent amusement that played through his reveries and his speech, and rested so impartially upon his own perception of himself indicated complexity, at least duality, in the web of his instincts. The nice sense of fitness, the taste that had made the tent and the dial so harmonious on the hillside, and took subtler expression in the infinite details of his unobtrusive adjustment to the life of the house and its various inmates — all this was far from simple. His eager, unhurried competence over his books, his unbored loneliness, the solid germinations of his reveries were all denials of simplicity. It was not simplicity that we came to see in him at last, but some happy equilibrium which had spun on in him longer than common and preserved certain elements of the boy in him undisintegrated, tiding him over until his own growing intelligence had caught up and preserved his instinctive reluctance to lean in any direction.

We had all felt it in our various ways — church and mission, summer colony, Katherine, Martha, we ourselves. He had resisted us, spontaneously, without aloofness, rejecting none of our experiences, but going on in serene response to some inner bidding of his own. Few as we were, we were a community, and we had tempted him with a fair array of the seductions of youth — pleasure and love and wealth among the indulgences, and religion and studious seclusion among the austerities. He had looked upon us all without taint of asceticism, and with a lurking amusement that had for some of us at least no irony in it; and he had retired into himself and waited. It is doubtful whether he knew, himself, quite what was going on in him — certainly not in the terms in which then and in the days that followed we were thinking of him. He told us all he knew, with a wondering gratefulness at our trouble and interest, and a humorous sense of his own unsatisfactoriness.

Behind the end of the summer the future was lurking for him; but meantime the moment had its rare charm. Perhaps he had caught the clue to his own dilemma, but if he followed it, as we guessed, in the unwearied hours that he passed lounging on the balcony, or seated with his arms about his knees near the sundial, it was in a serene mood, from which he would emerge at a word, lifting his frank eyes quickly to the speaker. He became for us the Charmides of our rustic temple. And if we could not, for ample reasons, play the Socrates to bring out the untouched harmonies of his spirit, it was not, I think, for failing to see in imagination the sunny upland meadows of the Arcadia in which he was lingering, or to catch behind his habitual expression the serious wonder with which he looked out beyond its borders.

What wonder that on the last morning, before the coach came to carry Hugh back to the pressure of the family — so typical of the pressure of the times, perhaps of all times — as we sat in our old places on the balcony, Philip should have broken out, in his poet's singsong, with the magic stanza of the *Grecian Urn,* touching by indirection the feeling that two of us at least had for the moment — the regret that it need end, the sense that its perfection was slipping with senseless equanimity into the nothingness of the past.

At all events, when it *had* slipped into the past the two relics, forgetting their tea and watching the sardonic shadow of the gnomon creep toward the moment when the shadow of the ridge should blot out all other shadows on the dial, had not the grace to be grateful to the gods for a sheer boon, but must sit and rail. For they had failed. They railed at the times. But, products themselves of their own times and people, they too, for all the perspective of their ironic aloofness, had failed to discover a path of fulfillment for so fair a promise.

III

DRAMATICUS LOQUITUR

III

DRAMATICUS LOQUITUR

I

NOT cynical (he protested). I hope you are mistaken, really. You say that my plays are bad — granted — that I can do better — even granted — but that I shrug my shoulders, say the public won't stand the better, and go on making the worse. You quote me with fine malice, but let it go at that. What you who sit here aloof, well bred and well read, have come to forget is a matter that is elementary to every playwright — so elementary that his instinct comes to take care of it for him, and so elementary that others looking in from outside come to scorn it.

There's a trite saw among the craft that the author proposes and the caste disposes, but I am not thinking of that. What I am thinking of is the thing that Dr. Johnson rhymed for Garrick — or was it for Goldsmith? —

The drama's laws the drama's patrons give —

You know the tag. That couplet has been ridiculed often enough since, and there are ways of taking it that are ridiculous. But at bottom, underneath the sense in which any panderer may quote it in his own behalf, it has a truth. It has a truth even more sweeping than the one Johnson had in mind — or at least was concerned with. Well, you have challenged me to defend myself for writing plays that are beneath my own standards and tastes, and my revenge will be to make you see, if I can, a measure of that truth even at the expense of damnable iteration.

You see, in my early obscurity I did write a play to please myself. It was my third attempt. The first two were the best I could do, but they were poor even to my own fond sense. The third pleased me. It even pleased a producer. And when I saw it on the stage I was thrilled. The dialogue filled me with exultation, the allusions found me richly responsive, the humor leapt with my answering humor, the pathos touched me home. I was rapt, I glowed, I smiled, I wept. And the house yawned.

I was desolate. The play lasted two nights. I don't say it was a good play. I only say it pleased me as the plays you know of mine don't please me — don't please me for your own reasons. As I say, I was desolate. I thought it over in chagrin for a year. And in that year I realized a number of things. At all events I put myself to school. Chiefly I steeped myself in Molière, and it was Molière that won me success with my next play, my fourth. You smile. But I assure you — to anticipate the language of your pedants — that it was what I learned from Molière that brought me to my second manner. Nothing could be more unlike, you say. And certainly my own plays scarcely resemble their godfather's. But I didn't speak of imitation. My enlightenment came when I saw the full measure of his conformity to the " laws " imposed by his patrons.

His problems, my problem, was one of utterance and understanding. It is everyone's problem, of course. But to the maker of plays it comes home to the quick. Poets and scholars and philosophers select their audience; besides, they may wait — they may accumulate an audience person by person, one here, one there, day by day. The playwright's audience is present all at once, and he can wait only till eleven o'clock. What he utters between half past eight and eleven must command a comprehension that is spontaneous, and for that little world universal. With him the problem is acute.

What I discovered, then, in that long winter of my discontent, as I pondered those bitter hours when the things I had uttered had so egregiously failed to command, from the rest, the response they won so thrillingly from me — well, what I discovered was that I had overlooked a great platitude. I had failed to build with old stuff. Oh, I had built with what was old stuff to me. What I hadn't done was to build with what was old stuff to them — that audience that yawned.

I see what is in your mind when I say this — that this is not a platitude, but only a touch of contempt for my audience, a shrug of cynicism at their expense. I assure you I have no contempt for my audience. And in a moment you will see why I say it is a platitude. You will feel let down when I repeat it. At all events here it is — that whoever you are and whatever you say, if you are to be understood you must build up what you say out of stuff that is old to those before you — old stuff and *nothing else*. Simple that I was, it touched me home first when a very young friend of mine came to me asking what one of my characters meant when he spoke of certain passing bullets as *ephemera*. I had tried to utter one little phrase, and I had used one little particle that was not old stuff to her — and the whole little structure fell, a house of cards. It didn't build at all.

You see the platitude — how the whole airy structure of communication — utterance and understanding — is built on credit. You are a dramatist and you use words. Well, every word has a meaning and that meaning you count on as old stuff. You build with other things too. You take certain knowledge for granted. You don't stop to explain everything — and even if you did you would use words. You make allusions, trusting a word or a phrase to call up an idea or a history. You try your wit, and in all wit there is a gap to leap. In every figure of speech there lies some unnamed association, and on that you count. All your audience will make out of what you utter they will make out of what is already theirs. You may build *up* something new for them; you can't build *with* something new. And what you build up is limited by what you build with. And there you are.

II

But I digress from Molière and his influence on my second manner and my first success. You smile again, and it *is* a matter of comedy. But I agonized over Molière. What I envied him most was a quality of precision, a bold confidence, a masterful celerity and certainty of utterance, an effect at once of bald economy and lavish riches — all this over and above his mastery of so many other things. Other things to be sure; but in Molière it is the qualities of his utterance that tie the last knot. Imagine him in the movie with everything there *but* utterance and you will see what I mean. Oh, the clue when I picked it up was threadbare enough. He knew his audience. But it was a thing *to be* known. It was of a homogeneity. It had attained to a quality such as comes rarely now to this people, now to that. The kaleidoscope of history had shuffled together the pieces of a coherent pattern. I suspect that the actual knowledge of that audience, the old stuff it had to build with, was very meager. But it was *theirs* — and theirs *in common*. It has been called an age of convention. Precisely. It was an age in which, in their consciousness, men *came together*.

I exaggerate for simplicity; I say a thing that can be true only to a degree. But here it was true to a high degree. I don't mean that men all agreed in their *explicit* ideas; I mean that they understood each other in their *implicit* ideas. Knowledge, traditions, manners, values, the very meanings of words

— all the things that were too trite to utter, were opulently *there* to be taken for granted, counted on, built with. Compared with my own task, Molière's was simple. When he tried to think of his audience he could know it without trying to think of it. The *honnête homme* was before him, a matter of course. And being himself an *honnête homme* he could, blessed man, write out of his own heart, and write for his own approval.

I took my lesson to heart. I had had my try at writing for my own praise. I had taken it for granted, simple that I was, that I was writing for my own likes — for you, for instance. But now, when I look even at you, I wonder, so to say, who you are, sitting here patiently listening to this tirade. Are you, I wonder, like a mixed grill I once sat among from one of our universities, men of infinite talk, learned men, but unable to converse? One of them could lecture on alkaloids, one on Plato, one on anthropoid apes. But when they sat together over their pipes and coffee they sank to the level of the village store. They had no old stuff in common to build out of. They were reduced to the lowest plane to find one where they all did live in common. They gossiped, they aired grievances, they talked politics. Individually intelligent, collectively they were stupid.

You — when I try to know even you, and say intelligible things to you all at once, I don't know, thoughtlessly and as a matter of course, what I can count on in common among you. Oh, you all put meaning to my words, no doubt — but the same meaning, umbra and penumbra, the same associations, the same suggestions, echoes, allusions? I don't know. Only, if you and your like were there to see my third play you didn't save it. You smile, and perhaps it was a poor play. But there we are. I am in the same dilemma. It isn't a matter of my intelligence, or yours, one by one. It is a matter of communication; and communication is a matter of community.

In that ill-fated play the little mosaic stones I used were old stuff to me — particles of my thought that I took each in a certain way. Each had its own character, value, color, tone, flavor, all that it meant to me. I called them up one by one, by means of symbols, and put them together into the new thing I tried to build in the mind of the audience. Well, that audience, I dare say, listened to those symbols, took them for what old stuff — if any — they were worth to them — each on his own — and built them into — into what, I wonder. They built them, no doubt, into what they could out of their own old stuff. But what was that? It was something tremendously different from what was in my own mind. And what I envied Molière he could accomplish because he and his audience were at one. He was an *honnête homme* among *honnêtes hommes*. The old stuff of his mind and the old stuff of theirs were the same.

Well, it was my play. And after all there was only one move on the board for me. I should have liked to elevate the stage — that ancient cry! But the drama rests on its audience — how shall I say it? — as a ship floats on the water in a lock. There will always be as good plays, I dare say, as there are audiences for them — audiences, I say, not individuals. Anyhow I wanted to write a play that would go — that says itself. But there was something more in my case. I was piqued. I had written a play that pleased me. Perhaps the world I had built — out of my own old stuff — was a fool's paradise, and I a lonely fool wandering within it. If my audience could have assumed that same old stuff would they still have yawned? I had no way of telling. Should they still have yawned I had been a fool indeed. It was my move, I say. I would use their language, see in their symbols of old stuff what they saw in them, count only on knowledge they all had in common, prune allusions to what would leap into all their minds at once. Then if I failed it would be because I was a very duffer.

III

I like our Americans. Perhaps that is why I had what is called success. Does it damn me to be partial to our countrymen? Still I have been much about at home and abroad, and here at home I've come upon what seems to me a disproportion of good human stuff — healthy natures, open dispositions, intelligences, clear minds, even cultivated minds. And yet I can't help seeing what makes some of our intellectuals a little sour. Our conversation, our theater, our pulpit, our literature, our politics, anything we do together through the medium of communication — oh, not only poor, but so much poorer than *we* are! Look you, I was following the clue of Molière and searching for a knowable audience, to address simultaneously in the idiom of their common mind. And there it was before me, that audience, one by one frank, informed, intelligent, but all together — ah!

I was baffled, but then I was curious. What I was looking for, of course, was the area where they overlapped. I set about it in deliberate search. I started out by looking for simple things — for songs, for legends, for tales, such as Homeric times, say, left for the Greeks of the great century, or the Middle Ages left for Shakespeare and his century — a common heritage, come into by every child at the fireside and painting the world to his fresh imagination. Of course we, we too, had songs and tales and legends by our own firesides, infinite in variety — but almost none in common. When I looked further I fared much the same. There was religion; but instead of age-old continuity of symbolic tradition we had a chain broken into innumerable links; we were a people of infinite sects. Even our Bible we no longer knew as Burns's simple Cotter knew it. Our schools? They had come, I soon saw, to value knowledge for its specific gravity, so to speak, its practical worth for this and that, and not for its community. Our reading? Well, everyone reads, but the press in its enterprise has kept pace with our diversity, and everyone finds literature to meet him where he lives.

What I found was infinite disparity; what the playwright must have is community. He must pare himself down to it no matter how much he has to throw overboard. Ah well! — you know how much one of them did throw overboard. It saved him from shipwreck at the cost of all the cargo he valued — he himself. Someone else might have got to port with more. This one saved all he could, and none of them do save much. Look at them! Even Molière would have had to pitch over the best of his — no less. He would have had to know his audience, and build on and out of what they had in common. And he would have found his materials devilish scant.

IV

Do I amuse you with my brave discovery of old commonplaces? I have another, to me still more luminous — perhaps still more old. All I had found so far was negative. Oh, I could put it the other way about jauntily enough. I could say to myself — Build with old stuff that is old to your whole audience in common. But, after all, that was little more than negative. It left me thinking with my own old stuff and then pruning my expression to translate it into theirs. But really if I were to communicate with them, build and have them follow with spontaneous understanding, I must have a look into the world of their minds. I must know how it felt to be there.

What was the world they lived in *like?* Lived in, I mean, in their whole consciousness of it. For the matter of that, what is the world any of us lives in like? My own, for instance? If I could see what my own was made up of I should have a clue perhaps. Bodily, I suppose, we all live in an identical world, along with the stones of the fireplace here, and the dog blinking on the hearth. That world is there, no doubt, and of course we share it bodily with the stones, and consciously, in a way, with the dog. But my world is distinguishable even from the dog's by at least the difference represented by what I've been calling utterance and understanding. At all events a dog never spread a civilization or wrote a play. And it is just what is implied in that difference that I was curious about.

When I looked, then, into my own I saw, over again, that the only world I could *talk* about, at least — and whether I was understood or not — must be built up out of particles of old stuff. Always, whatever I should say, I could only use words — words whose meaning I already knew. I couldn't go farther back than that. Words — that is, elements of idea I had identified with words — were the irreducible atoms out of which I must build the only world I could discuss. They made the primitive particles of the only world I could try to make intelligible. I could, of course, say something new with them, but I must build it out of these familiar pieces and out of nothing else. All that was new would be what sprang from relationships which I saw and pointed out between these familiar pieces.

All this I have said before till perhaps you are weary. But what I am after is this. Was this also the limit of the world I lived in — lived in in my consciousness, apart from any attempt at communication? And then I saw what was to me a light. For when I came to build up a thought, even for my own lonely understanding, all I could create anew sprang from relationships. Understanding *was* the grasp of relationships. It wasn't the separate particles one by one; that kind of thing even the dog could perceive. And if I were to grasp and hold relationships, they must be relationships between stable points or they would disperse and vanish as soon as they were thought. Perhaps a dog could go so far. No one can tell. The understanding I could retain and keep I could retain and keep because I could stabilize those points. And the points I had stabilized were the elements of thought I had identified with words. There was the fabric of my universe. What I could build it into was determined by the relationships I could detect between those stabilized elements as I conceived them. And there was the limit of my universe.

So much for me in my lonely world. And so much for anyone in his. But to me the final point of illumination appeared when I went on to realize how lonely those worlds might be. I had had the latent comfort up to now of the thought that we — those other worldlings and I — spoke the same language, had a pittance, at least, of vocabulary in common, and could so far enter each other's worlds in mutual understanding. And then even that comfort failed me. It wasn't words as words that those worlds were made of. It was elements of thought. And what any one poor gleaner gathered up into his sheaf of a word was a sheer hazard of his own experience. It disconcerted me to see how much one will have gleaned and how little another.

Crudely I utter the word *stone*. To Peter Bell it is a threat to his plow, or a thing to throw at a dog — and it is nothing more. But to another it brings up vistas by mountain or sea-shore, the windows of Bond Street and the Rue de la Paix, old rambles on the Acropolis, hours in laboratory and museum — an umbra of associations, too, of Mary of Magdala, of Ruskin and Venice, of Wilkie Collins, of Tower Hill. I might go on; I stop only for breath. And even so my illustration is unhappy; the term is a meager one even for the richest mind. Take words that are used to imply not things but thoughts, a word like *justice,* say, to cling still to commonplaces, and the chances of discrepancy grow rank. And when I remembered how many words there were, and how for each mind the meaning of each word hung upon individual experience, and how what they represented to each mind was what that mind built its intelligible world out of, I had my little hour of private panic over the possibility of any communication at all. It took only a grain of salt to rescue me from my panic. For all my reflections I was no worse off than before.

As for my actual audiences, I couldn't know what was in any given mind to make up the primitive stuff of the atoms it thought with. I could only get a hint of the gross discrepancies between one mind and another. Yet one hint I did get. Suppose, I said to myself, suppose I were forced to do my thinking in Latin. My Latin has grown dim with time, my vocabulary meager, and the meanings of the remnant terms thin. For the moment I caught the feel of an abject intellectual poverty. In Latin I should be an idiot. The most ignorant member of a Roman mob would have been a sage in comparison. And mind you, this poverty would be independent of my inherent mental competence; that is as it is. My mental poverty in Latin, just in the measure that it was more abject than it was in English, revealed the dependence of the thoughts I could think, the mental world I lived in, upon the number and individual richness of the particles of old stuff I had accumulated to build with. And I saw in principle the potential disparity between poor devils speaking the same tongue.

So much for the lonely worlds men live in in their own thoughts. But I was chiefly concerned with a common world they tried to come together in by communication. Well, when I saw where the discrepancy lay — what variation was possible in the actual associations about each term — and then looked out on the wide democracy I must draw my audiences from, I picked up a clue to things that had baffled me.

There have been glorious periods in the history of mankind, periods of high civilization, when the ideas of great minds won general comprehension, when a great literature flourished because it commanded an instant understanding, when harmony and justice reigned because men thought from the same ultimate premises. Have they been, I wonder, periods prepared for by a simple homogeneity of experience, a community of tradition, a community of meaning about the terms of a common language bred of a common familiarity with a few great exemplars of that language, before a heterogeneous life and literature broke down the clear import of each term? At all events if civilization is based on mutual understanding, the very possibility of mutual understanding is based on community in the ultimate silent premises of thought, the primitive old stuff posited unexplained, the meanings of the words we use.

Oh, I have spent covetous hours envying the mathematicians. They live in an harmonious world of thought and mutual comprehension. And they are no exception to the law. When they think they too must build with elements of old stuff and nothing else. Only, with them the primitive elements are very few and very simple, and so can be identical for him who thinks and utters and for him who hears and follows. This is the secret of their harmony, if it is a secret. For us the things we have to think about aren't, themselves, so few, so definite, so constant, and the primitive elements we think with can't be so either.

But you see where the hitch lies — and, too, where, had you the power, you would lay your hands. Not, heaven help us, by imposing ideas of your own. The world was never so full of ideas. Instead you would move to get men from the start born into the same world, giving them fuller and fuller community in those ultimate premises out of which each built the intelligible world he lived in. You would boggle for a moment, I dare say, afraid lest by imposing such uniformity you should thwart originality. And then you would see that even a genius can only build his thoughts out of old stuff, and can only be understood by those whose premises of old stuff are the same as his.

There, then, is my defense. You put me to it and you have paid — and with an infinite patience. You deplore the kind of play I write. Yet what did I do but do deliberately what that group of learned men I spoke of did by instinct and of necessity? In common courtesy I tried to make myself intelligible to all the company. I had had my try at building with old stuff that was old to me. It didn't build. If it was old stuff to my audience it was at least different; and if it built up anything in their minds, I didn't know, and they didn't care, what it was. I was living, don't you see, in an age when diversity of experience and education and reading was beginning to take community out of language — when the only really lively drama was one that dispensed with language altogether. All I could do was to approach that level. I did — and there we are.

IV

THE HIGHBROW IN THE DEMOCRACY

IV

THE HIGHBROW IN THE DEMOCRACY

I. THE HIGHBROW

THE Highbrow was nearing the age when tradition, slightly parodied, should dub him either a fool or a philosopher, and he was near enough the one in the estimation of many of his friends to make it desperately needful to be the other in his own. Unless he should turn out to be very much the philosopher he must turn out to be very much the fool indeed. The rôle he was in was not likely to win much gracious consideration from the box office or much applause from the audience. He must get his satisfaction from his liking for the part.

He acknowledged the need of haste. He knew that however common life was in the dreary collective sense, it was grimly infrequent for each one that took part in it; and the knowledge that his own one chance at it was getting on sent him, with an earnestness that his reviving humor smiled at, to a casting up of his accounts.

Old habits and old preoccupations had centered his sense of the one desirable thing in a knowledge of what the deuce it was all about. But he had lived long enough to have outlived a youthful expectation of ever definitely finding out. He had even had irreverent moments when it seemed as though in being thrust into a race in which the starting post, the course, and the goal were the three undiscoverable things there was a touch of divine irony. Still, indisputably, there he was. And to sit tamely acquiescent, not even to have won the right to fling forth a final opinion of it at the end, seemed to him weak-spirited. There were enough about him, indeed, playing a lively game with factitious and conventional values, but their prizes were so wholly in the external, enigmatic stuff of the puzzle itself that they seemed desperately irrelevant. For his own part, he felt a sharp duplicity in the situation, and he identified himself so wholly with the *consciousness* of the stuff as distinguished from the stuff itself that a mere accumulation of the latter seemed a kind of disloyalty. He felt his identity with a touch of defiance.

He was aware that this was the philosophic attitude, but there was little satisfaction in a mere posture. The question was whether he had arrived anywhere with it, and whether he could give some kind of explicit justification of what he was so defiant about.

That it was bound to be sporadic and unsymmetrical he admitted beforehand, for he had long discovered in himself a misgiving of that essay of the spirit that was known as systematic philosophy. He was obviously not a philosopher either in the technical or the professional sense. He remembered, as suggesting his attitude, with what crowing joy he had run upon a complaint uttered long ago by Mr. Frederick Harrison that he had sought vainly in Matthew Arnold for a system with principles "coherent, interdependent, subordinate, and derivative." If he felt in himself a like failure to pass a test so valiantly polysyllabic, he had for his solace the pleasure of the company he would rather have kept. Moreover, he had certain rational reserves about a thoroughgoing rational consistency. In the rarefied air beyond the earth, where reality could no longer interpose with its pertinencies, lay an infinite network of possible logical relationships out of which unnumbered systems could be built, equally symmetrical, and equally unimpeachable, and mutually incompatible.

Literature, therefore, at its best, seemed to him the justest reflection of the universe. It kept its feet on the ground even when it kept its eyes on the stars. He demanded of it indeed that it do both. And though what he valued in it was its view of the firmament, the view he wanted was from a known point. It was the connection that he prized.

Just now, however, he was groping for a sense of his own relation with the world. The thing to do, as he understood it, was neither to sit down wholly apart and think it out alone, nor to fling himself wholly into the midst of it and fight it out as one of the pawns. He must do enough thinking, to be sure. But his sense of duality made him aware that certain things were to be known deeply only through his own experience as part of the world — human nature in particular. And human nature was the principal thing that he cared about.

Years before, an elder friend of his, a Grecian, had said to him a few words that had clarified his own confused vision. From that time he had come to be aware of many rare men who sat in isolation, pursuing their reflections and studies in retirement, and looking out upon the world according to their various natures, but alike in this, that with Plato's philosopher they had been forced by the storm which the driving wind hurried along to retire under the shelter of the wall, content if only they could live their own lives and depart in peace and good will.

At first he had rebelled at their passive acquiescence, impatient at the dreary parallel, that one of them had drawn for him in an hour of humility, of those Mediaeval scholars who had kept the torch flickering through a thousand years while the gusty ages surged about them. He had never, for his own part, quite attained to their serene aloofness. But when he heard, listening to his own efforts, how thin and querulous his own voice sounded against the great roar of the world, as any single voice must in that tumult, he had alternate moments of chagrin and amusement, hardly wondering that no one would listen, or listening for a moment shrug shoulders and depart. What he had to say was too preposterous.

If he had been speaking on behalf of some established movement, the world would have understood him, taking his words in the right spirit as the aspirations and principles of a group, and not as the personal presumptions and scoldings of an individual. But so few, indeed, and so obscure were those whose principles he was in a collective spirit trying to proclaim, that it was, he knew, little wonder that he should seem detached and egoistic, supercilious, arrogant, boasting of his own merits.

He no longer, therefore, blamed the aloof for their aloofness, nor the world for its downrightness. But he had his own place to find; and when he tried now to be explicit with himself about his own relations with the world, he found that he too, in the measure of his sincerity, must be numbered with those who had got under the shelter of the wall.

Even there, as he found, there was a normal array of human nature, some of it not wholly to his taste. One evening as he was sitting in his library in glee over a sentence of Sainte-Beuve's there came a knock at his door. The sentence had no connection with his current reflections save, as he realized a moment later, that his detached enjoyment of it signified how shallow root his outer chagrins had taken. He glanced again at the sentence to fix it in his memory, so happy a criticism was it of an aspect of current thought and literature for which he had a vigorous dislike: "*At the risk of losing what credit I may still have with many of my contemporaries, and among them some who are very dear to me, I confess in matters of taste to a great weakness: I like what is agreeable.*"

With a smile still on his face he went to the door

and admitted one of his less intimate acquaintances. Such visits were rare enough to make him scent a particular occasion. But he was still enjoying his late find — it was the kind of thing that gave zest to his routine — and he tried to communicate his glee before inquiring into his visitor's business. He was unsuccessful; a look of puzzled wonder and preoccupation lay under the polite assent of his guest's face, and he gave over the attempt.

It was a cool spring evening, and the new moon, bright in a still glowing sky, was too beautiful through a long western window to deserve extinction. They sat, therefore, in the half light before the fire, and his guest talked. The tale was long, as tales of grievance are, touching from many sides the old story of merit and neglect. No doubt the case was real enough. The caller was a young man, an historian in the local university, of more than usual industry. The surprise lay in the note of humorless amazement with which the grievance was pursued. Wasn't history the chronicle of human injustice to the point of platitude? Our friend reproached himself with heartlessness without quieting his amused wonder at the way in which his companion summed up his own merits in definite lists of studies, courses, publications, and works in hand. There seemed to be something naïve and mechanical in such a casting up of accounts, something shop-like in such an auditing of the balance, something so curiously external and irrelevant that he was at a loss to reply without seeming priggish.

He rose instead and lighted the lamp. The bookshelves emerged from the gloom, and the soft colors of the rugs and draperies caught the yellow light of the shade. He noticed the restless eyes of his guest as they hovered about the room. Drawing up a table before the fire, and putting glasses and a decanter upon it, he poured out a modest bumper.

Upon reflection, indeed, he was surprised at his companion's lack of advancement. He put it down to accidental causes, for the man was of the type, as distinguished from his own, that both the big world and the official world of intellect were in the way of honoring, so close were the two grown in their animating spirit. Both worlds were of the same bent in demanding an external, estimable product. Clearly his friend was within the pale of their approval. The current humanitarianism had given a curious turn to the modern measure of a man. Its shibboleth of *service* was understandable enough; it wanted some contribution from everyone, and the specialist, measurable in lists of output, was the object and product of its admiration. What roused his wondering smile was the sight of a society that called itself humanitarian and was so out and out in its demand that every product obviously served humanity, and yet was so mistrustful of the attempt at perfection in the human product itself to which all this clamoring service must contribute. For it was clear that humanitarians had no patience for contemporaries who, by assimilating in their own spirits the significant things that had been thought and done in the past, summed up in themselves something of the human heritage of taste and of wisdom.

In a mood of momentary derision he set himself to contemplating the endless whirl of a service that was calculated only to accelerate the serviceableness of the servers. He went around and around in mental vertigo. There was no end to the circle, no stable norm to fix the ultimate aim of it all.

His guest's voice brought him back to the present.

"You dare do this?" he was saying, holding up his glass to the light.

"The laws permit it," our friend demurred. He smiled, catching in the question a long chapter in current Philistiana.

"I have heard — you will forgive my saying it — that it is held against you."

There was a tone of awkward friendliness in the other's voice that touched him, and he warmed toward the somber, distrait man who sat sipping his wine and gazing at the fire. For himself, he had no care to consort with the indirect and the scheming. The *esprit de politique,* which he had added in his own mind to Pascal's categories, won his frankest aversion. The friends whom he welcomed were those with whom talk could be free, recognized as tentative like a pleasant reflection, personal without personalities, spirited without effrontery — those with whom a look or a smile could relieve a mad assertion of its dogmatism or bitterness or malice, and take away from the utterance of a general principle the flavor of presumption. He wanted talk that was free from ulterior design. He loved humor without jests, and seriousness without solemnity. Of his present guest he knew little, but he thought he could detect beneath the harassed surface of the set face a lurking earnestness that went deeper than the personal disappointment of the moment, and he spoke as he would have spoken to a closer friend.

"I dare say," he replied to the other's allusion. "My trouble is that I've never caught the details of the life they want to create. They call it a life of service. And I want to cry out nonsense — that service means nothing until they define the end service is to go for. If we but knew that, what better could we do than try to reach it. If wine proves a stumbling block, why, we'll abandon it. Till then — " he smiled and held up his glass.

"Here's the eternal paradox of America," he went on, encouraged by a kindling smile and a response to his toast. "Our great experiment in individualism seems to me sometimes to have left us more sheep-like than the older orders left their victims. Service! Do our Americans really want it from others? The less American they! Honesty, yes, and honest work, and honest thought; but whoever wants more than that from others wants charity. No one else's services can make you the kind of being who embodies the life we are concerned about."

"Still," mused his companion, "wouldn't there be a kind of futility in the passive embodiment of it

— this ultimate being of yours? For life goes on and on, and the noblest ends seem to me those that in turn become means to still further ends."

"My dear," returned his host, touched and animated, "you have thrust home. But it seems to me that such a one here and there, moving and alive, would be a service in himself, a criterion for us, stable and stimulating, an invitation and a challenge. And I suppose, too, that since life is not a passive vegetation, we should find that our civilized product would not always be an object of vertu, stalking around with his attainments in his hands. If he had qualities of taste, and manners, and intellectual curiosity he could hardly keep from exercising them. They *are* an exercise. If he existed in varying degrees in a community, and we gave him his varying degrees of respect and emulation, we should get something out of him by way of service. He requires approval, for he has no easy life, and he needs the encouragement of respect. He has no arbitrary power. But the fact is that just that respect is what we grudge him. And here is the comedy of it — or the tragedy. We hate to think of anyone's really embodying the good we are working for; it seems unjust to the rest. The point, it seems to me, is this — that service, like happiness, is only to be attained as a by-product when some other end is pursued. Your teaching, for example, the most obvious type of service — "

He leaned over and drew down from a shelf a well-worn volume of Dr. Johnson and began to finger its leaves. But he caught in his companion's eyes a look that he had learned to know — a look of hurried impatience at the generalizations of out-dated authors — and he laid the volume on the table.

" Long ago," he went on, " a wise counselor and friend of mine warned me, in what I thought then was a cynical moment, that if a teacher was to keep his self-respect he must find it outside his teaching. I was a teacher myself, then, and have been one more or less ever since, and I rebelled indignantly. I hadn't yet learned the bitter lesson. I thought there was something disloyal in what he said. Teaching seemed the purest service there was. Since then I have found only wisdom in that saying. I am not referring to those clairvoyant moments when you see your colossal presumption in ever assuming the rôle of teacher at all. I mean teaching itself, with its eternal contact with immature minds, its over-simplified and over-dogmatic explanations, its dulling repetitions. The ancient scorn of the pedagogue has its ancient wisdom. There is nothing left for it but to make your life as you would apart. And then there occurs the paradox; incidentally you are the better teacher. You are no longer the intermediary puppet, the go-between. You speak from the heart of life itself. Your service is a by-product.

" And so, it seems to me, with service of all kinds. Given character, and intelligence, and taste; and then let a man do what appeals to him without thought of service."

"You assume a good deal — character, intelligence, taste."

"What kind of service is service without them?"

"Service itself is an aspect of character, isn't it?"

"A facile substitute, I sometimes think. It is so much easier than thinking, alas! The most hopeless part of it is the direction it tends to take. It tends to look outward and scheme for the control of external conditions. And conditions are made up so largely of people — other people — that it comes to express itself, as with our young intellectuals, in the itch to control others."

"You break, then, with the great ethical movement of your time. Isn't there a kind of futility in all reaction?"

"I dare say. But the faith in devices, in arrangements, in the management of circumstances, and the hope for some magic combination to make men both good and happy seems still more futile. It's a difference in temperament, I dare say. I can't believe in their devices and arrangements and their management of circumstances. There are so many such devices, all perfect. They *are* perfect. But being man-made they can all be man-unmade. Men aren't machines, and no magic combination can ignore the chief factor — I mean that incorrigible, self-willed animal man — especially the man who differs in opinion."

He refilled the glasses. In the silence that followed the coals settled audibly.

"Yes," the other said, somberly, his eyes on the

fire. " You touch off the great divergence." He looked around him and smiled. " This room — I feel like a youth to-night — you won't mind my speaking. I know that this room has grown out of your life here and your tastes, but it seems to me now that if I were to be given a room like this — fireplace, rugs, the quiet colors, the friendly books, the cool uncluttered stretches of writing table — the circumstance would remake me." He laughed outright. " It wouldn't do. I know the difference. I could never put my hand on a page with just the gesture that you used a moment since. I have books — more perhaps than you have here. Does it seem strange to you to hear me say that I've never cared what they said — *cared,* I mean — cared, for myself. There is the difference. I could use them in the trade of research and publication. That is the sum of their meaning for me. The thing for its own sake never called to me plainly; it was the trade that called. We are a race of shop-keepers, as they say of us in England, and we carry it on, this shop-keeping, even here.

He waved his hand toward the neighboring campus.

" Like shop-keepers," he went on after a pause, " we look for rewards, not in the thing itself but in something to be reckoned at the end of the transaction. We breed ourselves in this habit of irrelevancy, and we breed our youths in it too. It's America — or is it only human? At any rate we've invaded the seats of the muses; and now that we're resting there, or restless there, we despise them. We resent you, you who have caught their old serenity. We resent your presence, and we resent your aloofness, your seclusion, your quiet, your leisure, your books, your wine, your indifference to us. We blame you because you don't pretend that your work promotes either of the two great activities of the modern college — commercialism or reform, the commercialism that creates our miseries, or reform to relieve these miseries. We hate your concern for the past — as though there were any other place to learn from. Your culture exasperates us — and your Matthew Arnold enrages us. We are Philistines."

He laughed again, and was silent awhile before he concluded.

" Have I been bitter? I'm sorry; but we have only a single fling at life, and when we see too late the sorry mess we have made of it there is some bitterness in the first moments."

He rose to go.

" We know ourselves too well," said his host. " I suppose each of us could make out a bitter case against himself."

" Some of you, however, have done better; you have your compensations as you go — in the thing itself. It is all there. It accumulates with you. You pay, of course, in unpopularity, for you are disliked. You are undemocratic. But you have your reward."

When his guest had gone our friend returned to the fire, and filling his glass sat down alone with the sense of humiliation that comes from witnessing another's humiliation. Had he himself played the prig, strutting as the model of all the virtues they had discussed? He dismissed the personal question, however, as impertinent for the moment. The evening had not been altogether futile in other ways.

He had in general a grateful affection for the vine, knowing its humanizing power, and to-night he had seen it unlock in his guest generous feelings that had long lain pent in disused chambers of his mind. *In vino veritas.* And sometimes there lay in it too a solvent for the hardening effects of the world's pressure. Reflections crowded in upon him on this pleasant theme, but he put them off. The words of his guest had brought forward something closer to the heart of his current problem. He saw in them something of the world's attitude toward him and toward the aim he had set himself.

It struck him with force, when he had cleared away the irrelevancies of personal variation, that as his friend had said his thorn in the flesh of his local world was what they called his aloofness. He was accused of being indifferent to its militant causes and its sufferings, and scornful of its humbler pleasures and sorrows. There was enough justice in the charge to make him pause over it. But his habit of irony brought him quickly to an amused perception that when they accused him of futility and railed at his aloofness it was just their consciousness of his reaction upon them that stirred their ire. It was his descent from aloft that roiled them. His unpopularity was witness of his being in the thick of the fight.

To their accusations of scorn he could have retorted that the world was equally scornful of him, and that on the whole he was the one to suffer the most from it. But that was a return little enough likely to be effective, whatever the justice of it. Plainly he felt less irritation over the disparity than the world itself. He could not wholly acquit himself of an exasperating manner of letting the world know of his opinions of it. He had, on occasion, too little tolerance and too little urbanity. But there were other moments when he returned upon himself and admitted that perhaps it was he, and not they, who was mad.

For his own comfort, in the more general aspects of the case, he had long held to the old Platonic definition of the just man as the one who minded his own business; and though he knew with how much intelligence and humility so general a definition had to be taken, and how careful must be the supplemental definition of what his own business was, he tried to attack his problem in the light of it. The result was the curious discovery that the modern world seemed to have taken the opposite position, and to have reserved its admiration for those who minded everyone's business but their own. To his amused perception it seemed to have idealized the traditional life of the Scilly Isles.

II. THE DEMOCRACY

There was enough independent vitality in language, or in his manner of taking it, to make his habitual frankness with himself sometimes disturbing. Thus when he echoed his visitor's charge that he was undemocratic, he felt enough invidiousness in it to send him in search of palliatives.

He smiled at the Socratic homeliness of the defense that first occurred to him. He knew that he had no personal arrogance, but only a liking for those whom he liked, even to a preference in old days for a certain workingman's bar where he had often stood, squeezed in between plasterer and teamster, powdery and coarse, frankly liking it better than a more pretentious place frequented by the thirsty of a more elegant surface. It was not that his distinction in the humbler place had been more obvious, but rather that the thought of distinction had never obtruded there. He had felt more comfortably at home.

In his present reflections he enjoyed the impossibility of citing this defense among his respectable contemporaries, as much for the current feminine distaste for coarseness as from the current philistine distaste for other people's vices. But he was sitting on his own case, and made his own rules of evidence. If to be undemocratic, then, meant to have a sense of being generically superior and apart, he promptly acquitted himself. But the case was not so easily dismissed.

His attempts to define the current sense of democracy had always been unsatisfactory. He was not sure that definition of so connotative a thing was possible, but he knew that impossibility of definition was no evidence of unreality. He had but recently read a voluminous literature on aesthetics without, even in the end, losing his sense that there was such a thing as beauty. All the simple intuitions were beyond definition. No sage and no psychologist could begin to define the simple deliciousness of his morning coffee. Democracy was, of course, not a simple intuition, but it was made up of many subtle things to baffle explicit formulation. He set about inquiring into democracy, then, without much hope of getting at the thing itself, but with a reasonable hope of finding at least something of its force, and something of his attitude toward it.

The force of democracy was, as he knew who had felt its pressure, very real. It swept the main currents of modern life, and only in still backwaters failed to stir the depths and ruffle the surface. Equality was everywhere its capital word. And yet when he had pursued the idea with his democratic friends, in his favorite Socratic manner, he had no results beyond a renewed understanding of Socrates's death. Obviously there was no specific equality among men, either in natural gifts or in acquisitions. Politically it meant equality before the law; but the political aspect of the term was a small, almost negligible thing in the large vague force which it exercised in the current life. That force was still awaiting comprehension.

There was something real enough behind it all, however, to make him understand the exasperated resentment of those who clung to it without analysis. It had been too often the stimulus of generous thoughts and heroic sacrifices to be dismissed with a smile or disposed of ironically in the cloister.

He found a more promising mode of approach through certain avenues of his own consciousness. It seemed to him an internal matter bound up with the pathos and isolation of individuality. He put it broadly — that all the significance and all the value that life had it had because there was someone to be conscious of it; and so striking was that distinguishing trait, so tremendous was the possession of that one thing that cleft the universe in two, making of men the active knower over against the passive known, that other differences seemed to shrink into insignificance. In this ultimate equality, this common possession of a conscious autonomy, lay the essential dignity of men. Of that consciousness the largest unit was but the individual, and one man was an individual as well as another. In this all men stood together against the overwhelming mystery of the outer world.

For his own part he was poignantly aware of that individuality. For him, as for everyone, it was his one real estate. But for him, more than for most of his contemporaries, the absence of an alienating concern for possessions of any other kind threw an emphasis upon the simple claims of consciousness that made him peculiarly susceptible to them. The world lay about him — the grateful warmth and beauty of sunlight, the mystery of the stars, the fair colors of the marching seasons, the unwearying interest of the spectacle of life, the enhancement of life through friendship and love, the enlargement of vision and understanding through reading and reflection, the sense of companionship with those of other times who had shared his own way of seeing the world — there it was, the universe, embodied in the unique fact of his own consciousness. And as each man saw it in his own vision, that was, for him too, the universe. Here was the common bond, the human distinction; and here was the defiant assertion of the individual. Here, then, perhaps, in the dignity of this common distinction and of this self-sufficient individuality was the essence of the democratic faith.

He put his finger for a moment upon it, and smiled at the abstraction he had made of it. He knew well enough that he had rarefied the muddied and cluttered motives that had gone to the making of any real democracy. A good deal of lusty hate and envy, discontent, and swashbuckling adventure had got thrown into the balance at the lively and chaotic moments when such societies had been born. He knew, however, that this mixture of motives was universally human rather than distinctively democratic. But he was after some motive out of all that went to it that would justify and ennoble the cause. And it seemed to him that his finger was upon such a one. It looked to him real enough. Even in the envy and hatred that soiled the purer motive he could detect the latent question: "Why you and not I? I too am human, and what sanction other than human have you that you narrow the opportunities of this one chance of life that I have?" And with that question stripped of a discoloring malice he had an infinite sympathy.

Yet curiously, when he looked about him at the extant thing, what he saw had very little resemblance to what was beneath his finger. And when he had fixed upon the quality of the life about him it seemed to him dubious and contradictory. For the democracy as he saw it about him was not the assertion of this one namable equality. There were his countrymen, indeed, clinging to the old democratic phrases, the sturdy proclamation of personal independence and sufficiency. But apparently they did not want it. They did not want the austerity of that essential thing. When they saw it, or thought they saw it in his Grecian friend, for instance, they did not honor it. It roused their resentment. Had this aloof observer been less independent, had he *joined,* had he accrued to any group, he would have escaped their blame. His very self-sufficiency was the exasperating thing. He remembered how this friend of his had once stirred the anger of a fireside group of peaceable people by laughing that he was the only democrat of his time. They had seen neither his humor nor his seriousness.

The conflict touched rather than roiled him. He knew from inveterate experience the isolation of each separate soul, the horror of loneliness, the yearning for friendship, for love, for communion, for confessional, for absorption into some larger group, for some badge in the buttonhole. But he knew that however the confusion of tongues might shift the term, this loneliness was not the motive of democracy. No longing for particular sympathy would have prompted an organization of society whose essential feat was to do away with internal grouping, lifting all to a level that left each one unaccrued and alone.

No organization of society was so apt to keep chafed to the raw the sensitive spot of that longing for consideration as the one evolved by the democratic impulse. With no traditional limitations to the range of each wandering spirit, and no established relations to create a mutual understanding and a basis of intercourse, there was nothing left for it but a constant and particular discrimination on the basis of specific inequalities, silent reminders of actual deficiencies created by an impersonal and unjust Nature, chagrin at finding one's self too near the top of the table, pretension, rebuff, bitter uncertainty as to where one belonged — an unfair race in which each one started scratch.

Only a dominant spirit of independence could have longed for the individual isolation that goes with the abrogation of all groups and the equalization of all units. Essential democracy had won the battle long ago in a moment of heat. Even then it had been vigorously mixed with a group impulse against a common enemy. But when the consciousness of the enemy had died, and with it the common bond of the group, as he saw it dead now, so that each unit felt at last the isolation of the individual, the old nostalgia, internal enemy of the democratic idea, had crept back to its seat as one of the dominating motives of his time. In so far essential democracy was gone.

What roused his sarcasm was the perception of still another shift by which the term *democracy* was come to cover a range of motives twice removed from the nobler one whose prestige was still filling its sails. At first in the reaction from aristocracy it had meant in practice the assertion of men's common worthiness of certain things that the few had reserved for themselves. It had been unjust indeed to deny those who came knocking in the name of the spirit, asking to share in the full human heritage, and in the nobler work and responsibilities of life. There had been enough of restriction and oppression and maladministration to give appealing color to such demands. Few things were so moving as such generous aspirations.

But few things were so inveterate as human nature. And the democratic revolution of the Nineteenth Century had done little to change the normal run of human desires. There was still the old range of human qualities from bottom to top, from lowest to highest, and still the old distribution of numbers thickening in the middle and thinning out toward the extremes of better and worse. It was but natural, therefore, that when the say as to what should go fell from the hands of the few into the hands of the many a change should take place in what went. It seemed to him apparent that what had taken place, after the first outreaching for the specific things of which they had been deprived, was a gradual relaxation of the desire for the austere best, and a gradual sinking toward the normal desires of the middle run of men.

He paused over the triteness of this conclusion, inclined to smile at the easy patness of it.

When he approached the case from an angle a little more humane, however, he lingered over his judgment. What he saw about him in the way of taste and effective desire was not heartening. It was right enough that with their slow awakening to power the people should try to secure what they wanted. The distressing part of it was the kind of thing those wants turned out to be. Was he, indeed, become a fogy? Was he mistaking mere change for deterioration? Or was there a lowering of tone in the common speech, in the quality of the stage and of literature, in the dignity of public utterance, and in the activities of the church and of the schools? Was this reign of jazz instead of melody, and movies instead of drama, of O. Henry in place of Hawthorne, of economics in place of religions, of training in place of education only the supplying of new bottles for old wine? He tried to look at it so. And then he revolted. It would have been pleasant to acquiesce, to be good-natured and sympathetic. But his honesty, and the saving clarity of his humor held him back. He was too democratic to acquiesce.

III. HIGHBROW AND INTELLECTUAL

For our friend these reflections were a challenge. His own ancestors had fought to create and preserve the democracy. He knew, however, that whatever they had fought for, it wasn't that the people might have indiscriminately what they wanted; they believed that the people wanted a certain kind of thing. And for his own part he was restive at the thought of a democracy defined in any less spirited terms.

One day he presented his case to an arch liberal, a sociological friend at a " settlement " where in his own early days he had been tempted for a time to immure himself. And there they had it out, with the eternal inconclusiveness that belongs to the problem, to the clash of temperament, and to disparity of premises. He could never approach the place, and sniff its atmosphere, and feel the instinctive thrill of its immediate, intimate sympathies, without seeing himself suddenly as he must now appear to these modern Franciscans — as aloof, remote, scholastic, self-indulgent, shielded by a human philosophy, if it was a philosophy or was human, that let the world go by while he followed the life he preferred and the tastes he liked. He remembered how as a child, when he had cried till he had forgot his grievance, he had had to cast desperately back for it to keep his sobs convulsive. And now in this civic convent, with its rush of hopeful activity, its ardor of generous charity, its liberating freedom from the invidious distinctions of caste or culture, he had desperately to hold on to the point of view that in his own seclusion seemed so self-evident and right. Even to his own ears, therefore, as he thought back upon his conversation on his slow way home, his voice seemed to have been unwontedly shrill.

The two friends clashed at once, as they always did when they approached their tangencies.

"What I'd like, now that we are on our high horses and a little reckless of each other's feelings," he said, "is to get at the bottom of our differences. We're typical enough to serve for a general distinction — you here with your immediate sense of democracy, your quick sympathy for the unfortunate victims of it, and your vivid sense of an ideal future for it, and I off there aloof, a little critical of democracy itself, out of personal touch with the mass of it, and buried in what you call, a little scornfully, the past."

"We have something in common," his friend laughed. "You are called a highbrow and I'm called an intellectual. Take the current slang for what it's worth."

"Something else, too, I fancy," the visitor responded. "We're both forlorn hopes. The great inert mass isn't intellectual or highbrow, democratic or aristocratic. Rich and poor alike, it's a mass and inert."

His host demurred at that but he went on.

"You're less cut off from it, though. That's a

first distinction. I know the mass doesn't put through your Utopian schemes, but it does tolerate you — in its Sunday moods — as it tolerates Christianity. You touch its conscience, and it's Puritan enough to feel and respect the prick, even if it doesn't budge. You are the spiritual impulse of the times."

"You do us honor."

"Patience, and I'll undo it in a moment. The fact, of course, distresses me, but I can't help acknowledging it. Take, for instance, the two great touchstones of the period — of any period — current literature and current education. It is you who are the leaven. Your heroes and heroines of fiction, if they try to rise above Main Street at all, nowadays talk your talk. A few years ago — "

He crossed the office to a bookcase and drew down a *David Copperfield* that he had noticed there.

"You'll see what I mean," he went on, turning the pages. "Here it is. 'No words can express the secret agony of my soul as I sunk into this companionship [with Mick Waller and Mealy Potatoes] . . . and felt my hopes of growing up to be a learned and distinguished man crushed in my bosom. The deep remembrance of the sense I had of being utterly without hope now, of the shame I felt in my position, of the misery it was to my young heart to believe that day by day what I had learned and thought and delighted in, and raised my fancy and my emulation up by, would pass away from me little by little . . . cannot be written. . . . But I never, happily for me, no doubt, made a single acquaintance, or spoke to any of the many boys whom I saw daily in going to the warehouse, in coming from it, and in prowling about the streets at mealtimes.' "

He looked up.

"Half a century ago that was tremendously popular literature," he added, "written by the great champion of the common people. Your present sense of its snobbishness illustrates how sweeping the change has been in our fundamental silent acceptances. The shift, don't you see, is from us to you. Education strikes the same note. *We* used to be the leaven, and now it is you. Over against the mob-tendency of it toward the belly-interests, as Carlyle would have called them, you impose an idea."

"And are attacked and resisted for our pains."

"Naturally. But the attack is vital. You don't suffer from indifference. You are the troublesome conscience of the times. And I for one honor you for it. So much have we in common — the intention to put some idea and aim into the chaos of instinctive existence. And so I say we are forlorn hopes. Only, as the times go, I am the more forlorn, and that is what is troubling me, for I can't help thinking that my post is, in the long run, the only hopeful one."

"To us, of course," his host returned, "yours seems to offer still less hope, or none at all. At least it has been tried, and has left a very imperfect world, and a good deal of indifference to its imperfections. You tend to bury yourselves in the past, and work out for yourselves an elaborate, detached life, with costly institutions, numeraries and supernumeraries mulling over matters that time itself in its sweep has had no patience to settle, usages in dead languages that were never sure even when they were alive, motives in dead men that were never clear even when they acted on them, ideas in old literature that were caviar even when they were new. When I see all this, and the burden of it we still carry, and the prestige it somehow wins for itself, and the aristocracy it sets up, and its tendency to divert good minds from present and intimate problems, I can't help thinking that the impulse of democracy to ignore you is one of its happy instincts."

"You scrape bottom," his guest returned, "but in a shallow place, it seems to me. You mention excesses and abuses. Well, I dare say these irk me more than they do you. What does irk you, I think, is the real thing — a divergence at the very roots."

"Away back, certainly. I'm less and less able to see with you eye to eye. I used to. But the thought of these others dogged me; I couldn't get quit of them."

"Anyhow," our friend went on, "I want to have a try at the roots, and you can catch me up if I go wrong. I should say, then, that your sense of life starts with the individual and his personal impulses. Give him his animal needs, and over and above them a chance to exploit or express his own particular nature, and you have what you are after. Your sense of the fullness of life is in the widest range of spontaneous self-expression, of human originality. You thrill to the energy of life itself, and are restive at curbs and breaks and channels, lest something of that fine energy or some sport of originality be lost. And morally your sympathy goes out to the individual and his human worthiness of consideration, and his own aspirations and yearnings. Any humanly imposed standard that tends to condemn any man, if he is sincere and earnest, to a lower place in the general esteem seems to you an injustice. Do I touch you home? "

" You touch me home and you amaze me. My dear, what more can you ask? "

" For one jewelled moment I should ask a reasonable and not inhuman consistency. But of that in a moment. Just now I want to get at the point where we break in principle. For my part I look at your spontaneities, self-expression, originalities — the native energies of life — with a difference. They seem to me like a crop on which I have been set to work. They're the stuff I have to work *on* — some of it good and some not, and I sweat over it, weeding and pruning. They are all I have to work on, to be sure. But I don't identify myself with them."

" What then? "

" Why, then we come to the bottom, and if it seems a long way down, still I think it's the beginning of our difference and worth diving for. You identify yourself with these spontaneities, and I — you smile at my boast and so do I, but we are the puppets of our argument — I identify myself with the consciousness of something else. To me the spontaneities seem ultimately outside stuff. They come of themselves — pure gifts. I can take pleasure in them, but I can't always take pride. Do you see the difference? For I am something else behind. And there we are. It's the awakening of this something else that seems to me the real meaning of education."

"That dreary subject!" his friend smiled.

"I use the term for a state of mind. At all events where we divide, as I see it, is in the locus of our identity. And this is the great human cleavage. From here on we follow through, each on his own path, and get so far apart in the end that we lose touch with each other. We look out on different landscapes. As for you — everyone has his own spontaneities, and if you identify yourself there, and finally, why, one spontaneity is as good as another and one person is as good as another. As for me — if I identify myself with something behind — "

He paused.

"You feel your own vagueness," his friend laughed. "Do you expect a whole people to grasp it, or feel the force of it?"

"I don't. That is why I used the term *education* a moment ago. For the state of mind I want to imply comes hard. Do you think the worse of it for that? But that something behind — I know I am vague about it. I don't know what to call it. To reach it, and to set up shop there, is a kind of conversion. But I think I can appeal to you because you too set up a kind of fly-by-night booth there, as I'll take pains to say in a moment. You can see, though, that once consciously reached, such an identity imposes a new point of view, a more discriminating set of sympathies, and a new set of duties — selection and discrimination. I can't help feeling that what has been made of life has been made by a critical discrimination of the better from the worse out of the eternal stream of human spontaneities, and that what has been culled in this way is the human accomplishment *par excellence*. This tenuous accumulation out of all that human spontaneity has produced is the thing my final loyalty must go to. To preserve the lively remembrance of it, to further it, to bring up as many minds as possible on it, to cultivate and refine their judgment and taste by means of it — that seems to me to promise the only "progress" there can ever be. Aside from that we seem to be much like animals with *their* spontaneities. If we differ I dare say it is by virtue of what wisdom we get from this accumulation.

"There as I see it is the great cleavage. It trenches deep. Social theory is only one length of the furrow it plows. It separates romanticists and classicists, aestheticists and humanists, anti-intellectuals and rationalists, radicals and conservatives. And if you examine it you will see how fairly clean the furrow is. You romanticists, aestheticists, and anti-intellectuals are pretty generally radicals in political affairs, and the classicists, humanists, and intellectualists are pretty generally conservative."

"You are impartial, at all events," his friend nodded.

"Do those latter terms really seem to you terms of reproach? I was afraid I was boasting."

The two looked at each other and laughed outright in appreciation. Their divergence was thoroughgoing.

"I hate to quit at this point," our friend resumed, after a pause, "because from here on when I think of democracy and your special intensification of it I lose solid footing. What disconcerts me isn't that we should part here. I could understand that. The divergence is sharp enough. What disconcerts me is that you aren't content to part at all. And I have a notion that our confusion from here on, yours and mine, and most of the confusions in the large field of democracy in the world in general come from your sheer inability to be content with your choice. Frankly I don't see how you could be content with it; but then I don't see how you could make that choice at all. And now you must grant me a little bluntness. I'm speaking in good faith. You start with the impulse of those values, say — a sympathy with the spontaneities of the individual and his autonomous impulses. Well, you soon come to see that in the large social life of democracy these spontaneities conflict. It is their nature to. And you begin to clap on restraints. I believe you have rather outdone all history in that respect. Now that isn't consistent. Inconsistency, of course, mayn't bother you. You may well take it as the bugaboo of little minds. But I do want to know where your sincerity lies. Either you do or you don't believe that spontaneities are ultimate and self-justified."

They paused for a moment over that.

"You are wanting a landlord here, you say," our friend went on, "to improve a tenement. He objects, and you know that he is intending to cruise this winter in the Mediterranean. I said a little while ago that you were trying to put an idea into the chaos of life. You weren't displeased. What is an idea, however, but just the discriminating consciousness that I have been bungling toward — something behind and more authoritative with you than spontaneous impulse, and from which, as a point of view, you judge the impulse to improve the tenement as better, in this case, than the other impulse to cruise in the Mediterranean?

"Frankly, what right have you to any such discrimination if your sincerity is on the side of spontaneous impulses? Out of what do you get it in yourself that anyone should take it seriously as anything more than a personal whim of yours? If *you* go in for discrimination when you like you make out a case for those others who go in whole-heartedly for the cultivation of all that makes judgment good — acquaintance with human experience and thought and an intimate knowledge of the human mind and heart.

"We've touched here, haven't we, on the great divide. The worst and the best of judgment is that it does discriminate — calls impulses and the people that have them better and worse and does it frankly. You hesitate, kindly, to commit yourself. Sympathy holds you back. If you came over altogether you would seem to be abandoning a great mass of humanity who can be called equal on the ground of their autonomous and native impulses, but who aren't equal on the verdict of judgment. You prefer to come over arbitrarily when you please. But that preference seems to me to take away all the ground from under your feet. And as I said, I think it is the source of the great democratic confusion. You make of democracy a dodge."

"My defense is easily put," his host rejoined after a moment's reflection. "What I can't forget is that each one of these unfortunates that I sympathize with is as ultimate a unit as you, and that the ends they set up for themselves are as authoritative as the ends set up by you who are fortunate and cultivated."

"You mean movies, trade, newspapers, political oratory, vocational training, professional sport, automobiles, best sellers, total abstinence, advertisements . . ."

They laughed as the list grew.

"Part of those and those in part," the other responded. "And yet I think you would be the last to join a Primrose League for the promotion of the classics among the populace — Socratic Societies, Contemplation Clubs, Shakespeare Seminars. Forgive me, but don't you see that this list is really no more incongruous than yours. At the heart of these simple-minded people you'll find the universal love of happiness, and if they seek it in crude forms, still they want the best they know of. They aren't a mass when you know them. They are Robinson with his furniture store and his invalid wife, and his two sons and a daughter to educate, Kalematos with his fruit cart and his passion for Pericles and for America, Felix Goldman in his garret with his hack translations and his Utopian dreams, and MacPherson at his engine and in his labor union. They aren't a mass, but to themselves and to us they are as final personalities as your Burke or your Swift or your Socrates himself, each with his own one chance at life. Life offers little enough at the best for anyone, but for them too unspeakably little to deserve the scorn of the more fortunate. And your philosophy tends to ignore them. I have read a dozen volumes of one of your arch-humanists of the day, and never once a hint that in the world of his thoughts there were hungry children, or women hungry for life and thwarted by poverty, or men whose spirits have been robbed even of hunger."

"I see your point, of course," his guest replied after a pause. "And there is one part of me that will always go with you. The pathos of the individual, his one fleeting chance at life, his loneliness, his longing for happiness — they touch home. Still would your democracy have me do more than sympathize with these unfortunates, treat them with courtesy and consideration, see them if my eyes fall upon them, and speak to them if I know them? Would you really have me stop trying to spread the idea, for example, that as compared with *Hamlet* the moving picture show of even *Hamlet* itself is primitive and barbarous, stuff for inferior minds, and is supported by the unintelligent? I do sympathize with your simple-minded. But I can't help thinking that there is something false in an ideal that begins with a personal sympathy with thwarted longings and ends with idealizing whatever those longings happen to be for. Your sympathy may be the expression of your democracy, but if your democracy is also the denunciation of those who call the base base, and who praise the best at the expense of the second best, and who try to establish ideas of excellence, then I for one can see nothing worthy in it. It would mean the overthrow of all human values. Would you really have me cry up the ends these people aim at as the highest ends?"

"Not the highest, certainly."

"What then?"

" Simply the ends that come inside the range of their desire for happiness. For they are simple minds after all, and being human, and wanting to be happy in their own way, they deserve our sympathy."

" Ah, and is it you, then, who are democratic, and I who am undemocratic? "

" What do you mean? "

" Am I to say that those ends that I named are not the noblest aims, to be sure, but still are well enough for the lower part of humanity? The lower part of humanity! Isn't it the very denial of democracy to think of humanity in those terms? "

They were silent for another moment, and then his friend rejoined:

" The thing is, after all, to separate the objective from the personal, and keep the discrimination of better and worse from the weight of invidious blame. Who knows who is to blame? If sociology has done one thing of more value than another it has been to prick the bubble of personal responsibility. The young man who brought you up the stairs is the son of a harlot, and to blame him for the thefts he has committed when we know the childhood he has had would be pharisaical."

" By blame you mean malice and vindictiveness? "

" No, I mean the ascription of responsibility for the deed, and even for the motive behind it."

" I wonder," our friend mused, " whether it is possible, or even desirable? "

"There you are!"

"Is it possible to say that a man is a coward, and a bully, and a liar to boot without a touch of blame? What kind of a society would it be in which these things could be said of a man without raising a blush in him?"

"Ah, but when you consider that he is the result of forces, hereditary and communal, that he had no hand in shaping, how can you embitter him with blame?"

"I wonder whether your culprit wants to be let off on your terms. To call a man a cheat may make him ashamed; but I imagine there is less bitterness in that shame than in his feelings in response to your pitying: 'He can't help it, poor man — he's made that way.' There's less bitterness in being thought a knave than in being thought a fool.

"There's a more important thing, however. Moral values — we are speaking of moral values — are human values, altogether in our own keeping. Would you have us treat them objectively as we would treat a mole on a man's nose? They are values only because we value them, and only so long as we value them. Shame and punishment are a tribute to the culprit's humanity. They assume that he is a man and not an automaton. Shall I take it that you are here because you can't help it? Are you an automaton too?"

They laughed. Long ago they had had out together the old paradox of free will.

"I can't help the conclusion," our friend smiled

at last, " that it's only these poor devils that are automata. But then, where is your democracy? "

" In the end you've added to my confusion. Cromwell's wart and Charles's tyranny are to be thought of alike. Happily you wear that principle with a difference; you blame your enemies with a healthy sincerity. But just here is my trouble. When I try to think democracy through I'm repeatedly balked. Since the death and decay of *vox populi vox dei,* which may have been outrageous as a belief but was certainly glorious as a premise, I can't square the circles in which democratic thought seems to move. You seem to be wrestling throughout with inherent contradictions. And here is the sweeping one which troubles me most. It starts with a warm, instinctive sympathy with human individuals as such, with their spontaneities and originalities, and a sense that the fullness of life lies in the widest and freest range of self-expression. So far I can follow you. And then, presto! you hurl a sabot into the delicate machine. Certain spontaneities you yourself object to — undemocratic ones, for instance. Which means that you enter an idea of your own. Now that isn't playing the game. In so far you are offside. And you do, I know, want sanitary tenements, beautiful architecture, interesting books, and justice. If originality is your touchstone, architecture is good if it is original, regardless of its shape. If spontaneity is your touchstone, retaliation is just so long as it is spontaneous. If self-expression is your touchstone, books . . ."

"Your drift is plain enough," the other interposed, "but you chop logic."

"Like the White Queen, I'm trying to believe seven impossible things before breakfast. I can't take your fundamental idea seriously if you yourself abandon it whenever you like. And I can't take your objection to me seriously if you come over to my side at will. For after all the only distinction I claim is the privilege of discriminating the better from the worse, and overlaying a general sympathy for humanity with an intenser approval for some of it."

"The degree of that intenser sympathy," the other commented, "is the effective difference, I dare say. You tend, it seems to me, to lose sight of the rest, and forget that they are individuals. I come back forever to that."

"And my difficulty with democracy is that it seems to me to lose the advantages of a consistent discrimination without a real remembrance on its own part of the individual. That is not a paradox. In its public aspect democracy forces us to think of the people in a mass. We have the suffrage as a tribute to our individuality, but it can hardly be a tribute so long as everyone has it. It only means that we are over twenty-one. It is more common than the nose of which it is said scornfully to be the count. By comparison there is individuality in noses — large and small, aquiline, Roman, snub, bottle, and hook. I know that it is common to say that we have our proportionate influence in the affairs of government, and yet it is inherent in our very system that it is not the individual that counts, but the majority. And the majority is a mass.

"The distributive sympathy of democracy brings us, it seems to me, to a curiously impersonal, almost algebraic state of mind. For my own part, I've never been able to trace the individual opinion in that collective sense that you say ought to govern. Even I sympathize with the individual, being one myself. What I sympathize with in him, however, is his individuality, the subtle sum of all that he is. But when I realize how hard it is for one man to know what he himself thinks, even when he tries honestly to find out for himself; and when I see how much he has to give up when he comes, in the interest of action, to compromise with one other who disagrees with him; and how much more he has to give up when he has to compromise with two others, a thousand others, a million others — when I set my imagination earnestly to trace down what is left of that thing in him that I sympathize with, I can't find it. He is left to decide grossly between two gross alternatives; the nice delicacies of his own opinion, the things that give it the color of his individuality, are gone.

"You know the common verdict of our foreign commentators — even our most kindly one — that we fade, lose color, drift toward uniformity, lose the courage of individuality, scuttle to the cover of current opinion, deify the average. We all acknowledge the charge. Are we of inferior stock?

I hate to think that we are, and when I think of the history of our frontiers I am sure that we're not. I look for other explanations. Well, there is democracy, with its theoretic approval of majority opinion and the actual power of mass decisions. These tend naturally, it seems to me, to discourage the thing democracy starts out to champion. At all events democracy *does* seem to discourage individuality. And there I am."

"You would overthrow democracy then?"

"No," the other smiled at the inevitable question. "It's the idea that I'm concerned about."

"The idea that democracy is an evil?"

"The idea, among others," he concluded, waiving the temptation to launch into the defense of ideas as such, so dear to him, "that democracy has its peculiar dangers, that it solves no problems in itself, and that its most insidious danger is its tacit discouragement of a real individuality. This it does, it seems to me, partly from the force of public opinion, which democracy idealizes, and partly from another circumstance which democracy forgets — or you, at least, who theorize democracy — that individuality itself comes into its own only through development, through the enlargement of its consciousness, through being nourished on the best there is to know. Your current heroines of fiction, restive, hungry for self-expression, passionately hunting for their own souls — they are your type. Don't you see what they are sick of? They have no souls to find, so abstract a thing is the soul till it has fed on solid substance. It is this solid substance for the soul, if I may alliterate, the accumulations of the significant past, its experiences and its thoughts, that your highbrow at his best sets himself to preserve and further. And it is the democratic discouragement of this process that seems to me, sardonically, to menace the very end democracy sets up for its own.

" Have I abused you enough? Well, I'll return to my garret. I'm glad, for one, that there are people like you, here, remembering a side of life that some of us, perhaps, tend to forget. I suppose that neither of us is sufficient. A world of highbrows would be a terrible world."

" As terrible as a world of sociologists."

Our friend shuddered as they laughed their good-byes.

He continued in his old manner of life, of course. It was the only one he could pursue. He knew that in spite of the world's judgment, the best service he could render was to hold himself aloof, to perfect himself according to his own sense of life, and to react upon the world vigorously at his own points of contact. That was, Platonically speaking, his business.

V

AN HYPOTHESIS LET LOOSE

V

AN HYPOTHESIS LET LOOSE

HAVE the natural sciences ever been smiled at? They have been railed at by the ignorant and the stupid, girded at by the prejudiced, flouted by the misunderstanding. Even the brilliant have voiced temperamental antipathies; Disraeli on the side of the angels is one of the immortal jests. But they have rarely been smiled at — smiled at, that is, in frank urbanity by their friends.

The natural sciences are too intimate a part of the modern consciousness to be held thus at arm's length. Of all periods in history ours has — or at least boasts — the best right to the Terentian maxim, *Nil humanum*. And of all recognitions and acknowledgments laughter is the most human and the most humanizing. Not the laughter of malice, of course, or the laughter of derision — these are not enjoyments — but the hearty laugh of the frank intelligence. And whatever is not yet at ease in the gusts of sympathetic laughter is not yet wholly humanized.

Now the sciences are not an alien thing. They are not, for instance, physical nature, which is no laughing matter. They belong to us, and nature does not. They are ours altogether. All science is human knowledge and nothing more, and they can hardly be human without deserving a little laughter.

They are still, however, in a peculiar relation to us. Most men who have arrived at years of intellectual enjoyment date from a period when the scientific revolution was still grim enough to lend everyone, on whichever side, a straight face in all sincerity. The revolutionists were plain heroes or plain devils. The time was not yet come for relaxing the strained front of battle. Even a Clifford or a Haeckel in high 'Ercles vein was not occasion for smiles. Their voices were true clarion.

The revolution was successful, and science — to use the term for the sciences of physical nature *par excellence* — won to its side the intellectual world. Intelligence swore high allegiance to it. But even so science has not yet settled down to the amenities of civil life, and entered into the give and take, the banter, and the equalities of the domestic hearth of the mind. There is still a touch of stiffness in the family circle.

A little of the stiffness may be accounted for by the presence of an enemy outside the gate, and not a common enemy of the intellect but one particular to science. For though science has won over to its side the intelligence of the world it has not won over the unintelligence. And even now the unintelligent are lurking in the outskirts, threatening it with mediaeval interruption. It is not to be apprehended that science is in real danger, though history has its warnings. None the less the relations of science to this enemy are disturbing, and in nothing so much as in the fact that science itself is helpless against it. Science has only one weapon — the reason — effective with the intelligent but useless against the unintelligent. And until it is on terms of ease and laughter with its own family within, it can never be quite at ease over the enemy without. Only with the aid of its domestic allies can it effect a contact and offer battle. The time is especially ripe, therefore, for the general intelligence to bare the grounds of its sober amusement.

There is a degree of boldness, I know, in this suggestion of equality about the intellectual hearth — of something there with the right to judge science as a peer. A cat, of course, may look at a king; but the cat frankly remains a cat and the king a king. And a doubt remains whether any aspect of the intelligence with an itch to smile at science may not itself be the butt of whatever laughter comes last — a doubt whether there is anything there to which science is judicially answerable. Even if there is it is doubtful whether it can be brought to laugh with much gusto. Real laughter means a nimble leap of the mind over a gap of tacit acceptances. And the tacit acceptances at the intellectual hearth are all on the side of science.

None the less the venture is worth trying, however quixotic. It may be even more rueful than a tilt against the windmill; it may be a tilt against the wind itself. For the particular foibles of which science may be suspected are not embodied in any official creed or in the rubric of any institution, as the foibles which science itself tilted against in the days of its militancy were embodied in church and school and formulated tradition. They live in the atmosphere.

I

What is so intangibly elusive in the atmosphere, and none the less penetrating for that, is a prevalent sense that science is a sort of last word in the intelligence, a supreme court of the mind. Witness the ardor, almost the passion, with which, once the point of view became established, the most impossible things began to designate themselves as sciences — not in the older, homely sense of orderly knowledge, but in the special sense which the sciences of physical nature had gathered about them. Political theory, sociology, history itself, even literature, rushed under the scientific aegis, and assumed the gait and manners, together with something of the fine authority of their new liege. The comedy of these metamorphoses will some day be written.

Does common sense however — to start from there — place science in this supreme position? Following its somewhat casual methods we tend rather, I think, to feel that we live first and pursue science afterwards, that we find ourselves alive and then, looking about us for means of enriching the character of our existence, discover late in the day that a knowledge of the material scene we play our comedy or our tragedy in will aid us in this attempt.

After all, we are inclined to say, we do, collectively and individually, tolerate science or not, cherish it or not, pursue it or not, according to our prior judgment of its value to us. Thus common sense.

It is only right to state with nicer precision the distinction implied in what has just been said between science and that anterior judgment to which science is thus put down as subordinate. As already indicated I have used the term *science* in its popular sense to designate the natural sciences, physical and biological, those which are concerned with the material universe as it comes home directly or indirectly to our senses — the constitution of matter, the " laws " of energy, and the action and interaction of material phenomena under the goverance of these " laws." The sciences can deal, of course, only with what the mind is conscious of, but they hardly deal with all that the mind is conscious of. They select. Outside their selection is a field of other things that we are conscious of no less, notably the intimate feel of life as a thing lived — delights and miseries, appreciations and disgusts, sympathies and antipathies, aspirations and hopes and fears, impulses and affections. And in relation to all these there are our sense of perfections, our sense of relative values, and our judgments of things as they make for or against, or measure up to, these perfections.

The zeal of science, however, has sometimes gone so far as to say that only the former array of data, the sense data, are valid, and that the latter, the data of feeling and intuition, have no place among the verities out of which we are to make up our total conception of existence — well, that only a part of what we are conscious of belongs to the completed picture of all we are conscious of. Huxley himself yearned to such a view in his impatience with all thought but the thought of natural science. Some of his successors have been bolder. With militant bluntness the intransigent Haeckel bristles with the assumption. And tacitly or explicitly the assumption has been latent in all the literature of science that has crossed the border and dealt philosophically with the problem of life.

The right assumed by common sense to smile at science when it strides with this gait comes with the recollection that science itself is validated by data of the consciousness which belongs to the proscribed list — to an affection of the intelligence, to curiosity, to a value for knowledge and truth. We have other affections, but these are sheer affections none the less. And science takes its rank by their grace. Just now, happily, it ranks very high, but there have been times when it ranked very low, and there are people even to-day among whom it ranks very low. In so far, at all events, the dependence of science upon the turn of our affections suggests not its supremacy but rather its subordination. And common-sense tends to smile at the inverted reflection in the mirror of current acceptances.

II

It is a commonplace of human thought, however, that common sense, for all its stubbornness and inertia, has again and again had to yield to more precise reasonings. It has given up the daily course of the sun about the earth in favor of the earth's own revolution, and now, with Einstein, it may come to yield the earth's revolution to the mere relativity of that motion in which it is just as right to assert again the daily course of the sun about the earth. Clearly the early missionaries of science — I return to them, for it was they who established the implicit sense of the supremacy of science — had something in mind outside the scope of common sense. Did the lucid pleas, however, by which they put their case so compellingly really by their own logic place it in its supreme position?

They began by pointing out the importance of science. The very titles of those early militant essays and addresses point to importance as the dominant note: Spencer's *What Knowledge Is of Most Worth?;* Huxley's *The Educational Value of the Natural History Sciences;* his *Liberal Education and Where to Find It.*

> "Thus," concludes Spencer, "to the question with which we set out — what knowledge is of most worth? — the uniform reply is — Science. This is the verdict on all the counts. For direct self-preservation, or the maintenance of life and health, the all-important knowledge is — Science. For that indirect self-preservation which

we call gaining a livelihood, the knowledge of greatest value is — Science. For the due discharge of the parental function the proper guidance is to be found only in — Science. For that interpretation of national life, past and present, without which the citizen cannot rightly regulate his conduct, the indispensable key is — Science. Alike for the most perfect production and highest enjoyment of art in all its forms, the needful preparation is still — Science. And for purposes of discipline — intellectual, moral, and religious — the most effective study is, once more — Science. The question which at first seemed so perplex, has become in the course of our inquiry comparatively simple. We have not to estimate the degrees of importance of different orders of human activity, and different studies as severally fitting us for them; since we find that the study of Science . . . is the best preparation for all these orders of activity."

This is egregious, perhaps, but it is typical. The note of *importance,* of *worth,* of *value,* ran like a song through them all, explicitly in their utterances, and implicitly in the fact of their pleading before a reluctant humanity, upon whose verdict their success depended.

Importance, worth, and value! "That man, I think," says Huxley, "has had a liberal education . . . whose intellect is a clear, cold logic engine. . . ." This is but one in a noble array of requisites, but it is one. We may ask for logic, then, with frank insistence. Well, in the clear, cold logic of unbiassed thought *importance, worth,* and *value* are a confession. It is a more profound one than appears on the surface, and a more sweeping one in its consequences than I can hope to make appear. But it lies at the heart of these reflections, and I linger on it.

The profound revolution of the Socratic philosophy, it has often been pointed out, was affected by its return from natural science, as a center for the intellectual life, to a moral center. If that shift was momentous, the same degree of significance attaches to the revolution of the last century. For that revolution was a return — complicated and confused, it is true, by an intrusive theology — from the moral to the naturalistic center. The return was effected practically. Was it effected logically? For *importance,* and *worth,* and *value* are meaningless unless they imply an anterior judgment. They put science at the bar of a superior court.

III

The mere common sense of all this is so obvious that something must have been omitted from the claims of science as given in the previous section. No one thinking of science in the positive sense of that description would assert for it more than a high place among all our intellectual pursuits. Certainly no one would have thought of it as covering the whole of the intellectual life, since its subject matter is limited to the data of the senses, and its purely quantitative methods are appropriate to only that part of all that comes home to the consciousness. Not even the unintelligent would be hostile to it if all they had associated with it were the accumulation of knowledge about the physical universe. If there is unrest about the intellectual hearth and hostility among the unintelligent, something else will be found to account for it.

Anyone who knows human nature will know that there is not a great exaggeration in the paradox that matters of faith are more powerful with men than matters of knowledge. It was the old tenacity of faith in the account of creation contained in *Genesis* that made the fight of the first evolutionists, with mere knowledge for weapon, so bitter. And it was this perception that led the heroes of that movement to feel that, while their specific mission was to correct the current conception of the physical universe in the light of positive knowledge, they had a still more important mission — to free men from the tyranny of old habits of thought, of habits of belief without positive knowledge, of trust in sheer authority. "To take nothing for truth without a clear knowledge that it is such," was the new creed, accepted from Descartes and reiterated again and again in the stirring years of the last years of the century.

It was for this reason that they went so apparently out of their way not only to attack the prestige of the *Bible* but to sweep up in their condemnation the whole tribe of speculative philosophers. Plato, especially, suffered as he had not suffered since Aristippus, his contemporary.

"The Platonic philosophy," Huxley declared, "is probably the grandest example of the unscientific use of the imagination extant, and it would be hard to estimate the amount of detriment to clear thinking effected. . . . Platonism and its modern progeny show themselves to be at best splendid follies."

Herbert Spencer is even more contemptuous:

"Time after time I have attempted to read now this dialogue and now that, and have put it down in a state of impatience with the indefiniteness of the thinking. . . ."

The offense of these philosophers was that they had set adrift speculations which seized upon men's vision and led them to get their bearings in the world, not patiently on the basis of verified fact, but promptly at a stroke on the wings of imagination. The whole method was at fault. And the supreme virtue of science was that it inverted this method, satisfied to build only on the basis of verified fact, patiently, meticulously, step by slow step, taking nothing for truth without a clear knowledge that it was such. Science asked only one concession — that the whole universe was to be conceived, by a prior stroke of imagination, as a vast mechanism under one system of immutable, impersonal laws, which governed all that could be known by the consciousness and even the consciousness itself.

Really this was not quite fair! If the litany of "infinite patience, meticulous care, ultimate verification, skeptical progress step by slow step" had not been so often chanted, and its fine reasonableness had not been brought so utterly home, the congregation would not have been so credulous as they proved to be, when this same choir lifted their voices, and on the wings of imagination, far in advance of their verifications step by slow step, launched into the empyrean with a speculation of their own, whose fine audacity was unmatched by the tentative flights of a Moses or a Plato. If the prestige of its pedestrian sureness had not given an air of positive finality to whatever marched in the name of science, surely men would have smiled at the spectacle.

IV

Here was duplicity! It was not intentional, one may be certain. But the great ideals of the scientific revolution were positive verification and the cool impersonal use of reason. And here were the men of science flouting both — immeasurably in advance of verification, and ridiculing speculation with a speculation of their own.

A good many of the confusions of our time will, I imagine, when looked back upon in perspective, prove to have centered about one-in-chief — the confusion between science and men of science. Here at least such a distinction needs to be made. And if it is made, and we remember that men of science are men as well, their duplicity can well be understood. In their inseparable capacity as men their own imaginations were touched. Like Plato they dreamed. Perhaps they had not Plato's consciousness that they were dreaming.

They dreamed of a limitless universe, which none

the less their dreams could compass — a universe voyaging through time under the governance of a single system of immutable laws, impersonal and mechanical. In that perspective mankind appeared, it is true, but it appeared *in perspective,* an inconspicuous item, one among many species of living things, themselves mechanical automata, inhabiting one of the almost negligible masses in the scarce-affected emptiness of illimitable space. In this vision older notions long and dearly cherished were shockingly bouleversed. Men's ingrained sense that they were the ones for whom the universe was created, special protégés for whom the whole affair was run, was suddenly become nonsense. Their natural egotism, their sense that they were the heroes of the cosmic drama, the center of momentous issues, became promptly ludicrous. They had assumed that they and their ideal way of life were the points about which all that they could know took on its only possible significance, while all the time they and their way of life were but an insignificant mote in the magnificent vista of the whole. They invited laughter, and laughter was their prompt reward.

This, for men at large, was the scientific revolution of the last century. How much of it will withstand the revolutions of the future it is profitless to speculate about. Our question is its relation to the intelligence of the present. And as it stands it seems at one or two points a little awry. For if mankind are as insignificant as that, men of science are no less so, and this vision no less than they. It is their vision; they conceived it. It is not science, exactly. Even science is knowledge living in the human consciousness. But this is not even science with its objective equivalents open to scrutiny and verification. It is a dream, a vision, a creation of the speculative imagination. And its existence is in the imaginations of those who conceive it.

If men of science, when they launched their vision, had placed a consciousness outside and above the mechanistic universe, one to whom it was not a dream but a reality, they would have attained a greater consistency. But they pointedly excluded such a deity. As a consequence there was nowhere for it to exist but in their own minds. They were the center. Much use was made at the time of the term *anthropocentric,* and it is still a term of some force of derision. It is interesting, therefore, to remember that their chief antagonists did conceive an outer consciousness for whom mankind were poor enough creatures. But for themselves, they had no gods. With a little audacity and not too much seriousness one might ask which vision was the more anthropocentric.

V

It is an interesting speculation whether, if one could curve his line of sight about the world and behold himself in perspective at the end of the vista, he would thenceforth act in character with the proportions of the beholder, or the proportions of the beheld. The situation is open to comedy. Our scientific revolutionists, in something of the same dilemma, scarcely hesitated in their choice. However insignificant and helpless mankind became in their vision of the universe, and they themselves as part of mankind, and their vision as a product of their own, it became a thing of great importance for mankind to see this vision. Otherwise it would not exist.

One is more than tempted to fancy that they did, unawares, conceive an aloof, all-seeing intelligence that looked down on the universe of the scientific vision and saw as a reality what to the human mind was only an idea — saw humanity itself as but petty automata in the drive of immutable forces. Only so could the vision have attained a greater validity than the human minds that conceived it.

If one were to pursue this fancy one might detect certain telltale traits in the dreamers, vestiges of the traditional *odium theologicum* — championship touched with heat, for a matter of faith; an ardor for proselytes; and a certain humility mixed with a certain arrogance. They could not, of course, acknowledge a god into whose counsels they had been admitted. Yet the relative insignificance of mankind, and the mechanistic character of all life and consciousness robbed their gospel of any significance as coming from themselves. It could attain validity only from on high.

VI

Anyone who has had the patience to read so far will be irritated by a sense of unfairness running through all that has been said. The description of science already given, for instance, left out of account a factor that is as much a legitimate part of science as the material data with which it deals — the pioneering imagination. Hypothesis is the very means by which science marches over the border. And to fling at it a *tu quoque* when it ridicules the speculative philosophers is to leave out of account certain differences which men of science have always felt to exist between the two processes.

Hypothesis is, of course, a leap of imagination in advance of verified fact, and in so far an act of speculation. It is thought of by men of science, however, not as something of independent validity, but as a temporary agency, a technical means, a scaffold used in the building of a solid edifice. The solid edifice is the thing.

Master builders, however, tear down their scaffoldings before they turn over the completed structure. And it was the peculiar boast of the master-builders of science that nothing was to be accepted but the solid building itself. And just here is the crux. The hypothesis of a mechanistic universe has been turned over, in effect, as an organic part of the solid structure.

So long as it is kept in leash as a working hypothesis, it has an unquestionable function. It does something imperative for the working scientist in his laboratory. In the blank void beyond the frontiers of actual knowledge it blocks in a tentative pattern for further advances. And as a kind of shibboleth of the workshop it serves to screw up the courage and stiffen the perseverance of the workers in that dishearteningly complex field. It keeps them from stopping at any trying point with the easy excuse that from there on another order of factors, not amenable to mechanical law, become operative. As more and more is known, the field of science becomes more and more intricate, and its problems harder and harder. Without such a working tenet science might lose heart. As a scaffold in the actual operation of building it is useful, even imperative.

But when the leash was slipped, as it was from the first, and the hypothesis escaped into the world at large, among men who were not working scientists, it took on another color. The scorn of science for speculative philosophers left it no legitimate function in the world at large; its only function was in the laboratory among those who were pushing over the border of positive knowledge. Once on its own feet, so to say, it was on all fours with any other speculation.

VII

This shift has been the heart of the matter from the first. And the subtlest comment on it lies in the fact that those who were most active in effecting its release did not themselves believe in it in just that aspect of their own lives which they shared in common with those upon whom they were releasing it.

The sincerity of the Spencers, the Huxleys, the Cliffords, and indeed of that whole generation of militant scientists has never been questioned. In reading the essays and addresses of Huxley, say, with their clarity and their profound reasonableness, one is moved yet more deeply by the feel of their genuineness, the ring of their fine integrity. Yet this sincerity could not be real — and there is no doubt of its reality — if Huxley had genuinely believed in his hypothesis of a mechanistic universe — believed it, that is, as a humane philosophy and not merely as a laboratory policy. To believe it as a philosophy would at once imply that mankind themselves were but helpless leaves blown about in the winds of circumstance, blind automata whose least act and thought and feeling were but mechanical reactions determined fatally from the beginning to the end of time. To believe it as a philosophy was to believe himself also but a helpless puppet, a marionette babbling and jigging on the rostrum. To believe it was to nullify all thought itself. And the thought of education — Huxley was urgent in this matter above all others — was the last fatuity for one who held men to be in this plight. In the end it is incredible that Huxley believed in this utter helplessness, or that if he did he should not have looked at himself and laughed. He was a wit, Spencer assures us, as well as a man of science.

Mathematically Achilles can never overtake the tortoise; in real life he does. It is consistent with a perfect sincerity to hold both contentions true — one in moments of mathematical reflection and one in the practices of actual life. The folly would be to confuse the two systems of thought, and deny the actuality on the grounds of mathematical impossibility. It is consistent in the scientific workshop to conceive a mechanistic universe in which even the conceiver, looked at objectively as in a mirror, is a mechanism; and at the same time to know — as one knows that Achilles overtakes the tortoise — that in relation to life as a process of living such an hypothesis is unintelligible. Any conception that negates the mind that thinks it is unintelligible.

It is this shift from the workshop to the world that has been the source of our immeasurable confusions in the matter. The very sincerity of the great men who effected the shift is the best witness of how inapplicable the hypothesis is in the world into which they launched it. One understands how even a Huxley, with the emphasis of his attention and his ardor spent in behalf of the workshop, should forget the distinction — forget that as a man in the world propagating the scientific faith even he himself was acting on an assumption that contradicted his hypothesis. None the less there is comedy in the spectacle.

VIII

The most outspoken of the present enemies of science are intellectually so negligible that it is difficult to speak of them with sympathetic fairness. One aspect of their wrong-headedness is especially intolerable to intelligence — their stubbornness in pushing their religious credences into their explanations of physical matter. It was this stubbornness that made it necessary from the first for the knight-errants of science to go tilting in the highways and byways to win a place in the world for their rational processes. But the motto on the reverse side of the scientific banner, unfortunately, was "A Roland for your Oliver." For having won their way with the intelligent in the explanations of physical matter, they began to push their own credences into the explanation of morality and religion. The mechanistic speculation was there to give plan and significance to physical investigation and give heart to the investigator. What plan and significance could it give to men at large who were not investigators on the frontiers of physical knowledge? In the field of life as a thing lived, among the responsibilities and problems which all men have in common the mechanistic hypothesis offers no plan and significance. It specifically nullifies plan and significance there. If men of science voluntarily plodding in the laboratory need to be heartened by a vision of the whole — however visionary — lest they give over their efforts when effort seems to be fruitless, men in the world at large troubled by doubts not of their own seeking are no less in need of a vision to hearten their persistence in times of discouragement. And the mechanistic vision has nothing but discouragement to offer them.

Beneath the unintelligence and stupidity of the current revolt against science one may detect an instinct as valid as the logic which confutes *Genesis*. And one who sides with science in that conflict can only stand aside when science falls into stupidities of the same order. Only, being intelligent, he will not attack science, for the stupidity is not of science but of men of science. And against the foibles of men, on the one side as on the other, his best weapon is intelligent laughter.

IX

At the outset I spoke of a certain unrest at the intellectual hearth, a stiffness, an illness at ease of the intelligence as a whole, and I implied that the unease came from the maladjustment of science, its reluctance to take the position its significance logically placed it in. Now intelligence utterly at ease and at rest is all but a contradiction in terms. It is a fidgety member at best. Still the same impulse that makes it imperative for science within the bounds of its own province to erect an hypothesis which should tend to orientate and harmonize its data and render its principles consistent, applies no less to the whole intelligence. It too needs a center of orientation about which the data it surveys fall into some measure of steadying relations.

Men of science have assumed that the scientific hypothesis covers the whole scope of the intelligence, as we have but now considered, and a kind of tacit acceptance of this belief has got abroad. But science itself has never established this sufficiency. It has done no more than establish itself as one among many fields of intellectual interest — of great importance it is true, but by that very fact subject to a judgment that finds it important. And the conflict between this anterior judgment on the one hand — which looks out on life and finds science one among many pursuits — and the spokesmen of science on the other hand — by whose speculations all the data of consciousness come within the scientific net — this conflict marks the present impasse at the intellectual hearth.

Egotists though they are, children, in enumerating a company, will often omit themselves from the count. If we look back now on the militant revolutionists of the last century, it is not hard to perceive, with a smile, that they too, gazing out objectively upon their vision, which seemed so all-inclusive to the eyes of their faith, naïvely forgot to count themselves — forgot, that is, to count their out-looking selves. And the discipline which they imposed to enable men to share their vision, took care of the vision indeed, and even adjusted men's eyes to it, as to a telescope. But it neglected the other hungers and affections of the observers behind the instrument.

Neglected hungers and affections grow ravenous. And the neglected hungers and affections of the mind as a mind, the immediate love of life as an experience encountered and felt, not at the end of a telescopic vista but here and now — the love of beauty, of good, of truth, and the love of an understanding of life that compasses and harmonizes these most intimate and real experiences of the consciousness — such hungers and affections have stirred a counter revolution, both irrationally among the unintelligent, who have been but waiting for an opportunity, and rationally, if not among the intelligent at least among the intellectual.

And the sardonic thing has happened. It is not in the arena of science that the new phase of the conflict is to be fought out, any more than the old. Science has still to justify itself to the whole mind in defenders, and rebels, and spectators alike. And the whole mind is just what, since the triumph of the revolution, has been neglected. The old revolutionists and their antagonists too were brought up in a tradition that cultivated the mind. The fullness, the richness, the fine clarity, the sweet reasonableness of their old appeal were met by a fine clarity and reasonableness of understanding in response. For science is a human accomplishment, and its glory is the glory it attains in the appreciative mind.

The revolution was won. But the new conflict — its defenders, rebels, and spectators alike cultivated in the new discipline, a discipline that has forgot the out-looking mind in its vital reality for the sake of conceiving it at the end of a vista — promises a spectacle of bathos.

If there is laughter here it will be the laughter of the gods. As for us, though we can see now that in neglecting the mind and failing to see itself as but one coördinate field of human curiosity and pursuit, science has brought the threat of nemesis upon itself, there is little enough triumph in feeling that the glory of science is likely to be dimmed, and dimmed for lack of mind to see its glory.

VI

THE NEXT MOVE

VI

THE NEXT MOVE

I

THE drift of the intellectual atmosphere can sometimes be palpably felt. Among his other grave audacities, for instance, the late Henry Adams, as will be remembered, ventured into the field of prophecy. Like his New England forerunner, Cotton Mather, who looked into the wicked world about him and, despairing, felt that its end was hard upon the heels of the moment, Adams looked into the sorry state of learning about him and, not with a moral despair but with a mathematical formula, set a recently overpassed year for the end of the world of intellect.

He did not seriously mean, I dare say, that from this date we should all be keeping each other in madhouses, though he hints at the possibility; but rather that then we should have reached the limits of intellectual expansion, and should have to be content to mull over what we had already discovered instead of going on to the mastery of new provinces.

The precise date is of less interest than the reason why he foresaw the end at all. The prediction was a manner of speech, of course, a mode of approach, but the mode of approach to a very pretty problem. With his eyes resting chiefly on natural science, what he saw was the world of thought branching out in various directions, scholars burrowing farther and farther afield, bringing back what they have mined and returning for more, until at last it comes to a point where it takes a lifetime to reach the end of a single gallery. New knowledge may lie beyond, but life has its limits. No one else can push on for more, for it takes a lifetime to get so far. And no one can load up for someone else; mastery of the load is what it takes a lifetime to compass.

The vision is grotesque but not altogether fantastic. The full stop that for dramatic effect Adams put for 1922 is already foreshadowed in a slowing down here and there of the scientific drive. It is becoming harder and harder, for instance, for the physiologist to take over and use the physics and chemistry and mathematics into which his science tends to run as it advances. The sheer difficulty of mastering these additional sciences over and above his own threatens a limit to his actual progress just as the new vista opens out to his imagination.

Complexity of this sort is the commonplace of the moment. The old exuberance is gone. And the increasing difficulty of following down these divergent galleries and comprehending their drift naturally sobers the attempt. In a measure it has already discouraged the attempt; even the scientists themselves are disturbed over the accelerating shift from pure to applied science — from its intellectual significance to its incidental uses.

Reduced to these less extreme terms the drift itself is not quite shocking. To Adams perhaps it seemed so, as it probably seems to every thoughtful scientist or historian who has set his heart as Adams did on a mechanistic formula for the universe or for human experience. For the prospect down that vista begins to narrow in. But for others, as they watch the scientists approaching the end of their tether, there is a nice question whether such an end might not have been foreseen from the first — that is, whether in the nature of things the intellect in its positive or scientific vein — I use the term *scientific* in its somewhat colloquial limitation — should ever have been supposed to be the sufficient final evaluator of human knowledge.

So far as the large public is concerned the momentum of the scientific movement will keep fresh for a long time the vague comfort of a sense that the special branches of knowledge can take care of themselves; that the physicists know what the physicists are doing, the chemists the chemists, and so on and on; and that humanly all their devotions come back to the race from time to time in the form of engines and instruments, of hygiene and medicine, of higher explosives, and of more devastating gases.

This would be well enough if the intelligence were content to be naïve, grateful for a sop or a toy now and then, careless to understand, trustful, indifferent to the drift of the extraordinary intellectual currents which the scientific age has induced. There is a grain of comedy in the suggestion of such a paradise for the intelligence to have gone to at its death in the prophetic year. But whatever it is that the intelligence becomes when it ceases to be intelligent, so long as it remains intelligent it is skeptical, restless with the impulse of self-preservation. And self-preservation in this case means the answer to just this question as to where knowledge does come for its final authoritative evaluation.

The comment of "philosophy" on all this is obvious. One has but to choose his philosophy. But the case is hardly one for philosophy at all in its technical aspect — a point both curious and suggestive. For in spite of many a philosophic protest, something in the common consent of men, a gross and perhaps blundering common-sense, has now for nearly half a century given all the laurels to physical science — has made of it, in fact, *the* philosophy of the age. There is something, then, behind even philosophy. If this itself seems a gross assertion, the recollection of Socrates, pleading in behalf of philosophy to something behind philosophy itself in the minds of his young Athenians, will suggest its direction. At all events if this common-sense in its groping way has begun to detect an insufficiency in the scientific intellect to take care even of its own data, to say nothing of aspects of life with which science is not concerned but which are even more dear to men, the question of the next move of common sense is one of intense interest.

II

The incident which follows is a little gross and a little obvious. But it will illustrate a typical moment of unrest, and suggest the lines upon which such restlessness moves.

Five or six of us were sitting about a hospitable fireside. Our talk had been unwontedly spacious. In general there is no body of men in the world, I suppose, with so little in common as the group who make up a modern university. They are specialists. Their lines of divergence are the very reason for their being gathered together at all, and once together they go on cultivating their divergencies with all the virtue there is in them. And a physiologist who in the finest recesses of his mind is thrilled over the amazing transformation of hormones is reduced to anecdote when he sits next a Grecian whose vigils glow with the certainty that Homer was one and not many.

On this occasion, however — I speak relatively — we soared. We had begun thinly with Thucydides, thickened slightly with Grote and Gibbon, grown more general with Macaulay, and found common ground at last in Mr. Wells and his *Outlines*. We were an incongruous group, but we had all read or looked into the *Outlines,* and we now came to comparing impressions. They were trite enough, heaven knows. A geologist among us thought that while Mr. Wells was harmlessly superficial in his geological references, he was admirable in the rest. A biologist shook his head. The biological matter in the book was not biology; it might be political biology, if there was such a thing. The historical matter, however, had seemed to him beyond praise. An historian among us was incensed at them both; the survey of primitive natural history was the best thing of the kind he had come upon, but the human history was execrable, unscientific.

This phase of the discussion wound up in amusement. In the end the disputants compromised by agreeing that whatever the shortcomings of Mr. Wells as a scholar he had made of his work a piece of literature. Here a Grecian entered the discussion. Was a piece of writing that in the judgment of its contemporaries was false and shallow in its avowed substance properly to be valued at all as a piece of literature? The question was met with various degrees of puzzlement and amusement.

The point shifted. What was literature? The others committed themselves to two or three characteristics of it — that it was "pleasant reading"; that it was a thing whose values were "independent of what it said"; that "what it had to say was not what one went to it for"; that "it was not to be taken with the same intellectual seriousness" as the various branches of learning represented among them. It was essentially a matter of play, of relaxation, an indulgence of emotion, and clearly without the importance of serious intellectual pursuits.

It was with some malice, therefore, that the Grecian asked one of the others — a chemist — to state in chemical terms the value of chemistry. The request was of course an impossible one. The response when it came was first a protest and then a sober exposition in terms that were common to us all. The other men of science followed, each in turn rendering a judgment of his own branch of learning in language that was not the language of his own technique but such as all of us understood.

The historian alone among them caught the drift of this flank attack. The test was imperfect, he said; we were too diverse. But could any one of them, the chemist for instance, have told another chemist, or even himself, his conception of the *value* of chemistry in chemical terms? The chemist, still puzzled, acknowledged that he could not. The others made the same concession on their parts. And then all, a little more innocently than is quite credible, turned for an explanation of all this quizzing.

From what they had perforce acknowledged one conclusion was suggested — that branch by branch their science was a subordinate affair. Instead of a center about which all human knowledge revolved, as somehow it had come to be conceived in the course of the last half-century, it was a subsidiary thing, justifying itself, even pleading for its existence, before a higher court. And when its spokesmen pleaded before that court, as they had just now done, they must abandon their sciences and the language of their sciences, and appeal to its judgment in terms of its own idiom, its own premises, and its own logic. They were on sufferance before a higher jurisdiction. The conversation ended on this sobered note.

For some such jury, self-conscious enough to have solidarity, objective enough to be envisaged and acknowledged, and definite enough in its qualifications to determine for itself an effective discipline — for some such supreme bench of intellect the common sense of the evening seemed to us, by a hearty stretch of imagination, to be vaguely groping.

III

The incident was hardly a straw in the wind that was blowing in the world at large. It was floated by too consciously induced a draft in too private a chimney corner to be significant of more than its own conclusions. But its own conclusions were intelligible so far as they went. And if, as one forever hopes, common sense is to follow the lead of intelligence there was a clue held out there simple enough to be of promise.

It was evident that in justifying chemistry even to himself the chemist — to use the poor chemist again — appealed to something in his own consciousness that was not in the field of chemistry. Instinctively he abandoned chemistry and chemical language and spoke in the common tongue. The point, of course, was not linguistic. He was dipping into the real thing behind the language he used — into a seat of judgment in him to which his chemistry acknowledged itself subordinate. And in using the vernacular he was pointing to what kind of wisdom — knowledge and judgment — it was that sat at the center and determined the weight and worth and final significance of things.

Obviously the vernacular is vernacular by virtue of responding to what is common to the minds of men, vocabulary and idiom representing elements of thought shared by the generality. Men differ widely in their contacts with the outer world, my tailor and my lawyer and my doctor, for instance, each having familiarities outside my range and outside each others' range, and vocabularies to match. But what we can't escape in common is human nature. And when there is talk of values — well, value itself is in its final analysis a direct relation to some affection of this human nature. Men will differ, of course, in their affections and the consequent values which they hold — for olives, for Giotto, for truth. But this is the field where final values are held and where they are compared and fought out. For there is no one else to hold values but men themselves. And so men when they speak of values speak in the vernacular, and the quality of what they say will hang upon their wisdom in this ultimate center.

So much, perhaps then, may be said for any natural aristocracy of intellect — that first and last they will be well found in this ultimate and common thing, human nature. Their competence will be a competence at the center where all things come at last for their final weighing in. And indistinguishable from this competence will be their mastery of the vernacular. For the very mark and measure of their minds will be the fullness with which they can make intelligible to humanity itself in the idiom of its own thoughts the human meaning of experience and knowledge.

If this conception ever comes to seem reasonable to that very common sense that is being so sedulously invoked, the corollary problems of conscious solidarity and effective discipline are relatively simple — simple, that is, to the understanding, however arduous in the less amenable field of practice. For conscious solidarity comes from a common discipline. And the common discipline here is too clearly indicated to need more than allusion. Common sense itself is the essence in heart and mind of the immediate experience of life; and common sense fined and refined, heightened in degree without loss of identity, will derive in the nature of things from the enlarged and deepened rendering of life that common sense in its fullest development and finest balance has recorded. I mean, of course, literature — not literature in its mad ephemera, but literature in the lasting accumulation which the broad common sense of mankind has saved from oblivion just because in its native idiom it has most perfectly embodied the central outlook of common sense itself. And if this conception ever does come to seem reasonable to common sense we shall come again to an understanding of that discipline by way of the languages and literature which has never quite disappeared and never quite lost its association, however vague, with the idea of the highest culture.

IV

To go on is to undertake the real hazard of this adventure. To aver that in our free intellectual community, the open supreme court to which all the specialists and their world are subordinate will find its personnel among those whose minds have been formed and informed by humane letters — to say this is to challenge every instinct and justifiable pride that has given momentum to the main intellectual drive of the age. To the specialist — there are exceptions of course — even to the specialist in philology and literary history — literature is the flaunting banner of all that specialization is not — of play instead of work, of relaxation instead of discipline, of emotion that plays hob with judgment instead of intellect that dominates emotion. In a word it is the flaunting banner of dilettantism.

This is a common enough point of view. There are few vaguer words in the language than *literature*. It means all things to all men. And much of what goes current under the term deserves worse things than the tolerant scorn of the specialists. But the crux is not between good and bad literature; bad literature, like bad science, is out of court. It is a distinction between an intellectual temper and balance that can be called central and those that are radial and subordinate. And I am venturing the assertion that in kind literature is the expression of what is central, and that a mind rightly founded here is qualifying for a central place in the intellectual life.

The silent acceptances of the time are all to the contrary, and the gross organization of the intellectual life is based on these contrary acceptances. None the less, and in spite of all this, when the specialist is held to it with ironic insistence to put the final value on his own field of learning, it is to the idiom, verbal and mental, of literature that he is forced in the nature of things to resort. Not because literature, for casual convenience, also happens to use that idiom, but because literature is itself, *par excellence,* the expression of just that central thing, human nature, to which all things come home at last for their final evaluation.

The case of the specialists against literature, however, is not to be dismissed cavalierly. It is a real case, granted the premises upon which it is built. And these premises I should like to examine. If there is much bad literature there is also much nonsense written about literature. It will behoove this examination, therefore, to step a little gingerly and a little soberly.

Starting then with its use of the vernacular, we may say of literature at least this — that in thinking in and using the common idiom it looks out on life, pictures it, and reflects upon it from the point of view of what is common to all men. And in taking human nature for its subject, not abstractly but in the concrete after the manner of common experience, it stays at home in this aspect also. It remains at the center. But this center is a very complex thing, made up of all the motions of the mind — sensations, instincts, affections, imagination, feeling, thought, all working together, not like a case of discrete instruments but like a lens of many blending curvatures. So that looking out on human nature in all this complexity and dealing with it with the mind itself active in all this complexity — not sensation alone, or feeling alone, or reason alone, but the whole intelligence in its complete temper or balance — literature may be said, a little abstractly, to represent the complete human reaction to the full spectacle of life.

This is its peculiar feat, and in this it stands alone. No other expression of the spirit attempts to do just this complete thing. The fine arts occupy each a meager niche, music confined to the senses and to only one of them, addressing sounds to the ear and stirring emotions that respond to sound; painting and sculpture producing sights to the eye and stirring emotions that respond to sight; and so on and on. Each field of learning occupies its single gallery, gathering data and formulating ideas that hold within those bounds. Literature alone looks out from the center all round. Nothing is alien to it — the whole panorama of the senses, the whole play of the intellect, the whole play of the emotions responsive to sensation and to ideas. It brings them into a kind of synthesis and harmony and proportion, and interprets their significance to the whole consciousness.

It is this centrality of literature, indeed, that often betrays it. One may know no chemistry, and know that he knows none, and modestly desist from chemical judgments. But he can not be so modest with his common humanity; he cannot put it aside. Let him be deficient here and he cannot escape being a fool or escape exercising his imbecility. And literture, unhappily for its good name, is the expression of this aspect of the mind that may be a fool. That is inherent in its nature. Accordingly many things are done in the name of literature straight from the unplumbed depths of foolishness. Other things are done which are not — a discrimination delicately to be perceived. But the discrimination is a nice one. And the inevitable association of all literature with the processes of the mind that are common to everyone gives it, to the undiscriminating, an air of the casual, the amateurish, the off-hand.

To compare the restive mind where fancy and passion and instinct are old hearthmates of the intellect, with the austere mind where intellect sits alone, undisputed master, by a fireside neat, ordered, and controlled, and to say that that and not this is the authoritative superior — to say this must seem to those who have devoted themselves to the clarifying processes of science like proposing a return to chaos, a fear not hard to understand.

And yet the facts of life, and the reasons of the intellect itself, do confirm the heresy. It may be too bad that life is not subordinate to intellect alone. If so, life itself is too bad. The rational sciences themselves come at last before the court of the whole mind here at its center to justify themselves. It is judgment in this field that has the last word. And so it comes about that the vital question of the intellectual life is whether this aspect of the mind shall be cultivated or uncultivated.

But to cultivate it with literature, the field of the dilettanti! There is no doubt it is the field of the dilettanti, and so much, indeed, the worse for literature. But they hardly represent literature more than the quack represents science. They take it as a matter of play, a pleasant indulgence, using it to touch off an emotion for the pleasure of feeling it go. And here is a touch of the current comedy. In so far as the specialists in intellectual pursuits look upon literature obliquely in the same way, they present the solemn spectacle of serious men accepting seriously the dilettanti whom they contemn, and taking them at their word.

This, I think, is the false premise that has invalidated literature as a serious thing in the intellectual life. And I cannot abandon it without calling attention to a further comedy that has developed out of the situation. So seriously have our dominant intellectuals, the specialists, taken the dilettanti that the dilettanti have ended by taking themselves seriously. For yearning after the current fashion they have made a science of dilettantism itself. It is called aesthetics. And — last tribute to the age of specialization — aesthetics has developed its own specialists.

I cannot help recalling that Phidias and Velasquez and Raphael and Mozart with their appreciative publics antedated aesthetics, and that Cubists and Futurists and Vorticists came after. But whatever aesthetics may be among the fine arts, whose aim in the nature of the case is to address and please the sensations immediately and on the spot, its relation to literature reveals an essential difference. For in addressing the whole mind and not simply the sensations literature enlists other responses that in their nature reach beyond the moment — understandings that have a dynamic value for the mind itself. So that by gathering literature within its scope and allying it with the fine arts aesthetics has tended to elevate a single aspect of it and sink the rest. This distinction is of prime importance.

It is possible, of course, to take the imaginative thrill of literature as an end in itself, just as it is possible to take the spectacle of life simply for the thrill of it. As for life, no doubt there will always be many to take it so. But there is a touch of futility in such an attitude. For life itself does not stop; it goes on and on. Its ends do not end but themselves turn into means in generative perpetuity. Hence a kind of triviality attaching to play as a sufficient human pursuit. It is by a transformation of ends into further means that life is humanized, the reason playing its part in lifting life above the brute level of incoherent sequences through its vision of consequences.

If life itself asks for this ampler response, literature does so even more unequivocally. Both are alike in this, that they present themselves before the same full array of the mind and engage all the arms of the mental service. In so far as they differ, however, they differ in that life is a spectacle without an excess of intelligence, often with none, and may be responded to in kind. But no one holds that literature can be produced without intelligence. Its very analysis of fluid reality into discrete words, its rendering of elemental emotion into articulate form, its liaison of cause and effect in story and epic and drama, are all intellectual processes. Even more than life itself, then, it asks for an intellectual response. And to take it neat, as an aesthetic indulgence, is less to respond to it in kind than taking life so. For literature *is* the intellectual response to life, tempered of all the motions of the mind in their finest balance.

This is not to conceive a separation between literature and pleasure. To take literature as a task, to forego the delight of a good book, to miss the zest of it, to lose the pleasant benediction of a quiet library, would be to say farewell to literature itself. But that is only to say that a very pure pleasure is to be had in the full play of the mind. That the frivolous, and the voluptuous, and the sentimental shrink from the exercise of the intellect, or that the tired specialist goes to literature as an outlet for starved emotion is hardly reason to think of it in emasculate terms. If we have gone so far as to think of literature itself as specializing in emotion — as naïvely correcting the one-sideness of pure intellect by offering the other-sidedness of pure feeling—well, that is the last straw, a final oblivion of what is the central balance of the mind.

V

I say a final oblivion, but happily or unhappily nothing is final, as I have only now been concerned to point out. The present moment itself begins to show signs of packing up and moving on; a healthy discontent and skepticism are urging it after a new center. The old one of physical science has begun to reveal itself as not quite central. For all the authority it has attained by the common consent and silent acceptances of the times, the perception grows that all along it has been subordinate to common consent and silent acceptance; and that behind, animating and directing them, is the high court of the intelligence, the complete and balanced temper of the whole consciousness. And the question of the moment is whether this court, this final common sense that lives at the center, will again delegate authority to some subordinate aspect of the intellectual life, as it has done to natural science in the age that is passing, or whether it will do the harder thing and assume authority itself.

Delegation is tempting; the parts are so much simpler than the whole, each one more sharply definable, more exclusively and selectively manned, less cluttered with the presence of those who have never consented to join. Common sense on the other hand pays the penalty of its universality; it is shared by everyone; it is bound therefore to be looser, vaguer, more indeterminate. But loose, vague, and indeterminate as it is it cannot escape being final and having the last say, wise or unwise, being as it is the very verdict itself of how much humanity values the pursuits and products of all the activities of the mind and all the activities of life. And its quality will depend, in the nature of things, upon the success with which it finds for itself an effective discipline in the native stuff of its own judgment, and creates for itself a nucleus of those who embody some measure of its perfections.

It may of course be a question whether literature is a sufficient medium for such a discipline. The very cunning of the synthesis it offers to the mind is so much after the manner of life itself that like life itself the discipline it affords is a hazard. It tends to fail, perhaps, in one essential — the exercise of the intellect unentangled. And like life itself literature offers so many lures to the lust of pleasure that unless the intellect that comes to it is elsewhere informed and rectified and strengthened it may succumb. No need to point examples; the world of the dilettanti has captured literature even now and gelded it.

But if literature does not offer the discipline that alone will create such a judiciary as has been desiderated, still an intimate knowledge of it, a quickened appreciation of it, and a critical judgment of it are indistinguishable from the requisite qualifications. For though literature is neither life itself nor a mere replica of life, it is a sense of life rendered by the whole intelligence and interpreted to the whole intelligence. And the ability to see life from the center, and to interpret it there are the ends of such a discipline, whether that is called a critical love of literature or an intellectual grasp of life itself. For to be richly and articulately conscious at the center is to be master of the final value and significance of all knowledge.

VII

LITERATURE

VII

LITERATURE

I. A POINT OF VIEW

THE desire to bring literature back from the esoteric regions where our coteries and our critics have all but succeeded in putting it, to see it again in touch with the large common sense of mankind — Molière testing his comedies upon his housekeeper, Racine addressing the *honnête homme,* Swift an open book to both philosopher and child — and to have brought to bear upon it again in homely wise the frank free play of intelligence — such a desire must now and then, I imagine, attack every simple lover of literature and sanity, as he returns to them both after a sojourn among the mountebanks — often desperately sincere — of the lyceum and the academy, of the agora, and the groves of Eleusis.

In one such lover, at all events, the desire has come to the point of eruption. And with it has come a voice that says, "Don't." Whether this is the voice of the true Socratic daemon, or the voice of the immortal Punch, its advice is golden. After all, there is only one true thing to be said about literature. Literature is to be *read.*

But come — there is something constrained and ascetic in any unmitigated negative. Here is the past, for instance, with its intricate pattern and its bright pageantry; no one suggests that it is not to be written *about* — discussed, criticized, interpreted. But then the past was real. It was, once, it is true, but what is it now? All its reality has gone from it; it is only literature in the end, stuff for the consciousness and nothing more. Whatever has not come to that has come to nothing. And in the courts of the consciousness, who has now the better of it, Hector or Alexander, Antigone or Aspasia, Falstaff or George the Fourth? Allow the impulse of literature at all — to say out what the mind conceives — and if lief is granted the historian, it goes by the same token to whoever has it in his mind to say his say about that other pageant — the less equivocal of the two.

And besides there is the eternal interest in *shop* — that common shop of all the workmanship of the mind, where all things of the mind are made, and all things are repaired, and all apprenticeships are served — where the stuff of the mind is turned over into communication. At all events it is this interest chiefly that has led me to fling golden advice to the winds, and add one more voice to the tumult of the bazaar.

I

"The critic's main duty," says one of the most appealing of critics, Mr. Spingarn, "is to interpret literature and make its purpose clear to all who wish to love and understand it."

These terms are at once so just and simple, and so free from the Corinthian turn of much current criticism, that I seize them as a sort of permissive text for an inquiry to be undertaken in a wholly Doric vein. I dare not say laconic. And I borrow another sentence of his, because in its last words it puts the particular bounds — if they may be called bounds — that I have proposed for this Doric venture.

" Now while the critic must approach a work of literature without preconceived notions of what that work should attempt, he cannot criticize it without some understanding of what all literature attempts."

" Some understanding of what all literature attempts." This is the boundary that I hope, with a good-natured allowance of freedom, to keep within. It ought not to prove difficult. The real difficulty, I imagine, will be in justifying the attempt to wander over so much ground. But the very sweep of it beyond the horizon of a single glance is a perpetual and provoking challenge to the mind. Here, indeed, the sky is the limit. The fields beneath it have all been surveyed over and over again, it is true, but these surveys are the chief provocation of all. To say nothing of the winds that will be blowing at all hours, playing eternal havoc with the fences.

At all events the chart has been complicated enough by this time to excuse any hearty attempt to clarify one's own ideas of it. And with that high hope I am setting out. Such an attempt, however, may not be taken lightly; and I may be forgiven for first spending a little time in clearing a space to begin from, and indicating at once something of the base line and the point of view.

This is especially necessary because in the nature of literature there are no constants. In this it is unlike natural science, say, which until yesterday at least was felt to have a constant in the physical universe, however variable the minds that tried to grasp it. Literature, on the contrary, is itself the product of the mind, so that the mind that creates it, the creation itself, and the mind trying to understand it are all in the drift of what we aptly term "Movements." Even now, for instance, on the side of literature we are conscious of being somewhere in the backwash of a wave that we call the Romantic Movement, and on the side of the mind in the cross-seas of the Scientific Movement and the Anti-intellectual Movement. One of our variables, however, we do have the power of stabilizing in a measure and for a moment, and by selecting and maintaining a point of view for it can at least steady our vision.

To this point of view, then. In a phrase that has been quoted, I suppose, as often as any other from his very considerable utterance, Wordsworth refers to the intellect as

> *— that false secondary power*
> *That multiplies distinctions.*

No other distinction of his own making comes so near as this to the heart of the literary movement in which he was so prime a mover, and with which, a little helplessly, we are still moving. It involves both aspects of what, to me at least, seems the impossible paradox of that movement. For with a blithe inconsequence, apparently quite unconscious, it adds a distinction of its own — a distinction, moreover, that ought to be false by its own acknowledgment, but one which the poet himself must have put faith in. The other aspect of the paradox may at first sound petty, but will not prove so, I think, on reflection. It lies in the fact that to express his misprisal of distinctions the poet — hands crimson with the dye of words — was forced to use some seven distinctions that in its slow development the race had painfully evolved. Without them he could never have expressed his misprisal — which seems, therefore, a little ungrateful. Nor could he have written the ten volumes of verse that lie here on my table, a prized possession, without the inheritance of some thousands of other distinctions that subtly mark the discrete concepts of his mind out of which he built them up.

Language — word and statement — is so frankly the product of that power of the mind that multiplies distinctions, and is so wholly the working substance of literature, that a literary impulse which bases its own distinction on a contempt for that power deserves at least as careful a scrutiny as we should be tempted to give a school of painting that misprised a sense of sight, or a school of music that misprised a sense of hearing.

Now most of us who have grown up since the early nineties have, first and last, done a good deal of groping in the matter of literature. What is literature? Is it an intellectual criticism of life? Or a moral interpretation? Or an aesthetic presentment? Is it instruction? Or is it play? Is it a fine art? Or is it a liberal? The current answers are various to the point of hostility. They spring from funds of vitality, indeed, and permit us no doubt that literature is important, but they leave us in utter doubt as to what that importance is. Is it too much to ask whether this confusion may not be due to a certain virtue in our contemporary spokesmen themselves, a certain fine consistency — whether in misprising the intelligence they have not sometimes scorned to bring it to bear in any notable force? At all events here in these informal excursions and rebellions in the neighborhood of literature it will not, to them, seem a boast to propose carrying on without such a misprisal.

2

From this point of view, then, I suggest that the first step in reasonableness will be, not to define but to refrain from definition, or at least to go no further than the very liberal and very literal sense of literature as anything in letters. Perhaps it might be added — anything in letters *that lasts,* for whatever has no persistent value is not worth lingering over. And whatever in letters does last will last by virtue of just such values pertinent to all letters as I dream of capturing.

There are other current usages of the term, I know. In the commonest of these certain types of writing are mechanically segregated from the rest and called literature *par excellence* — epic and lyric verse, drama, discursive fiction — the touchstone being a certain personal freedom of the inventive imagination. But *poetry,* shorn of its clinging antinomy to *prose,* is perhaps a better term for these *genres.* And while it is poetry in this sense that lies at the very heart of all I am concerned about I cannot help thinking that is is just this sharp segregation of poetry from literature in its larger scope — these Romantics are old multipliers of distinctions! — that has cut poetry adrift in our apprehension from the source of some of its richest values, and exposed it to a multiplicity of distinctions too vague to fly the banner of intelligibility.

I pause over one of them. What literature, for instance, is art? All writing is an art in the liberal sense. But in the esoteric sense what literature is art — indeed what is art itself — has never been intelligible to two persons at once. No two have been able to agree; and perhaps no two have been able to comprehend one another. The term is still madly current in literary discussion — a tomb-of-all-work, to use Henslowe's locution, in which much unrealized meaning has been buried, perhaps forever. For lack of point its use has remained a gesture of legerdemain. It has done little to clarify the idea of literature. Rather by its esoteric character and its irrelevant associations it has tended to waft literature out of the light of common day and make of it a thing less serious in the degree to which it has made of it a thing less intelligible.

Now of all things the considerations that affect the judgment of literature are intelligible or they are nothing. And so I return to a sense of literature that has the advantage of simplicity — everything in letters that lasts. Everything in letters has at least one characteristic in common — that it attempts to express something conceived by the mind. And if it lasts it will be because the particular conception of the mind to which it gives utterance has been of too much value to be let die. Whether as in poetry it exercises the imagination in the interpretation of a subject in which our interests are at their liveliest and our sympathies at their keenest, or as in other kinds of writing in which, whatever our interest our sympathies are less intense, its essential feat is the same: it puts for the appreciative mind, in a form that is clear and just, a conception which the mind values.

Have I used the term *value* here with some of the vagueness I have railed at? It is the term which I have set out to fill, if I can, with significance. And so, for a time, it may stand empty, a jar by the winepress, as Ruskin might say, ready for the harvest. But something of its shape and capacity — its legitimate expectancy — I may indicate at once.

I have used the term *values* in its simplest and most Doric sense. If literature is of no importance the irony of that fact will sufficiently laugh us all out of court. But if it is of importance it will be so by virtue of the values which it has for those who read it. The problem that comes home to the intelligent reader, untouched by current sophistications, but unspoiled too by any democratic love of commonness, is not whether what he reads is literature, or whether it is art. Whatever he has read — Spenser or Spencer, *Utopia* or *Endymion,* Shakespeare's *Hamlet* or Boswell's *Johnson* — the question that does come home to him is the simple question of its worth, its values in the range of values of which it is susceptible. Of course it is literature — it is in letters. Of course it is art — it is the product of knowledge and skill. But what are its values? That question remains.

Literature is written for the reader — so much, of course, will go without saying. Even saying, however, will hardly suffice to put it beyond question that some of the values he may look for are beyond the pale. For readers are of all kinds, and cherish all manners of affections. Walpole found Burton sovran for sleep; and the old alliance between trunkmaker and publisher is notorious. But suppose the intelligent and serious reader with mind normal and lively; and suppose him coming to literature with open curiosity and ready receptivity for whatever things of worth the writer may have to say to him. With such a supposition — is it too much to say?—it is legitimate for literature to offer him whatever values it has. For if they are actual values is there any reason why it should withhold any of them?

If the reader values beauty, for instance, and it can offer him imaginative pictures of beautiful things, I cannot see why it should not do so unless beauty itself is a poor thing. If he values truth, or the distinction of good and evil, and it can bring these things home to his apprehension, I can see no reason, except in so far as they in turn are poor affairs, why it should refrain. Or let me put it still more sweepingly. If he values such a reflection of life as should embody all its values in just proportion and nice subordination, and literature should reflect such a synthesis, I can see no reason why such an embodiment should not be its most consummate achievement. This is not to say, I hasten to add, that literature can offer such a synthesis; on the contrary it quite obviously can not. Literature is not life; it is a thing in itself, limited, and governed by the laws of its own nature. Some things it can do and some things it can not, and some things it can do more effectively than others. Just what its native powers are is the point of doubt and inquiry. But I am concerned now with a general principle—the plenary liberty of literature to offer the reader whatever values it has—and with a general point of view—that since literature is a contribution to the common culture and the large life of mankind, it is from there rather than from any point within the circle of literature itself that its values are to be most justly legitimized.

3

It is the orthodoxy of the moment to look upon literature wholly from within — at least from within the circle of what is a little vaguely called the aesthetic. Even Mr. Spingarn, with whose appealingly simple words I have begun, plunges promptly into a realm twice removed from the intelligible values of the larger world. "The critic's main duty," he will be remembered as saying, "is to interpret literature and make its meaning and purpose clear to all who wish to love and understand it." Now nothing, it would seem, could be more catholic than this. And nothing would be if he had not in the next moment gone on to say: "The first need of American criticism to-day is education in aesthetic thinking." And but a moment earlier he implied that to understand literature one must bring to it, not a mind tempered and composed of all its powers in nice interplay and balance, but some particular readjustment, some suppression of normal sanity, by which he is to think of it, and value it, as "always a kind of divine nonsense."

This is so characteristic of aesthetic criticism — of that criticism from within as I have called it — that it is worth lingering over for a moment. In what special frame of mind is a reader to approach literature? What are his legitimate expectancies, his allowable curiosities? Is Mr. Spingarn so far wrong as I have implied in asking of him a particular re-adjustment of normal sanity?

For it is true that as we come to the appreciation now of this and now of that object of attention and interest, we do alter the mind's proportions, so to speak, bringing forward some of its powers, dismissing others to quiescence. For instance, we recognize a difference between the faculties used to appreciate a painting, on the one hand, and those used in mathematical calculation on the other; and one who listens to music with appropriate responses may read Spinoza in vacant despair. To this general rule literature is no exception. The reader brings to it a frame of mind subtly altered from the one he brings to science, say, or the one he brings to business, or to sculpture. Even within the bounds of literature itself he adjusts his mind differently to the appreciation of *Othello* and the appreciation of the *Tale of a Tub*. And perhaps in the absence of any constant standard it is but a reckless and loose procedure to mention any normality in a thing so protean as the mind.

Still in the rough experience of life we do attain to such a sense of normality, of balance, of temperance, or just proportionment of the mental powers. We watch their focus not upon one object alone but upon many and varied objects. And we award the praise of highest sanity to the mind that has all its powers developed and ready, with one power in unremitting operation — the power to proportion all the rest to the demands of the situation under scrutiny.

Now literature is the situation I would scrutinize. And the prior question as I read, if I ask it at all, is just this question of proportionment. Should I bring with me only some specified part of my mind, asking of literature the satisfaction of some one curiosity or affection and judging it according to some one response? Should I bring to it only the love of vivid imaginative picture, or only the love of beauty, or of reason, or of moral values, or of technical virtuosity? Or should I bring to it a mind framed like the mind I bring to life itself, as to a thing infinitely various, now addressing this faculty, now that, now these — a delicate balance, a mobile proportionment?

In saying then that literature is written for the reader, and that its values are as many and as various as he may get from it with a mind cultivated and alert and unconstrained, I have put my own sense of the matter. Literature, however, not being life at large, but a thing in itself, is obviously limited by laws of its own. The parallel of life, therefore, is not altogether just. Some of the values of life it may reflect and some it may not, and some in large measure and some but meagerly. Still, to bring to it a mind harmonized by the discipline of experience, and framed to the temper induced by reflection upon life itself, seems to me, for one, to promise for the reader the richest returns, and for literature the strongest safeguard of its high sanity.

4

In returning thus to an older fashion, I know, I have seemed to give up certain things which have come to be very dear to many lovers of literature, a certain glamour of mystery, a certain magic, that comes from a sense that the poet — to use the term in the widest sense — inhabits a different plane from that of normal humanity, a fourth dimension, in which he is to be apprehended only by the abandonment of the sanity that suffices in the world of three. I linger over this charge with some regret, for it seems to imply — what I do not for a moment wish to imply — that the poet has no distinguishing mark — genius if you will — which sets him off from those who are not poets. And quite clearly if some men are poets and others not it will be by virtue of certain differences. I acknowledge the miracle. And I acknowledge it the more heartily that these differences lie in a field where whatever happens is a miracle. No man knows how a thought occurs to him. It occurs. The most rigid logic does not make it occur. At most, logic puts to it, after its occurrence, the question whether it will fall in with the assent of normally composed minds. If we know a poet by the special variety and happiness of these occurrences, that does not lessen the miracle. On the contrary. But the miracle is of the same order as our ordinary miracles, though a happier one. We are all magicians.

Yet another tie links the poet's mind to the minds of those who are not poets. If we ask where it is that a poem comes to its consummation, it is clearly not in the poet himself but in his readers. Wordsworth could not distinguish his poetry from his bathos. Milton held his *Paradise Regained* higher than his *Paradise Lost*. To many a poor scribbler in his garret his own lines seem to embody the poetic miracle, though no one else will acknowledge it. When all is said, it is the happiness with which the poet's " occurrences " come home to his readers that makes him a poet. He has found a kind of logic and followed it; that is, to all the occurrences that flood upon him he has put the test, and has selected those that will meet with a happy assent.

This is not, of course, all that there is to be said about literature, or all there is to be said about the magic of it. But it will serve to indicate what I mean by protesting against a sharp separation between literature and the normal sanity of mankind, even at the point where it seems miraculously to transcend that normal sanity.

I am the more content to forego here the special magic of literature because, however real it may be, it belongs to the reader in the moment of reading rather than to the critic in his attempt to " interpret literature and make its meaning and purpose clear." Real magic can not be explained. What can be explained is by definition not magic at all. If when all is said there is a residuum of magic for a balanced sanity to thrill at, that is over and above the "meaning and purpose" which it is in the critic's power to make clear. Besides that very magic itself may be heightened when all that is comprehensible is disposed of.

II. LITERATURE AND THE AESTHETIC CANON

At the beginning of his essay, *The Aesthetic Hypothesis,* Mr. Clive Bell has cleared the heavy air about that subject with a genial gesture.

"It is improbable," he says, "that more nonsense has been written about aesthetics than about anything else; the literature of the subject is not large enough for that. It is certain, however, that about no subject with which I am acquainted has so little been said that is at all to the purpose."

I repeat this disarming remark because, whether one agrees with his conclusions or not, it must be admitted that Mr. Bell has himself written about aesthetics in a way that is not nonsense. He has shown, on the contrary, that the term is to be suspected of a real meaning.

Still, for my own part, when I was recently brought to a halt once more by the term — this time in the utterance of Mr. Spingarn from which I have already quoted — and saw it used as it often is nowadays in connection with literature, my own first response was to question its intelligibility. If it is often vague in its application to the sensuous arts, it is more often vacuous in its application to letters. And Mr. Spingarn has used it without further definition, as though it carried with it a very clear import.

"The first need of American critics to-day," I quote again, "is education in aesthetic thinking."

Aesthetic thinking! Clearly not that. But since his subject is literature and criticism, his probable meaning is that literature is primarily an aesthetic matter, and that the principles upon which a right judgment of it is to be founded are the principles of aesthetics. What then are these principles of aesthetics? The Schlegels theorized them for the German Romanticists, and Hegel wrought them into the body of metaphysics in his day as Croce has done in ours. But these translations of an idiom of homely thought into an alien idiom of transcendent metaphysics are hardly clarifying. For literature, above everything else, is the common possession of all cultivated men, and its real philosophy will stop within the confines of their common-sense. Explanations that step outside the normal sanity to which literature is addressed — the normal sanity which in response acclaims and establishes it as literature — do not, I should say, explain it at all.

No one that I know of has tried to question, in terms of common-sense, just wherein or how far literature is an aesthetic art. And perhaps it is no wonder, for as Mr. Bell has implied, the term *aesthetic* is very vague, and the "much nonsense" that has been gathered about it has made its neighborhood precarious footing.

It is possible, of course, that the term may imply only a loose aggregation of arts, a mere sackful, wholly unrelated, and that what are called the aesthetic principles are only the independent principles of each one. In that case, however, it will have no validity of its own, but now mean the principles of painting, now those of music, and so on to the bottom of the sack. About such a use of the term there is nothing to be said. If there *is* something to be said, it will be because the several arts do have something essential in common. And the part this common factor plays in each will be the extent to which aesthetic principles have valid significance for it.

The only part for common sense to play in so vague a field, I think, is the part of the skeptic — not a disposition to find no points of contact at all, but a spirit of dispassionate scrutiny, as alert for points of identity among the arts as for points of difference, and a willingness for the argument to lead where it will, not unaware of the little ironies that lie in wait for the pedestrian who trails on the heels of Pegasus.

I

The first cautious step to be taken is to examine the grounds of association by which literature has come to be linked with certain other arts that are to be called fine, and lays its first claim to be gathered under the aesthetic wing. For clarity and simplicity I shall take music and painting as sufficiently representing the fine arts outside the one whose candidacy is in question. About them, at least, there is no doubt.

An accident of language, if it is an accident, has made the association easy and natural. We think with language, and when we do not think, language does something for us still. The word *art* covers, among its multitude of processes and products, both literature and the fine arts *par excellence*. For literature is obviously an art, at least in the primitive sense — skill and knowledge brought to bear in the adjustment of means to ends. And the term was so used of literature, no doubt, before Horace gave it eternal currency. This alone, of course, does not make of literature an aesthetic art, for there are shoemaking also, and medicine, and swimming, and many another that hardly lays claim to be fine in that sense. But it does form a bond, and within the bond of this liberal term we instinctively, it is safe to say, feel a closer alliance between literature and the fine arts than we feel between literature and the others.

Between literature and painting, moreover, there has long been recognized at least one common intention. Both have been concerned to flash pictures on the mind — one through the imagination and one through the senses. Both have been said to " imitate " life, to use an old-fashioned phrase. And both have used the opportunity that imitation offers to heighten and deepen by a process of selection the impression that heterogeneous reality makes on the mind.

With music, on the other hand, literature has also a traditional alliance, however slender. The old association of word and melody in song oversteps the bounds of history into the dim past. This tie, to be sure, is chiefly a mechanical one rather than deeply organic, since the sounds of words are not what make them literature, and it is by this common property of sound that literature and music fall in with each other. None the less they are linked easily together in the mind by virtue of their long companionship in this matter.

Between painting and music, on the third side of this triangle, the connection is neither by a traditional association nor by a common element. It is made by yet another tie — in that both painting and music address the senses directly, though they address different senses. And this suggestion seems to be borne out by the ready inclusion among the fine arts — though with so loose a term it makes wary treading — of sculpture, architecture, ceramics, and other products all immediately sensuous in their address.

The outer range of the fine arts has never been definitive. Tolstoi went so impetuously far as to include the epidermatic contact of human beings. But the range is somewhat beside the point here, since the three arts of painting, music, and literature will easily contain all the elements of the problem. In the end we have an association of three arts bound together not in a straight line but triangularly, literature with painting by the link of imitation, literature with music by the second link of song, and painting with music by a third link — the address to the senses. We have not as yet the basis for an aesthetic common to all three.

2

If there is among these three arts a basis for a common aesthetic it will be by virtue of some organic trait which they have in common. And after all this is not very far to seek. For by whatever method they go about it each one has in view the creation of something permanent that in itself shall bring a disinterested satisfaction to one who apprehends it. They exist for that satisfaction and are valued for it. This generalization is good as far as it goes. Its difficulty, however, is that it is broad and vague, and formulated into a definition it would cover a good many objects of human design hardly to be thought of as among the fine arts. But sweeping as it is it may have an adumbration of the truth we are after, and will serve as a starting point, however far we may have to depart from it.

If all this sounds remote from the warm poignancy of the fine arts themselves, it will be remembered that aesthetics is not the enjoyment of the arts but an attempt to rationalize them. Its stint is to render them intelligible to the understanding, to afford a basis for critical judgment, and to true them up in practice to the standards of a critical taste. And its inherent difficulties are great. The various arts are incurably headstrong; each one goes about its task of producing something "in and for itself"; and each one goes about it in a way appropriately different from any of the rest. This mutual isolation tends to make common definition precarious. And the point at which they do seem to come together in the disinterested satisfaction of these who apprehend them — involving many of the incommensurate differences between mind and mind — is in a very elusive region.

With so much identity in mind as the basis of a common principle, we may catch the spirit of such a principle and some suggestion of its features by looking again at the three arts just glanced at. First of all, then, music. It is hardly to be supposed that the aesthetic principle — whatever it may turn out to be — first developed with music affectionately in the foreground. In fact it did not. But music would seem to have less power, and hence less temptation, than any of the others to be diverted to any end other than the immediate gratification of the hearer. It is freest of all from the coil of outer circumstances; it is intangible; it represents nothing; it is a means to no end outside itself. It may imitate the sounds of other experiences, but in so far as these imitations are used not for their value as sounds but for their representative values they are felt at once to be cheap and tawdry, sheer violations of the spirit of music itself. Our direct appreciation of the timbres, the rhythms, the melodies, the harmonies of sound are felt to be enough. The lover of music may find in his responses something of the whole gamut of the feel of life, and yet find there something of a release from the heavy and the weary weight of life itself. If this is the direction in which the aesthetic principle would guide all the arts, music would seem the one which conforms to it most closely on its own sheer impulse. It has little power and little temptation to transgress. The principle governs there without government.

When we turn to painting, however, something of the discriminative force of the principle may be observed at once. Painting differs from music in a point that promptly breaks from the fine isolation occupied by the "purest" of the arts. Painting takes a tangible, material form; it appeals to the eye. Now in the non-aesthetic world of experience what appeals to the eye is a substantial part of the world, and it has there other significance over and above its sheer appearance. It is one of the powers of painting, a power traditionally exercised by painters themselves, to create by line and color the illusion of some aspect of this outer world — a power only scantily possessed by music. But there is also another power of painting, no less traditional, that corresponds for the eye to the sheer appeal of musical sounds to the ear. I mean the harmonious disposition of line and color irrespective of imitation. That is, there is a value for us in form wholly independent of its resemblance to other forms. We take delight in the lines of a well proportioned vase; we compare the Greek column with the squat hogsheads of its Egyptian prototype and we thrill with the sense of its exquisite rightness. Our pleasure here is in the shape visibly before us — not as an outline which we identify with the shapes of other things, but in the direct simple appeal to the discriminating vision. And it can be readily perceived how this, in its own field, corresponds to the direct simple appeal of musical sounds to the discriminating ear.

Thus painting and music are linked by a tie yet closer than the one already observed — a tie which brings painting more obviously into harmony with the aesthetic spirit as it has been vaguely adumbrated. The point, however, is too important to be accepted without further examination.

For the pleasure traditionally taken in painting has been mixed. Part of it has been a pleasure in imitation and part in sheer form. On the one hand there has been a pleasure in the connection between the painting and the object represented — in recognition, in a sense of latent beauty in the object perhaps unrealized until now, and in the endearments of old association or the discovery of new.

On the other hand — "Let no one imagine that representation is bad in itself," says Clive Bell in the essay already quoted; "a realistic form may be as significant, in its place as a part of the design, as an abstract. But if a representative form has its value it is as form, not as representation. The representative element in a work of art may or may not be harmful; always it is irrelevant. For to appreciate a work of art we need bring with us nothing from life, no knowledge of its ideas of affairs, no familiarity with its emotions. Art transports us from the world of man's activity to a world of aesthetic exaltation. For a moment we are shut off from human interests; our anticipations and memories are arrested; we are lifted above the stream of life."

Still — "There are those," says Sir Sidney Colvin, "who declare that painting must appeal to the eye and visual emotions only and stop there — that any sign of mind or meaning behind the visual effect is a positive blot on the picture and makes of it 'literature in two dimensions' and the like. Stuff and nonsense! Of course, and it should need no saying, the primary and essential appeal of every picture must needs be to the eye by its harmonies and rythms of line and color, its balancings and massings, and proportions and contrasts of light and shade, and by their direct effect upon the visual emotions. If such appeal and such effect are not forthcoming, or if they fail, the picture is naught, but if they succeed and the picture is a picture indeed, then the more of mind that can be felt behind it, the richer the associations and suggestions it conveys, the better."

Now what pleasure we shall actually take in a painting before us we are free to decide for ourselves. The aesthetic principle carries with it no onus of obligation. At most it discriminates. We choose in freedom, or by the tradition we have fallen in with, or in humility by the quality and character of those whose sense of values we most respect. Whether we ignore all but the representation, or say intransigently with Mr. Bell that we must "bring nothing with us from life, no knowledge of its affairs, no familiarity with its emotions," or mediate with Sir Sidney — whichever choice we make we can, I think, make the aesthetic discrimination and allow that from whatever elements we derive our pleasure and in whatever we place our sense of values, the harmonies and rhythms of line and color are alone the values legitimately to be called *aesthetic*.

Here is a province wholly detached from the world of affairs. Here is a province created by the art out of its own proper substance. Here is the one point of contact between painting and music for a common principle to cling to. And if we can acknowledge this I think that we can go on to say that what we may call aesthetic enjoyment, as distinguished from any other enjoyments we may derive from a work of art, are found in the appreciations with which we respond to these elements in isolation from the outer world of our experience. So much at least is a common meaning for *aesthetics* applicable to the two arts that we have examined.

3

The initial difficulty confronting us in the third is obvious. For while music does in its harmonies and sequences of sound provide a sensuous substance of its own for our disinterested appreciation, and while painting likewise presents a sensuous substance for our disinterested appreciation, literature has no such substance to offer. It does, to be sure, like music, record itself by pothooks on the page, but the shapes of the pothooks are not the creative substance of either. Like music too it expresses itself in sounds, but while sounds *are* the creative substance of music, they would never of themselves create literature at all. Like painting, on the other hand, literature may, to be sure, flash on the consciousness pictures of the world of experience. But just this is the *non-aesthetic* aspect of painting. In the end the refusal of literature to present a sensuous substance that corresponds organically with the sensuous substances in music and painting is the source of all the difficulties which lie in the way of an obvious alliance between them.

Lest I be guilty of adding another difficulty, I hurry to correct an overstatement just made in the pursuit of the main ones. In saying that the sounds involved in reading would never of themselves create literature I have said what is obviously true. None the less it would be wrong to say that the sounds of literature as read aloud or echoed in the silence of the imagination are not important aspects of it.

"In his loneliness and fixedness he yearneth toward the journeying moon, and the stars that still sojourn yet still move onward; and everywhere the blue sky belongs to them, and is their appointed rest, and their native country, and their own natural homes, which they enter unannounced, as lords that are certainly expected and yet there is a silent joy at their arrival."

Who is there that can read such a passage and not feel that the rhythm and cadence of those phrases are a significant part of its utterance, or that if they were marred by change, or slighted of their sonorous undulation, or ignored for the sheer intention of the meaning of the words, the effect of the passage would be other than it is? One aspect of style itself, over and above the cardinal virtues of clarity and significant continuity, is revealed in the writer's success in making the sounds and sound rhythms coöperate with the sense of the words. And versification is just that and nothing else — its rhythms, its meters, its assonances and alliterations and rhymes are nothing but sensuous music, a singing obbligato to the meaning of the phrase.

In a coign of the cliff between lowland and highland,
By the seadown's edge between windward and lee,
Walled round by rocks like an inland island,
The ghost of a garden fronts the sea.

Or —

Under younder beech-tree single on the greensward
Couched with her arms behind her golden head,
Knees and tresses folded to slip and ripple idly,
Lies my young love sleeping in the shade.

Here in these sensuous echoes and undulants of sound is one element of literature, at least, that may be rescued pure for aesthetics.

Still on reflection one is forced in honesty to acknowledge that in literature, prose or verse, however contributory the music of its utterance may be, and however its music deepens and endears the meaning of its communication, this musical obbligato is ancillary, and not the chief substance of the art. There is a simple test here; no one long reads either prose or verse in a tongue he does not understand. There it is with all its music; but its music is not enough. One reads translations of prose for its ideas, though the music is gone, even translations of verse. But when one's primary desire is for music he goes to the source where he may have it pure — to music itself where every sound is selected for its musical value alone.

If it were by this musical thread that aesthetics had bound literature to its car, there would not be much more to say. It could be averred at once that aesthetics had its jurisdiction over one aspect of literature, and that in so far literature was an aesthetic art and subject to the aesthetic canon. At the same time it would have to be added that this aspect of literature was a secondary one, however important, and of a kind that, like music, could hardly help conforming to the aesthetic canon since there was nothing for it to do but conform.

It is obvious, however, that when Mr. Spingarn, in his indictment of our American appreciation of literature, says that our first need is education in aesthetic thinking, neither he nor those whose sense of literature he voices have this musical matter chiefly in mind. He himself rails with refreshing scorn at a conception of literature as " an external thing, a complex of rhythm, charm, beauty without inner content, or mere theatrical effectiveness, which goes back through the English 'nineties to the French 'seventies, when the idea of the independence of art from moral and intellectual standards was distorted into the merely mechanical theory of 'art for art's sake.'" For him, quite apparently, the aesthetic aspect of literature lies in what it says.

4

With this, however, we are back again in our initial dilemma. The term *aesthetics* has either a common meaning for both literature and the sensuous arts or it has no valid meaning for literature at all. I confess that the term is difficult. And conscious of this difficulty I have, perhaps in error, gone to Mr. Bell for its meaning among the sensuous arts. He has, however, given it a meaning for painting that is intelligible, one that is susceptible of a common significance among all the sensuous arts, and one that does not clash with the vague aura of intention that clings about the word from its vagabond experience in the usage of the language. At the worst his definition will serve as a stable basis for a discrimination that is worth making in behalf of literature.

This discrimination is brought to a point by a sharp conflict between his explicit sense of the aesthetic canon and Mr. Spingarn's implied one. The one avers that the essential substance of literature lies in what it says to mind and heart. This, says the other, is just what the aesthetic canon has nothing to do with. "To appreciate a work of art we need bring with us nothing from life, no knowledge of its ideas and affairs, no familiarity with its emotions. Art transports us from the world of man's activities to a world of aesthetic exaltation." Now as has just been said, neither the pothooks on the page, which symbolize a word, nor the sounds by which it is uttered are the substance of literature. The substance of literature lies in the meanings which these arbitrary and indifferent symbols call up in the mind. And here is the rub. So far are these meanings from "bringing nothing from life, no knowledge of its affairs, no familiarity with its emotions," that they cannot possibly bring anything else to mind. For the words in the vocabulary of a language have evolved in the midst of life, and are nothing at all but the expression of its affairs and its ideas. Their whole power is limited to the bringing up of just those things and nothing else. As each word sinks into the consciousness of the reader of literature it calls up, not the thing itself, but a conception generalized from his past experience, with all the feel about it that has been aroused in him from his former associations. And whatever is said — for all language construes into statements true or false — adds its significance to these conceptions gathered from life and its affairs and its ideas. There is nothing else for it to do.

What is left, then, for aesthetics to do in the government of literature? Or to put it conversely, how far is literature responsible to the aesthetic canon — in how far is literature an aesthetic art? Music addresses the ear; painting addresses the eye; literature addresses the imagination and the intelligence.

Each one, it is fair to say, is good in its own kind in the degree to which its own substance embodies the peculiar perfections appreciable by the part of the mind it addresses. The creation of beautiful appearances on canvas, then, is the aesthetic function of painting. The creation of beautiful sounds and rhythms, then, is the aesthetic function of music. Literature is more complex; it addresses both the imagination, which compasses the stuff of all the senses, and the reflective intelligence, which entertains truths about what the imagination conjures up. If we should follow the aesthetic canon, therefore, we should have to say that the aesthetic responsibility of literature in its major aspect is to present adequately to the imagination the semblance of the things of experience about which significant truths may be uttered, and then to utter those truths.

All of which, I am tempted to add, goes without saying. For all this is implicit in the character of literature itself. The aesthetic canon has added nothing of its own.

Will this analysis satisfy those who have been so passionate to bring literature under the aesthetic canon? It is doubtful. It is possible to suppose that once the term *aesthetics,* with its close affinity to the sensuous arts, has become associated with the peculiar delights of those arts, it has suggested for literature limitations and prescriptions appropriate to *them,* but not at all native to literature itself. This confusion seems to be especially centered about one power which literature cannot help exercising and which the other arts cannot exercise at all. For while the other arts cannot utter thoughts about what they present, literature cannot help uttering them. This address to the intellect, with all that it has of a moral implication, is apparently a stumbling block to those who, by their frank professions, and perhaps naturally, seem to scorn the intellect itself. They are all for emotion. At all events there still remain to be confronted those bugbears to the aesthetic mind that go under the names of intellect and morals, to say nothing of that other affair — that

Serbonian bog
Where armies whole have sunk.

I refer to the emotions.

III. LITERATURE AND THE INTELLECT

I

Literature is expressed in language. I state this fact modestly, with the aestheticists in mind. They have been lively claimants in the field for now more than a quarter of a century, and they have won to their side if not the world at least the spokesmen of literature. They are, apparently, aware that literature is expressed in words, but not that it is expressed in language. And between these two perceptions there is so wide a difference that a sense of literature based on the one is scarcely akin to a sense of it based on the other. For while words designate detached concepts of the mind, language cannot avoid the expression of thought. And thought is a bone of contention.

The disparity I have just mentioned is probably temperamental at bottom, and temperament is not to be gainsaid. One's temperament is one's castle. Literature, however, is a freehold in common. And if, by the aestheticists' own canon, an art is good in its own kind in the degree to which it embodies pure the perfections appropriate to the aspect of the mind it addresses, it will in some measure have proprieties of its own independent of the various tempers that approach it. And these proprieties, after all, are the only things worth communicating about it. Our tempers are our own. The things in literature worth making common are those inherent in it by virtue of its peculiar medium and the peculiar stuff the medium embodies and conveys.

Literature is expressed in language; but there is a further discrimination to be made in adding that it is expressed in that area of the language called the vernacular — not, of course, in the blithe ephemera of the street, but in the idiom, however refined above daily wear, that has got its substance and its color from the common experience of life itself, and the reflections that the thoughtful have brought to bear upon it. There are other patois in our possessions, other idioms responding to and expressive of other more localized kinds of experience and thought — the language of mathematics, for instance, and the technical vocabularies and idioms of science and law and the like — but these are not the language of literature. For literature speaks from the area where everyone is at home.

Idioms of whatever kind spring up to take care of the data of experience, and the thoughts of those who reflect about that data. And each idiom — patois, jargon, vernacular — renders up again in communication the kind of data and the kind of thought it has evolved among. And just as the language of mathematics has sprung up to designate the data of abstract quantity and reveal the cursive logic of quantitative calculation, the vernacular has sprung up to meet the needs of garrulous man as he responds with the full array of his faculties to the full spectacle of puzzling life.

And what is literature that it should express itself

in this vernacular, but an attempt to present just this vernacular view of life, so to speak, to which its medium is sib? What is it, in contrast with other affairs that use other areas of the language for special ends of their own, but just the rendering of any aspect of the whole protean spectacle and the protean response of the whole mind to it after the familiar manner of daily experience?

It is true of both literature and life that the moralistic mind, say, will naturally, and in the very sincerity of its preferences, find its chief interest in certain responses, just as the dominantly aesthetical mind, or the dominantly rationalistic mind, or any mind that is chauvinist of some province of the empire, will find its chief interest in other responses. That each one finds in literature something worth contending for is significant. Men do not clash over this issue in music; music is clearly aesthetic — nor over mathematics; mathematics is solely rational — nor over sermons; sermons are moral or religious. But over literature from age to age the battle goes back and forth in endless campaign.

The deduction is that literature, like life itself, is neither solely aesthetic, nor solely rationalistic, nor solely moralistic, nor solely responsive to any single predilection of the mind, but that its distinctive achievement is its fine synthesis of them all. There is an art or a science devoted to each separate predilection. Literature is the only one that can attempt a synthesis. Quite apparently, however, it is not obvious that literature *should* make it. And

Mr. Spingarn, now that the tide of battle goes in favor of the aestheticists, can set up his banner in triumph and utter his proclamation that literature is not subject to intellectual standards. "Not subject to intellectual or moral standards," are his words, but for the moment the one point will suffice.

That literature is an aesthetic art in so far as it has no ulterior motive — no desire to prove anything, and no desire to urge anything, but only the desire to embody the perfections proper to its own materials and its own means — so much we have already seen. But to say that it is not subject to intellectual standards is to forget, as I say, that the means of literature is language. And whatever is expressed in language is, do what we will about it, inescapably intellectual. And this is not a matter of choice, either, any more than to say that color is visual or that sounds are auditory. It dwells in the nature of things.

At all events it is just this substratum of intellectual content in all language that I wish to point out. I know that the term *intellect* is a vague one, as, curiously perhaps, all our terms of the mind prove to be on examination. Consciousness is the most baffling subject of consciousness. But here in the discussion of literature where technicality would defeat its own purpose, and where the only value of words lies in what men normally understand by them, it will be enough to say that in using the term *intellect* I have intended to imply an aspect of the mind distinguishable from sensation, from imagination, and from emotion, and confined to those operations of understanding by which we perceive the relations between things.

2

I begin, then, at the bottom with one sometimes-forgotten fact — that words, taken individually, have no creative power, and properly speaking can *convey* no new meaning to the reader of them. It is conceivable that a painter may put a color or a form on his canvas never before seen or imagined by a given observer, and so may be said to *convey* the impression of that color or form to him. But with words as words the corresponding feat is impossible. A writer may, of course, use a word which a given reader has never seen or heard before — *meconic, pernocation, cachetic* — one of these will catch most of us — but it will convey nothing to him. The only power of the word is to call up in the reader's mind a meaning already there. The word is not the creative element of literature.

The creative power of language — that is, the power to convey something new to the apprehension of the reader — lies elsewhere. It lies in the power of language to take old concepts already planted in the reader's mind and put them into new relationships. And here in this primitive creative gesture of language is enlisted the critical faculty of the understanding. The perception that emerges is a motion of the intellect. Not just any beautiful words culled by hands from the heap in the dictionary and strewn together in gorgeous procession — *medlar careen cellardoor, lunate rounceval gambit.* From such a procession we may catch, one after another, sounds which the ear may joy in, a rhythm that sings, and bright concepts which the imagination may vividly picture. And if literature were chiefly an array of beautiful words, as one might suppose from the words of many a commentator, a matter of rhythm and cadence, a flashing appeal to the imagination, here might be a notable line of literature. It is not; it is nonsense. And what it lacks — it need not be said — is that congruous relationship which is the essence of language, the intellectual congruity that is the chief creative substance with which the writer of literature works. The aestheticist can blithely say that literature is not subject to intellectual standards, that it is "always a kind of divine nonsense." And may it not be answered that here is nonsense, and if it is not divine it is because the divinity he really has in mind lies in the intellectual perception he is at so much pains to deny?

If we may think of words as the filaments out of which all linguistic discourse is spun, and then remember that when these are put together it is the perception of relationships which makes them cohere, we shall have caught the intellectual character of the process with which we are dealing. But we shall not even yet have arrived at the smallest unit of linguistic discourse. Let me return to the fine arts. One of the most striking differences between language and the objects of sense, and so between literature and the fine arts, lies in the non-committal character of the latter. Forms and sounds appear before the senses, are apprehended, and there is an end of them, save for the feelings and thoughts that each of us, out of his own nature, brings in response. These latter are our own, of course, not uttered by the objects themselves. Literature, on the other hand, is forever committing itself; it does nothing else. Its web is forever created by the compliance of two strands — warp and woof — something put forward for our apprehension and then something asserted about it, predicate forever passing judgment on the subject. The painter may picture

Waters on a starry night

and leave it at that. But the poet may not; he must interpret, commit himself to a belief, reflect about waters on a starry night, ask us to accept an opinion about them:

Waters on a starry night
Are beautiful and fair.

Not that the majority of sentences in even the austerest of literature are themselves very profound in this intellectual appeal. Yet even at their simplest we are not indifferent to the logic of their congruity. If but now with careless fingers we had turned two pages instead of one, and had read —

Waters on a starry night
Are yet the fountain light of all our day,
Are yet the master light of all our being,

the grammatical technique of our web would have been flawless, but our minds would have been taken aback. For acquiescent as we normally are to the vagaries of the writer, we none the less sit in unremitting critical judgment, upon the rational congruity of the two essential elements of the web.

It is not hard to understand how this or any character of language slips the perception of many whose concern for literature is sincere. Our power of sophistication to all matters of instinct and habit is great, and not all the oblivions that follow are evil. In the process of reading, for instance, an ardent speller — if there is such a thing — might remind us that in our callousness to the printed page we grow oblivious to the miracle of translation by which the intricate permutations of the little shapes that fall under the eye call up sounds to the mind — sounds which are never sounded, never even consciously imagined, yet which by a further translation call up the meanings that alone occupy the conscious attention. It is, of course, on reflection, no bad miracle, and illustrates not only the tendency of our habituation, but also the fact that oblivion may be a virtue. To indicate, therefore, that language forever engages the intellect will of itself mean nothing to the point. Oblivion may be a virtue here as well.

In the presence of anything presented to the judgment it is always a nice question how far back among operative causes to carry the liveliness of conscious appreciation. A sunset is a sunset in undiminished grandeur though we know nothing of vibration and refraction, and a primrose by a river's brim loses nothing for most of us from our ignorance of botany. But there is a distinction between the products of nature, which operates in fine disregard of our responses, and the voluntary products of human skill, which artfully builds for the sake of those responses. Unlike the conventional collocations of letters which make up the words he uses, every collocation of words and every predication is an act of particular choice on the part of the writer. Out of these collocations and those predications he creates whatever he creates. And to make a virtue of oblivion at just that point where whatever is just and fine springs first into subtle embodiment is both to miss what has been done with infinite delicacy of perception and tact, and to relax the very fineness of our demand to meet which the finest voluntary products are created. No conscious product of the writer is irrelevant to the appreciation of the reader.

3

In the larger aspects of literature are there any addresses to the intellect that are inherent and inevitable? By the larger aspects of literature I mean the patterns — over and above the web common to all expression in language — by which we recognize the product as poetic — as drama, tale, novel, lyric. If in these very differentia by which poetry is known as poetry and not as something else some address to the intellect is inherent, the question will have some kind of answer.

It is too simple to be dwelt on at length. A very

great proportion of all literature, prose and verse, takes on the pattern of experience; that is, it is either drama or narrative. Is it too much to say that in all literature of these types intellect is the chief designer of the pattern? All experience is strung on a thread of time. Not mere sequences, however, but *con*-sequences, are the determining thing — the liaison of cause and effect. Not that one must read for this particular interest. What one reads for is his own affair. A proofreader reads for errors. Browning's grammarian read for the enclitic *de*. But after all it is this liaison that creates the *genre,* making the five acts of *Othello* a single play and not five one-act plays, the eighteen books of *Tom Jones* a novel and not eighteen novelettes.

And even the lyric, which confessedly comes as far as any form of literature from intellectual intentions, is not hostile to reflection, so naturally among the spontaneous responses of the consciousness does thought arise, and so wholly is the lyric devoted to the spontaneities of the mind's responses. Even frank generalizations may take lyric form without offense.

> *"Beauty is truth, truth beauty," — that is all*
> *Ye know on earth, and all ye need to know.*

> *The Rainbow comes and goes*
> *And lovely is the Rose;*
> *The Moon doth with delight*
> *Look round her when the heavens are bare . . .*
> *But yet I know, where'er I go*
> *That there hath past away a glory from the earth.*

I do not mean that generalizations like these are the essence of lyric poetry, or the end toward which it moves, as an argument moves toward its conclusion. And it is quite possible, I think, to feel in the case of Wordsworth a little too doggedly the shadow of the argumentative intention. Yet over-sharply as it defines itself at times, this shadow is not out of keeping with the lyric spirit, when it falls, a natural incident of the picture, in a scene illumined by the poet's mind.

Specifically and concretely as the imagination may body forth the forms of things, our spontaneous response to them may well gather a part of its endearing intensity from the poet's sense of a wider significance in them than comes from their bare existence. And it is to be doubted whether — apart from a sense of beauty, which painting ministers to so much more purely than literature — the significance for us of any scene or situation lies simply in its vividness in the imagination; and whether for those other significances, which literature can render to us so much more purely than anything else, some element of generalization is not always involved. At all events the intellectual process is not alien even to lyric expression — or where would the sonnet be, or the elegy, or the ode?

After all, thought has its sheer delights; and if literature were of no other worth to us than as a passing pleasure, there need be nothing in its appeal to the intellect to lessen the pleasure as it passes.

Even mathematics, brought home to the heart, may have its poetry.

Now of my three-score years and ten
Twenty will not come again,
And take from seventy a score
It only leaves me fifty more.

And in literature of every kind, where, if ever, the mind strikes its natural gait, and sings in the full harmony of all its registers, nothing, I venture, but incapacity can account for a reluctance to fall in with blithe, unhalting step, and join responsively in the appreciation of all its antiphonal notes. Whether we approve or not, music is composed of sounds; and whether we approve or not, literature is woven — web and pattern — with appeals to the intellect. That these do not account for all our responses goes without saying. But that these are inherently there, and that it is they in the main which make of literature more than a passing pleasure — make of it an interpretation of life itself — though it may not go without saying, makes the saying of it forever worth while.

IV. LITERATURE AND MORALS

To pause at this, and let literature stand for a moment as a feat of sheer intellection is perhaps a salutary exercise. Most of the pressures of decadence bear destructively and hostilely at this point. But a picture of literature as sheer intellection is grotesque, after all, as a skeleton is grotesque — apart by itself a caricature of the living thing.

Pure reason has its pleasures, and even in literature, since it is there, it is possible to enjoy its presence with selective attention. But in normal experience intellect is usually a means rather than an end; and in literature, though literature is more rational than life, intellect takes on something of the same relation. It is not, however, an insensate machine in any relation. It is a protean thing, infinitely adaptable, having in it an operative principle of sanity to rescue it from the stupid invariability of the mechanism, which is your true Bourbon, learning nothing and forgetting nothing. It is forever sensitive to the subtle variations of the matter under its eye, and fluently readjusts its own play to the needs and values of the changing situation. But for all this it takes on its full significance only in pursuit of some other end.

I

What is still to be disentangled, then, is the special kind of object at which the intellect, exercising its high sanity, aims in the service of literature — the special kinds of value which it contrives to capture there, and which have made of literature so invariable an accompaniment of civilization and so intimate a companion of all civilized minds.

Surely it is far more intimate and invariable than any of the sensuous arts. And I cannot, for my own part, help feeling that literature is nearest in kind to our most human qualities. It is the only one among them, at all events, that speaks to us of humanity in intellectual terms. And our intellect and our gregariousness are our most humane characteristics. To ally it to the sensuous arts, therefore, as do the aestheticists, is, it seems to me, a little to dehumanize it.

For the sensuous arts are, at bottom, still phenomena. Each object of these arts is a bit of external reality — matter or energy — for us to come into contact with. Fine as it may be to our appreciation, a painting or a statue or a symphony is, when created, still of the phenomenal order. Its materials are physical and enter the consciousness by way of the physiological senses. If one of these arts contrives by selection and arrangement, as blessedly it often does, to create something far more beautiful than such materials are likely to become in the rough haphazard of unmodified nature, and thus show the operation of mind upon it, still it never ceases to be a sensuous object in the material world, any more than, say, a trowel, which is also a sensuous object showing the operation of mind upon it, or a sundial, or the garden that lies about it exquisite in the sunlight. The animals, too, modify phenomena. The spider spins his web; the bee moulds his comb, the bird shapes his nest and sings his song. In this respect, at least, they are artists in the things they do; they rearrange the materials in the outer world and leave them there. But one intensely human thing they do not do.

The character of the material things of the outer world is that they are *there.* They exist. The human observer in contemplating them may have his thoughts. But they are his own thoughts. The phenomena are without. It is a happy thing that he should have objects so exquisite to contemplate. It is the human thing that he should be a thinking being. It is no wonder, then, that he should thrill when he is made aware of something in him of a sort that only human kind can experience. The sights and sounds of the outer world, indeed, are no meager gifts; nor are the smell of grateful odors or the taste of nectar. All these, however, he shares in kind with brute creation. What he does not share, sheer creation of his human brain, is what he thinks *about* his experience with these phenomena. And when he feels the stirring of his thought, and realizes that these particular thoughts are his own, not shared as yet even by other human beings, it is no wonder that he should leap with the impulse to embody them, to realize them, to expose them to the realization of others. In language he has an instrument ready to his hand. And what he creates, when he does give expression to them is, in some form, the kind of thing we call literature.

Our present concern, however, is with poetic literature, and these reflections do not quite bring us to its door. All literature is expressed in language, and language is shaped in an intellectual mould. But there are differences in the uses to which language is put as it piles its sequent statements one upon another, and some of these uses are not the distinctive ones which belong to the more exquisite thing we call poetry. For of a truth if both *Othello* and *The Origin of Species* are expressed in language and in so far are intellectual in their character, yet they look at us with very different expressions, and serve for us very different ends. And our search is for the end which the intellect serves when it wears the livery of the poets.

Among the things which catch our disinterested attention and lure us into recording and communicating our observations and reflections, there is one chief line of cleavage. On one side the line is the great *donné* of the drama — the stage, the scenery, and the properties of the setting — the material universe conceived as a closed mechanical system in which mankind (*homo sapiens*) appears as a species of animal and no more. I mean natural science. On the other side the line there is a kind of interest which natural science ignores — an interest in the peculiar fortunes of humanity. And among the factors which determine these fortunes are some which are not to be dealt with as the intellect deals with the phenomena of physical nature. Here are desires, impulses, affections, aspirations, the very intellect itself — the whole armory of human self-consciousness, in virtue of which mankind is concerned for its own ends — in virtue of which, indeed, it is concerned to amass its knowledge of the universe it inhabits.

If the natural sciences deal with the mechanics of the universe and what happens there according to laws in which men have no say, here is a situation in which we do seem to have a say, and in which the eager heart of our interest is in what we make of it by exercising this say. Stimulated by this interest we scrutinize the terms of the situation we find ourselves in — the stage, the scenery, and the properties. We evaluate them in relation to our own humanly conceived ends. We ponder and analyze the baffling human nature we find ourselves possessed of. And we try to catch the particular go of life as it makes for or against the ends we set up for ourselves. For this particular interest there is only one word. It is moral.

Is it too much to say that of all human utterances that special kind which we call literature *par excellence* is the one which most intimately and exclusively deals with the factors which make the situation a moral one — with mind and character, thoughts and impulses, affections and aspirations, let loose in the midst of the human struggle to make the best of the human plight? So far as subject can determine the matter, at all events, literature can no more help being an affair of morals than astronomy can help being an affair of natural science. The statements of which an *Oedipus* is compiled have no more license to belie the situation they purport to reveal than the statements of a *Principia,* and if the links of association which determine the sequence of the statements in the *Oedipus* are different from those which govern the sequences of the *Principia* — less the logic of mechanical things and more the logic of human nature — that is the evidence of an intelligent adjustment of intellect to the nature of the subject and the kind of truth pursued.

2

There is an ambiguity in the term *moral,* however, which probably accounts for much of the current antagonism in the matter; and the lively comedy of the 'nineties — the battle between the heavy ranks of the Philistines and the bright battalions of art for art's sake — was almost wholly beside the point.

There is no activity, of course, that may not on occasion do what, from the point of view of the world at large, may for practical reasons be found intolerable. The architect in his study may draft a wing which, in the hands of the builder, may cross the property line. But the question is not one of architecture; it is a question for the police. The novelist may write of scenes which to society may seem, when published and circulated, to cross the line of propriety. But this is not a question of literature. For all the literary problems are solved and the manuscript has left the author's hands before the act is committed which has given dudgeon.

In this great battle beside the point, however, the Philistines raged that nothing should be put into the hands of the public that traversed public morals — in which they were right in principle, there being a line somewhere beyond which police jurisdiction begins. The Aesthetes countered that literature had nothing to do with their public morals, in which they were so far right, since as literature it is a completed thing before the offensive act is committed. The Philistines, innocently generalizing, cried that literature must be moral. The Aesthetes riposted that literature had nothing to do with morals, and as innocently carried their militancy into another signification of morals, and denied for literature a character which is the one thing which makes it literature at all.

For both sides fought over morals in the homiletic sense. And obviously literature is not homiletic. The maker of literature is a moralist, but he is not a moralizer. He is a moralist as an astronomer is a scientist, both steeped in knowledge, one of his earthly data as the other of his heavenly data, but neither, in his special capacity, intent on the particular application of it. Both are addressing the mind, the human apprehension and comprehension.

3

The difference, however, is not altogether one of ambiguity. Even after all ambiguity is cleared away, and literature " in itself as it really is " proves objectively to deal with a moral substance, temperamental differences will still tend to divide the lovers of literature at this point, some finding the values they seek in one variety of their responses, and some in another, and both passionate, since the sanction of their values is in their indisputable feelings. There are moods in which one is inclined to say that these are sacred precincts. Literature is there for every comer, and every comer — to literature of all things — is welcome to whatever he may find. Only the moralizer indeed, intrusive meddler, will be bold enough to thrust into the privacy of personal preference with his own discriminations of better and worse, of ought and ought not.

To respond without discrimination to this mood, however, is to take the wind from the sails of all criticism, and discredit beforehand the aesthetic moralizer who here is urging us to ignore the intellectual and moral character of literature. For the critic's frank function is to speak to, or in behalf of, the reader, and if the precinct is sacred there is nothing for him but silence. But the critic, after all, has his place. He is essentially a reader, as every reader is, implicitly or explicitly, a critic. And for readers to be garrulous, or earnest, or amused, or indignant among themselves over the books they read is the frankest of privileges. Even the critic prepense comes to literature first as a reader. And it is only in the measure in which he gives utterance to ideas and judgments and tastes which seem valid to other readers of literature that he has any point at all with them.

In the very nature of things he belongs, in spirit, not to the craft of letters but to the world outside the craft. It is from the point of view of that world — the cultivated reading part of it — that he speaks. What are the tastes, ideas, judgments, reflections, responses justly to be brought by the reader to the literature he reads? The critic communicates his own, indeed, but in the measure of his intelligence and sincerity he communicates his own just because in the end they seem to him the ones best worth becoming common. Is this presumption? I dare say; but in the large tolerance of the world of thought it is the allowable presumption behind all utterance. And the judicious reader discriminates between what belongs to the writer and what belongs to the subject, and gets his reward when the one throws light upon the other.

When the aesthetic critic, then, says of literature that it is not subject to intellectual or moral standards, he need not be speaking of literature itself, but only be saying to those who read it that they should not bring intellectual and moral appreciations to bear upon it. The distinction is understandable. But to me at least it suggests rather the critic's own temper than anything inherent in literature itself.

It would mean for the reader the withdrawal of his appreciation from many of the things that are scrupulously said by the writer — from the recognition of truth, from the justice of portrayal, from the validity of cause and effect in the interplay of human forces, from the whole correspondence between literature and human experience.

What, if anything, would be left would be a picture in the imagination, to be appreciated perhaps for its beauty, but shorn of the distinctive things that only literature, by virtue of its peculiar medium, can add to the picture. Withdraw these things from literature and there is little left for the critic — or reader — to reflect upon but the technique of the writer. Which accounts, perhaps, for a principle which the aestheticist has commonly substituted for the intellectual and moral standards which he has banished — that the writer of a work of literature is to be judged not at all by the thing he has chosen to do, but only by the effectiveness with which he has done it.

But here is comedy. The critic has turned pedagogue. For the pedagogue, indeed, the method, the technique, the way it is done, is the only thing; it is the only thing teachable, for what the writer conceives in his own imagination is his own affair, not to be taught, not even to be known by the tutor before it is communicated. And for the critic to say to the reader that he too should not care what is said to him but only how it is said is to ask him also to play the pedagogue — all the world the pedagogue!

The aestheticist, however, has not left himself quite without a critical standard of a kind that belongs to the reader as a man of the world, and I have done him, in so far, an injustice. " Literature is imagination, not thought or morals," says Mr. Spingarn, voicing the aesthetic spirit. Now of imagination in literature there is no question; literature is of imagination all compact. And perhaps it is because in pure imagery stripped of all intellectual and moral implications literature comes near to producing in the reader's mind something comparable to the sensuous substance of the sensuous arts that the aesthetic critic clings to it as the one matter legitimately to be appreciated. But to withdraw from imagination all intellectual and moral enrichment is to let it hang solely upon the vividness and beauty of the image — to pare narrative to the dimensions of the *tableau vivant,* lyric to the picture book, and drama to something less than the cinema.

The point is not one for dogma. Still one may feel a little sorry for one who, in loyalty to a self-denying ordinance, rules out from his appreciations Othello's

Oh, the pity of it, the pity of it!

There lies the tragedy. But he has not brought to the play the intellectual perception to see it focused there, nor the moral apprehension to feel with sympathetic poignancy the depth and force of the dilemma that has come to this. He should be as well content had Othello cried with the king in the nursery rhyme, " There, there! Oh, deary me! " The imagination without intellectual or moral enhancements could vivify that exclamation as well as the other. And as for beauty, the only meaning it can have in the apprehension of moral passions springs from the sympathetic — hence in this case the moral — echo of them in the reader's heart.

If to our apprehension human beings were automata, like the waves of the sea or the swaying branches of the forest, and our only interest in them were in their physical motions, we should have a literature not subject to moral standards, though it is hard to imagine why we should have any interest in such motions not amply taken care of by the natural sciences. But we take humanity with a difference. The interest that sends us to literature comes from a sense of the human consciousness, a thing compact of impulses that we call affections, that attach to certain things which the consciousness compasses; a cunctator which evaluates and balances the consequences of many desires; and a force which sets us going toward what, in view of all this, we desire most. Our interest in watching the interplay of these elements in the human world about us is eternal — and we look on with sympathy and antipathy, good and ill will, love and hate, curiosity and jealousy, anxious or amused as we wait for the outcome.

As for literature, looking into the springs of my own interest in it, I find that I prefer dramas that are peopled with people rather than with crystals and clothespins. Crystals and clothespins have their adventures. But my interest in drama is clearly in something that such adventures do not reveal. They reveal no consciousness to catch my sympathies. Nor do I care for dramas peopled with lower animals. Yet all animals have what correspond to consciousness, to desire, to will. What they do not have, in sufficient force at least to engage us seriously, is intellect to weigh and evaluate the objects of desire. Without it in fact they may plunge the more headlong after the immediate object; and if our chief interest were merely in animate movements toward desired ends we should no doubt find their less hesitant actions the more engaging.

But our interest does not center there. It centers sympathetically upon the moral dilemma created by the presence — in the protagonist and in us as we read — of intellect. Without it men confront us as automata. With it and its interim of hesitation, when present desires are faced with other desires conceived in more dispassionate moments or moments of other passions, and when they are weighed and balanced over against each other, there comes a running current of suspense, and your Hamlet — exaggerating to the verge of caricature the typical moment of all drama — sits down and has it out with himself. There is the heart of our interest — richer than the gambler's zest in the sheer hazard of the outcome, and richer than the sportsman's zest in the matching of wits, because here are gathered all the elements of the human situation. The choice, when it comes, is the expression of character; and character, wise or foolish, good or bad, as we see it through the synchronous play of our own sympathies and intellect, is the center — though not, perhaps, the sum — of our value for literature. Not the sum, for human nature is complex, and no element of it but may, on occasion, be the chief subject of our interest, and this or that piece of literature concern itself with but one or two. But the center, none the less, for even these engage us for their potential share in the moral drama of life.

V. LITERATURE AND THE EMOTIONS

I

Ever since the Romantic Revival at the end of the Eighteenth Century, the chief commonplace of literature, especially of literature at its most poetic, is that it is at bottom the expression of emotion. At all events, one of the counts in the indictment of Pope at the time, and one of the most frequent characterizations of him still, is that he, with his age, was of the essence of prose intellect, more concerned to address the mind from the stores of reason than the heart from the wells of feeling; whereas real poetry has no other function than just that of conveying emotion.

It is not upon Pope and the Augustans that I am here intent, but rather upon a nice point of human nature. I mention Pope, however, because the nicety of this point was involved in the rebellion of the next age after him, and he was the most characteristic figure of his own. Between him and Shelley, for instance, a great gulf is fixed. It is hard to imagine a greater disparity than they present, or a greater shift in appreciative taste than took place in the century between them. We ourselves are far from Shelley, but we belong to him rather than to Pope. And this is not a matter of time, either, but rather of spirit, as one may see by realizing how much nearer we seem to Shakespeare, and even to Chaucer, than to the wits of Queen Anne's reign. Nor is it, on the face of it, to be explained by the peculiar temper of our era, for this is the age of science *par excellence,* and hence of reason. On that score one might guess that we should find Wordsworth as intolerable as Jeffries ever did, and should read Dryden and his followers with avidity. None the less, when we turn to the literature of the past it is to Chaucer and Shakespeare, to Wordsworth and Shelley that we go. And when we try to explain to ourselves, if we do, why they seem to us so much more poetical than the Augustans, we cite from some angle, as the Romantics did a century ago, the disjunction between mind and heart, reason and feeling, intellect and emotion, and seem to ourselves to have captured in the distinction an essence that inheres not only in particular poets but in all poetry.

And I dare say that we should have done so if we had treated the distinction gently, in the delicate spirit of poetry itself. But ours is, after all, an age of prose, and such essences are hard to keep in prosaic hands. In their nature they are subtle and evanescent, and when one of them is put into words, fluidly at first in a large gesture of speech, it tends, if held too fast, to harden into a crystal. A crystal is dear to pure reason for its clarity; but it is the nature of crystals to develop many facets, and hence many sides to " take off " from besides the one from which the original essence is reflected. This is, of course, the eternal hazard of language, and because it is the hazard of language it is the hazard of ideas. Thus an antithesis of mind and heart, true from one angle and richly confirmed in the many intimacies of experience, where emotion seems to twist and distort the rectitudes of thought, and reason seems to cool the genial glow of feeling — this antithesis, reflecting so pure and authentic a light from one face, reflects from others half-lights not contemplated in the first moment of capture.

One of the secondary facets of this antithesis has been accountable, it seems to me, for a certain wryness in our current ways of thinking — about life, incidentally, but more particularly about literature. And so, as I have suggested, I should like to look with some care at a nice point in human nature intimately involved at this crossroads where life and literature, creative imagination and appreciative response — those ancient couples — come together in more or less happy conjunction.

Perhaps I should use the term *psychology* instead of the humbler *human nature.* The current designation has power as a charm or spell. But I am eager for the simplest clarity. And it seems to be the peculiar feat of psychology, even for those to whom it is an open book and no magic, that instead of clarifying the unknown in terms of the known, it rather lures the known out of the setting of life where it has its bearings and where it may be met and recognized, and puts it, briefed and labelled, into categories never encountered on the open road.

Now from the point of view of poetry this dilemma seems gratuitous. The subject of psychology is the consciousness. As a science, therefore, it ought to render the consciousnes intelligible *to* the consciousness. But after all, we know the consciousness only in terms of what it is conscious *of*. And the intimate rendering of the consciousness in terms of what it is conscious of is poetry itself. Human nature is its subject.

2

I keep to the homelier language of poetry, therefore, and speak simply of a point in human nature. When I mention, then, the old antithesis between mind and heart I speak of something which, I imagine, was very ingenuous in its first intention, and carried very little baggage with it beyond its immediate apparel. It is apparent now, however, that what began as a loose contrast has come to be fixed into a four-square logical premise. Two things that were held up in general opposition have come to be taken as, in the nature of things, coördinate. And mind and heart are spoken of as two alternative sources from which to draw when one comes to make a poem — or for that matter a sonata or a philosophy.

I do not know that this sense of two coördinate, alternative, mutually exclusive sources in the consciousness, from which to draw and to which expression may be given, has anywhere been explicitly put. Rather it seems to be taken as too axiomatic to need putting. At all events it finds too many echoes in current criticism and formal review, public controversy and private conversation to leave doubt about its prevalence. Yet a little scrutiny of the relations of mind and heart will show that they are not coördinate and alternative, and that to speak of literature as the expression of emotion is to expose it to infinite confusion.

I hasten to prelude that emotion plays its Hamlet's part both in the making of poetry and in the apprehension of it. It plays there without interruption. But then — and here is the distinction, or absence of it — it plays without interruption in all the conscious moments of life. And just this fact about the consciousness makes it as false to say that literature is the expression of emotion as it would be to say that a sunset, or a cup of tea, or a vision of Como under a summer sky, is the expression of emotion. If we step outside literature and look at our feelings as they respond to the accidents and incidents of daily existence, we see at once that they play an unceasing obbligato to all experience, and are to us, simply, *the way it feels* to be conscious of what, from moment to moment, we lend our conscious attention to — whether our present sensations, our absent thoughts, our sleeping dreams, or our waking recollections and imaginings.

Oh, we know the heat of the sun and the cool of the breeze on the mountain slope, and the aching thighs and the throbbing pulse on the high trail, and in response the heart sings with the zest of the road. We throw ourselves on the grass by the roadside and watch the spider dart and murder on his web, and in response the heart recoils, somber at the sight of ugliness. We push on to the top and look down to the lake below, Como calm and iridescent in its setting of purple hills, and the heart grows still with the hush of its loveliness. On the long road down we recall the tilt of the hat and the cock of the eye of the beggar we had bribed with a lire in the last village, and in the recollection we laugh again. And at the gate of the villa by the shore we hear the welcoming shout of our host, and in response we feel the glow of friendship, and of welcome, of rest, and of quiet.

Our emotions, that is, are secondary and consequent — how it feels, as I say, to be conscious of these things. We are first aware of them and then respond with our feelings — each one with his own. For our companions may not feel as we do about the same experiences. They may complain of the steep trail, laugh at the spider, remember the beggar with anger, and grow boisterous at the sight of the lake below. It is the emotions that conform, and conform in each one out of his own nature, after he is aware through his senses, in his memory, in his imagination, in his thoughts, of the things present to his conscious attention.

Later in the evening three of us sit on the terrace looking at the sunset. We all see the same colors, crimson and gold below, then lucid lemon, shading through tender green to azure at the zenith. The sunset is alike for us all — but our feelings? They may be alike, indeed, if one may guess, but what is not a guess is that they need not be alike. And here as it turns out they are not. One of us is sad and silent, one radiant and silent, and one indifferent, only half attentive. Does the sunset convey emotion? Whose emotion? All that can be said of it is that it is there. What is conveyed, science tells us, is vibrations, or whatever. What is palpably ours in common is the sensation of colors. But how it feels to each one of us to contemplate those colors is a thing determined, not by identical but by disparate factors. The sources of feeling are not in the common object but in the several diverse observers.

3

Now to speak of poetry as the expression of emotion is not as unintelligible as to speak of a sunset as the expression of emotion, though it is nearly so. Poetry does not put life itself before us, but it does an equivalent thing. It builds up the semblance of life for the imagination, scenes and situations which we picture in inward seeming, and it expresses the thoughts and reflections and understandings of the poet's mind. But how we feel in contemplating these scenes and situations, these reflections and interpretations, is a matter of our own responses. We may feel as the poet felt, or we may not. We may feel as other readers feel or we may not. What is expressed and conveyed is, like the sunset, approximately the same for us all, but the emotion comes, not from the poem, but severally from us.

"Oh my dear Dickens!" wrote that dour Scotch reviewer, whose ruthless "*This will never do*" will be forever associated with Wordsworth and the Romantics, "what a No. 5 you have given us! I have so cried and sobbed over it last night and again this morning; and felt my heart purified by those tears, and blessed and loved you for making me shed them. Since the divine Nelly was found dead on her humble couch beneath the snow and the ivy, there has been nothing like the actual dying of that sweet Paul in the summer sunshine of that lofty room."

I am a lover of Dickens, and struck by this letter I have read again in a long-neglected passage, of the death of "that sweet Paul." I speak of myself because my own emotions are the only ones I can know with confidence. But I cannot believe that mine are those that Jeffries says were his. I know that they are not the emotions with which years since I first lived in imagination through that scene. Yet what Dickens wrote, and what Jeffries read, what I read as a boy and what I have read again to-day are identical. And so I repeat that in any accurate sense literature does not convey emotion.

Inadequate as the statement may seem at first sight, in view of the high place that literature occupies in our affections and our scale of values — to me the highest place of all in the whole opulent range of human accomplishment — what must be said of it is that essentially and fundamentally it is the expression of thought. Yet I do not know what higher human praise could be given it. Thought implies two distinguishable elements, and these are the substances which literature, by the special genius of its medium language, expresses and communicates — what the thought is *about,* the things posed for the imagination to contemplate, and the thought *about* it, the reflections and interpretations proposed to the understanding. So much the poet expresses.

The cloud-capp'd towers, the gorgeous palaces,
The solemn temples, the great globe itself,
Yea, all which it inherit, shall dissolve
And, like this insubstantial pageant faded,
Leave not a rack behind. We are such stuff
As dreams are made on, and our little life
Is rounded by a sleep.

With what emotions each reader responds, whether with exquisite melancholy, or glad relief, or with angry protest, or with weary acquiescence, these are his own affairs, brought by each of us out of our own several natures, our dispositions and prior reflections, after we have realized what the poet has posed to our imagination and understanding.

It goes without saying that the poet has his own feelings like another as he conceives the scenes and thoughts which he presents. Perhaps his feelings are more intense than those of men who are not poets. But it is not the intensity of his feelings that makes him a poet, or the mad-house would be the temple of Apollo. He is a poet by virtue of the infinitely delicate perception of just what articulate elements of consciousness — stuff of imagination and significant thought — have stirred his own.

And though it is not his emotions that he proceeds to express, but rather the stuff of imagination and reflection, his emotions serve him of course. In them he knows how it feels to be conscious, and specifically how it feels to be conscious of those things. Prompted by his feelings he selects and rejects. And more than that, he counts on sympathy, a community of responsive feeling among others when they have imagined the scenes and understood the thoughts which he has conveyed. He does not always get it. But when he does he gets it by bending all his judgment and plying all his art to the presentation of the things and thoughts that have stirred his own feelings, and he gets it from those who, in their common humanity, their common breeding and culture, their common experience and reflection, have come to feel as he does about the same things.

Is all this a desperate laboring of the obvious? I should say that it was if the confusion were not so ingrained in a wide range of contemporary thought. Music, for instance, still more commonly than literature, is said to be the expression of emotion. Can those of us who do not enjoy the Tristan music be confidently said to have missed what Wagner expressed? Is it not truer to say that having got all that Wagner expressed — sounds, their pitch and timbre and harmony, their rhythms and their melodies — we do not respond with the same feelings with which the composer probably conceived them, or the same feelings with which many others hear them? Are these latter the same among themselves, or the same as those of the composer? No one can confidently tell. It is just the fact that these emotions cannot be more than grossly specified in communication of any kind, and never clearly compared, but rather are private and incommunicable stirrings within the breast of each separate person, that makes it a source of confusion to discuss the arts of expression in terms of them.

It is intelligible — if we come back to literature — to speak of Shelley as more imaginative than Pope. The stuff of the imagination — the semblance in the consciousness as of things apprehended by the senses — is one of the products of the mind which language gives explicit voice to. It is intelligible to speak of Pope as more intellectual than Shelley. Thoughts, understandings, generalizations, are things which language gives explicit voice to. But it is unintelligible to say that Shelley's verse is more imbued with emotion than Pope's, for emotion is not in the verse but in those who read it. Now those who read Pope in Pope's day read him because what he said to the imagination and intelligence came home to their lively appreciation, and to imagine and understand what he conveyed to them was a stirring delight. Their emotions responded in that way to that kind of thing. It was so far from failing to stir emotion in them, that it won for Pope a larger public in his day than Shelley won in his. We read Shelley to-day with more feeling than we read Pope with. Is it not rather we who have changed? What Pope expressed and conveyed is the same now as it was when it flowed from his pen in the grotto at Twickenham. If our emotions as we read are of other kinds and milder than those of his contemporaries, is it not simply that our spontaneous affections for his imagery and his thoughts are less than theirs? And if Shelley stirs us more deeply, is it not that our spontaneous affections for his imagery and his thoughts are greater?

4

This distinction gains what importance it has from the fact that poetry is a human product in human hands, not only in the hands of the poet but in the hands of his readers. It is well enough to say, "Give genius its rein; take what it offers and be thankful." But who is a genius? And which are the works of genius? These questions are answered by those who read. Genius is a designation accorded by mankind. So that criticism, tacit or overt, the judgment of him who reads, whether he reads and tells or reads and is silent, is forever copartner in the fortunes of this exquisite product. Literature is in the keeping of human judgment, and just in the measure of our value for it is it important to keep our judgment of it delicately clarified.

The confusion that arises from the assumption that literature is the conveyancer of emotion is the confusion that always intervenes when the judge confuses with the object he is judging the feeling it stirs in him — simple to detect when the petulant man kicks the inoffensive stool he has stumbled over, ancient source of comedy in a Sir Anthony's " Insolent, impudent, overbearing reprobate, can't you be cool, like me? ", and pathetic fallacy at all times.

Not to detect the fallacy, but to proceed on the supposition that the emotional response is part and parcel of literature itself is to attribute to it an infinite variety of answering spontaneities, incommensurate and incalculable — the trival emotions of the trivial, the vulgar emotions of the vulgar, the sentimentalities of the sentimental, and all the limitless rest. Only when we disentangle from our total experiences as we read such elements as are conveyed by literature itself can we disengage what is there for common judgment, and bring to it an intelligent consideration.

This disengagement of literature as a subject of judgment from the private and disparate feelings of those who read it and write about it would clarify our endless talk about it. Not until we remember that the emotions are simply or richly the vital flavor of experience to each one of us as severally we lend our consciousness to it — the feel to ourselves of each awareness of sense or imagination or thought as we bend our attention upon it — the unceasing obbligato of our waking moments — or our sleeping dreams for that matter — whether they are filled with an awareness of the outer world of actuality, our own memories, imaginings and thoughts, or the memories, imaginings and thoughts of others conveyed to us in literature — not until then shall we be able to speak of literature in significant and intelligible terms. For only then, when reflection has for its subject the thing that is identical for all of us — the thing our diverse feelings are about — have we a common subject for discussion at all.

VIII

THE TEMPER OF THE NEW POETRY

VIII

THE TEMPER OF THE NEW POETRY

THE distinction of literature is its unlimited liability. In comparison every other preoccupation — except living, and that only in its finest moments — and every other form of expression seem meager, hedged about, confined to a narrow range of subject and a narrow range of faculties. Even the fine arts, of which much of a mystical sort is made nowadays, dwindle under examination to the straitest of bounds, each confined to a single sense and its emotional responses.

Literature, on the other hand, confronts the whole of life, and reacts to it with the whole of the mind. Nothing is alien to it within or without. If the point were to make the contrast with the fine arts it might be related how easily literature adds smell, taste, and feel, and pain to its repertory, and adds memory besides, and aspirations, and fears, and the emotions of thought, and abstractions, and causes and consequences, and reflections, and reason. Literature, in short, is commensurate with all the dimensions of the world, and all the dimensions of the conscious brain and heart.

And poetry is literature heightened. Only, in poetry there is this reserve — that while in prose with its colder deliberation there may be an explanatory launching of the baldly new and alien, poetry demands a spontaneity of emotional consent that is not likely to be given to new facts or to strange ways of thinking or feeling. Poetry, as a consequence, is a more telling measure of the minds it comes intimately home to. It comes home to where the mind lives, or it fails. And the poetry of an age puts us into closer touch with the whole temper of the age than any other index can.

This is seen best, of course, in perspective. Our own mental balance, being ours, seems natural and finely sane — the norm from which others vary. Thus to the temper of Queen Anne's time the temper of the Elizabethans, as seen in their poetry, appeared gothic, and a little barbarous, wearing a complexion in which fancy, imagination, and passion flamed up garishly, and intellect, taste, and restraint bore down but lightly. To the Victorians, in turn, the Augustans, as reflected in their poetry, seemed arid in fancy, in imagination, and passion, and tamed by a frigid excess of intellect, commonsense, and decorum. Later, to the *fin de siècle,* the Victorians, as plumbed by their poets, seemed soft through a surfeit of sentiment, and immured in moral tenderfootedness.

By the same token, then, what is the temper, the complexion, the balance or overbalance of mental weights borne by our own peculiar poetry? The question is not yet to be answered in full; the perspective is not ripe. And this is not, I dare say, to be called an age of poetry at all — of poetry matured in its own genius and met half way by the spirit of the times. But there is a poetry, and it has a very articulate public, both of them provocative.

I

Thus it was in a spirit of irony with a holiday touch to it that a radical friend of mine should have given me a recent anthology of what is called the "new" poetry. The collection was not utterly recent as anthologies go, but it was recent enough as poetry goes, and the copy that came to me was of a third printing eloquent of currency rare for poetry of any kind in the last two decades. It was with a counter-irony, therefore, that playing up to a holiday mood the book should have taken its revenge by yielding up a certain charm, as the phrase is. And from other collections, which after a reluctant start began to threaten both purse and shelf, I found the impression confirmed.

The new poetry has uttered its challenge, and it is only good sportsmanship to take it up. But the challenge comes, it must be confessed, a little equivocally. For the anthologies, which may be taken, I suppose, as fair and representative selections, offer so much that is indistinguishably of the old. Anyone much traveled in the realms of the *Golden Treasury* or the *Oxford Book,* frank exemplars of the older tradition, if he should come one day upon Miss Davies's *Cloistered* within those covers, would find nothing to startle him but the shock of wondering that he had not remembered it there.

Tonight the little girl-nun died:
Her hands were laid
Across her breast; the last sun tried
To kiss her quiet braid;
And where the little river cried
Her grave was made.

There are two more stanzas equally simple and equally rhythmical. And there are so many selections no less fresh, but no less of the old dispensation, that in a moment of skepticism one may find himself questioning whether the charm of the volumes may not have lain in the taste of these priming waters rather than in the draught of the new fountain itself. Even among poems that could never have found a place in the older anthologies, there are some of a kind that the world, with its terrible capacity for bathos, could not have waited until now to conceive. The reader is left as a consequence, with a problem of his own — apart from his inevitable quarrel with the anthologist's choices — of distingushing what it is that is new.

In point of form, however, the new is often detected in the guise of *vers libre.* Of *vers libre* much has been said and more has been bitterly or scornfully thought. Two of its differences come home at once and insistently to the lover of the older verse — its reluctance to sing, and its frail hold on the memory. And he rebels. He misses the rhythmical undulations that croon an obbligato to the voyaging thoughts, lulling to drowsiness his keener responses to the accidental, the temporal, and the ephemeral, but stirring the immemorial emotions that lie below the level of our developed differences, and seeming thus to universalize the articulate message of the poet. And he feels that the greater ease with which metrical lines flow into the matrices of his memory implies something yet more telling in the poignancy with which they speak to him, weaving their thoughts more organically into the subtle synthesis of his mind and his heart.

These losses of *vers libre* are the commonplaces of conservative rebellion. They are real enough to be grievous to certain tempers. But they are, after all, only negative; and the very frankness with which they proclaim themselves is a fair claim upon an equal frankness in the search for compensations. All virtues cannot be compacted in a single poem. But when I, for one, come to examine the chief compensation that *vers libre* proposes for itself — I mean freedom — I am confronted by a paradox. For I cannot help thinking that not the least loss of *vers libre* is the loss of freedom itself.

The point is at least curious, and if it leaves *vers libre* still room for many virtues, it throws a certain light upon the temper of the time that has produced it, and upon those criers of the newest poetical shop who have made much of freedom in their defense of the new.

II

"Law," remarks Mr. Brooks Adams out of an inveterately legal and political mind, "is nothing but a series of regulations imposed on the strong for the protection of the weak." The idea is prevalent, and it is given a kind of official stamp as the attitude of the *vers librists* in a pronouncement of one of the criers of the new verse — that they "are doing pioneer work in an heroic effort to get rid of obstacles that have hampered the poet and separated him from his audience."

Whatever of political truth there may be in the conception of law as an obstacle, it is certain that in the province of the mind *law* has a subtler significance. In the expression of thought, for example, the possibilities of chaos, the possibilities, that is, of stringing together inconsecutive ideas that no one else can follow, are so infinite that the strong themselves quite voluntarily hunt for a law to guide them, not for the protection of the weak, but as the condition of their greeting anyone on the way. For the laws of the mind are not moral impositions, but rather a description of the tenuous paths over which if one leads others may follow. In this region, where the trail is so narrow and faint and the wilderness on every side so vast, far from separating the voyager from those who come to meet him, the trail is the only assurance of their coming together at all.

As for freedom, it may be possible to apply the term to a total disregard for reasonable consecutiveness, but in that sense *freedom* is not an intelligible thing. To make freedom intelligible there is needed the criterion of an underlying pattern from which it takes appreciable departures. The pattern makes it intelligible by making it measurable.

I do not know how far the lovers of free verse would agree with me in saying that this principle of the pattern holds for verse form as well as for rational statement, and that by giving up the law they have given up a freedom that is intelligible and for the reader, at least, enjoyable. Yet I venture the suggestion. I am at a loss, for example, to feel the added felicity that a lawless freedom has contributed to such a typical passage as this:

No man shall ever read me,
For I bring about in a gesture what they cannot fathom in a life;
Yet I tell Bob, and Harry, and Bill —
It costs me nothing to be kind: —

For I can never know whether the actual cadences there on the page are the result of a peculiar mastery or a peculiar helplessness. The criterion is missing, and the result savors of accident. The result is there, indeed, to be enjoyed for what it is. But one peculiar source of enjoyment is foregone — the enjoyment of freedom itself. On the other hand it is hard to compassionate Swinburne, say, for his metrical fetters:

In a coign of the cliff between lowland and highland,
By the sea-down's edge between windward and lee,
Walled round by rocks like an inland island,
The ghost of a garden fronts the sea.

Here, over and above the slumberous echo of the croon, the alert faculties respond with the constant leap of pleasure caught from the recurrent play of the poet's masterly liberties — liberties spontaneously appreciable because each one is a measurable departure from the pattern. There is surprise just because there is expectation, and delight in diversity because the spirit of unity is never violated. The best manners are free; but the free manners of those who have no manners are hard to bear. In affairs of intellect and of taste freedom indeed spells life. But a freedom that acknowledges no constant loses the touchstone that makes it either intelligible or enjoyable.

Can it be just possible that the champions of free verse scan their older poets in the sing-song of doggerel that they find their liberty so straitened by the bounds of meter? Or, still to be unkind, is it that they find themselves poor craftsmen in need of an easier medium? The laws of meter are exacting, it is true. And it is the definition of doggerel that it follows these exactions with pathetic fidelity.

Dogs delight to bark and bite;
It is their nature to.

It is possible to imagine the droning schoolboy doggerelizing something better than that:

When *to* the *ses*sions *of* sweet *si*lent *thought*

But the intelligent reader of poetry knows better. And just in this better knowledge he finds its peculiar felicity. Cavalierly, and ostensibly ignoring the schoolboy sing-song, he reads more nearly thus:

When to the *ses*sions of *sweet si*lent *thought* —

If he accounts to himself for his explicit pleasure in the haunting music of the line, he will find that it derives in part from the foreseen cadence of the croon, but even more from the variations which, without violation of its spirit, yet with nice adjustment to the current thought, bring it nearer still to the temper of the enveloping mood. A rebellion against the laws by which such happy ends are gained he understands only in the ironic compartments of his mind.

In the light of such considerations the compassion of our champions of free verse, and perhaps that of the poets themselves, would seem to be all for the poets and not at all for their readers. To "get rid of the obstacles that have hampered the poet" may be kindly meant. But the exigent reader is likely to feel that poetry made easy is poetry made a less exalted thing, that the difficulties of poetry are the inherent difficulties of a rare and high accomplishment, and that to evade them is to aim at a lower kind of product.

III

There is another point of approach that perhaps comes nearer to the sense of the *vers librists*. If the pattern of conventional meter is abandoned, there are other patterns short of pure chaos that the poet may be guided by — a cadence appropriate to each utterance, inevitably right for the poet and recognizable, once uttered, by the sensitive reader. This, I think, is the avowed defense of the genre, and the validity of it is apparent in the fact that it has always been the animating ideal of prose.

This perception would at once throw *vers libre* into the level sea of prose discourse, and would warrant the unsympathetic reader in demanding straight margins and normal capitals, but that *vers libre,* once put into prose form, is evidently not prose according to the canon of prose taste. A nice ear and a rational mind would be shocked to find in unbroken format this curious assertion:

> I saw in Pamplona in a musty museum, I saw in Pamplona in a buff-colored museum, I saw in Pamplona a memorial of the dead violinist; I saw in Pamplona a memorial of Pablo Sarasate.

This is not prose. Even at its most impassioned and most poetic, prose is governed by certain rational principles of concision and continuity.

For prose as well as verse has its pattern. But because prose in its nature is more preponderantly rational, the pattern lies rather in the architecture of the idea than in the undulations of its sentiment, and imposes on the expression a different economy, a rigorous articulation of each part into the structural logic of a more angular whole, a hearkening to the colder voice of sense which tolerates sentiment only so far as it does not interfere with rational clarity, an allegiance to the form of the fact even when the fact is fanciful, and to the lines of the thought even when the thought is passionate. The freedom of prose is also a measured freedom, intelligible and appreciable through never being out of touch with the pattern of the idea which it creates.

When an idea is suffused with feeling, it is true, the rational pattern tends to be overlaid; and in the lyric plane, where it is suffused to the point of saturation, the prose pattern tends to disappear. It is at this point that, in metrical verse, the other pattern, the musical pattern, in its close rapport with the emotions, steps in to give appropriate form to the sentiment of the poet. And it is just here in this fluid region of feeling that *vers libre* seems to fall between two stools — between the rational pattern on the one hand and the musical pattern on the other.

The results are sometimes curious. The effects of verbal cadence are partly, even largely, matters of association. If the poet, therefore, selects his cadences in the whim of a perfect freedom, he abandons them in an equal measure to the chance impressionism of the reader. And when the reader wanders errantly into associations of his own out of the store of stray cadences that the accidents of experiences have sung into his mind, he is doing nothing that is not allowable by that freedom that is the first and last law of the genre. He has been abandoned to the hazards of just such accidents. Thus one reader finds himself helpless before such stanzas as this:

Therefore
I have renounced my kingdom;
In a little bronze boat I have set sail
Out
Upon the sea —

helpless, that is, to resist the memory and the tone of that earlier *vers librist* whose compositions in this kind have escaped the anthologists:

Errands gone
On with fi
Delity
By Ladies and Gentlemen
Your humble servant
Silas Wegg.

— or of Mr. Boffin who, if he *is* illiterate, promptly falls into the infection:

A literary man —
With *a wooden leg —*
And all print is open to him.

The elements are all there in their immeasurable freedom — the breaking up into strange lengths, the emphasis thrown upon the odd particles of speech, and the forced breathing at stertorous intervals, like the sophomore at his maiden speech:

"Why do
You thus devise
Evil against her?" "For that
She is beautiful, delicate;
Therefore."

Such responses are indeed eccentric; but eccentricity is their natural heritage. For here, in the appeals of the cadence, the common ground of the pattern, which to the *vers librist* seems an obstacle which separates him from his audience, has been done away, and the chances of their coming together are by so much the less.

Whether *vers libre* will win to an important place among the resources of English prosody will hang, in the event, upon two human factors — the genius of the poets who use it, and the enjoyment of the readers, who have it in their hands to immortalize it by their affections or to mortalize it by their neglect. If it wins it will be pure gain, for it cannot destroy the old for those who prefer the old. But its way is rugged with difficulties — not the explicit forces of hostile criticism, but rather such silent forces as work in unconsciousness among the judgments of those who need render no account of their affections or their prejudices. For it has consciously surrendered many of the qualities which endear the poet to certain constant factors of the spirit. It has given up the ground note of the rhythmic beat, and with it the matrix into which the flowing thought pours its stream to haunt the memory. It has foregone the melody that sings to the coursing blood and releases with its magic the latent passions of the heart. If it has the advantage to the poet of an unfettered freedom, it loses the advantage to the reader of rendering that freedom constantly measurable and so constantly pleasurable. If there are compensations in that freedom, they are such as still must be explained even to the intellect — so far are they as yet from striking out spontaneous responses from the seat of our spontaneous enjoyments.

Meantime, while we wait for the poet who shall compel our affections, the genre is hampered by the mob of those writers who are attracted by its relaxations, who have nothing to say, or no gift of expression, or who, with a passion for purple, can find no market for purple prose. As for them, and, indeed, for the bulk of those who now write *vers libre,* the final comment is perhaps that of Dr. Johnson on the not dissimilar Pindaric inundation that followed in the wake of Cowley — that "all the boys and girls caught up the pleasing fancy, and those who could do nothing else could write like Pindar."

IV

It would be comfortable to stop at this point, letting our delight be the arbiter in a matter that is so largely one of delight. But the interpreters of the new poetry are eminently just in insisting that the substance of verse is of deeper importance than its outer apparel. If they needed defense in this it would be enough to remember that no one reads poetry in a language that he does not understand, though all but the meaning is there for him to enjoy; while many go to translations — of Homer, say, or even lyric Sappho — for the substance of their thought, though the charm of the form has evaporated. The fresh power of expression, therefore, to be won for the new poetry by the freedom of a less restricted craftsmanship, is the thing of chief significance, and becomes justly the thing of chief interest.

" The new poetry," says one of its principal interpreters, " strives for a concrete and immediate realization of life; it would discard the theory, the abstraction. . . . It has set before itself an ideal of absolute simplicity and sincerity — an ideal which implies an individual, unstereotyped diction; an individual, unstereotyped rhythm. . . . It looks out more eagerly than in; it becomes objective. . . . In presenting the concrete objects or the concrete environment, whether these be beautiful or ugly, it seeks to give more precisely the emotions arising from them, and thus widens immeasurably the scope of the art."

How reverently this Muse is to be taken will depend finally upon her acolytes, as has been said. Meantime her heralds have taken her seriously enough, and a touch of exaggeration is to be forgiven them in their enthusiasm. I am at a loss to believe, however, that this exteriority, objectivity, and concreteness are really new, or that this reluctance to look inward will widen the scope of the poetic art. Even the older poetry tried, in Milton's phrase, to be sensuous. It was objective and concrete in its method. But it did also look inward. And as one sweeps over the range of lyric and dramatic poetry, and realizes anew how many of its deeper harmonies are plucked from this inward string, his simple arithmetic will hardly let him conclude that by ignoring it the new poet has added another octave to his lyre. The new, on the contrary, seems to lie not so much in an added range of poetic substance as in a special convention in the way of taking a limited part of the old.

As for the older poetry, the impulse that produced it was essentially reflective. I know that this assertion may sound strange — a contradiction to what has just been said. But I believe that a moment's reflection will show something of the consistency and justice of the assertion.

We are at best in a sardonic relation to the world. We find ourselves here where we have not asked to come, instinctively curious and emotionally concerned for the point of an experience whose normal bitterness is an affront unless we can find in the situation some rational plan to satisfy our intelligence or some aspect to satisfy our affections. All literature in its broadest sense is an attempt to interpret some phase of this human scene, to put it in order, to build it in to one or both of these orderly structures. Prose accepts the responsibility of building-in its materials to the understanding. But poetry accepts still another responsibility — to build its materials into the orderly structure of the feelings as well. It is these cumulative structures of thought and feeling that make up the house we are trying to put in order — tentative structures, it is true, forever subject to intelligent, or unintelligent, readjustment, but none the less the home we have made for ourselves, in relation to which the outer world has for us the sum of its significance.

The inward glance of the older poetry was a glance at these patterns of the mind. Its substance was concrete; and it too had an abhorrence of abstract theorizing. But it was stirred by a lively sense that its reason for being was to find a significant place for this concrete substance, and it tried, implicitly or explicitly, to *build-in* its materials, to interpret them. The reluctance of the new poetry to look inward, therefore, would seem to be a reluctance to concern itself with the patterns of these structures. And a sensitive reader, ranging through volume after volume of the recent anthologies, will be struck with the perception that with a large consistency the poems that impress him as new among them will seem new by virtue of their bringing into the province of poetical *ideas* something of the same temper that has rebelled against the patterns of meter — and that here too the freedom that is gained by ignoring the patterns of the mind is an unintelligible freedom.

He may come, in grateful surprise, upon this metrical poem by Scharmel Iris, a little obvious in its close, perhaps, but momentarily the better for that:

The pale day drowses on the western steep;
The toiler faints upon the marge of sleep —
Within the sunset-press, incarnadine,
The sun, a peasant, tramples out his wine.

Ah, scattered gold rests on the twilight streams;
The poppy opes her scarlet purse of dreams.
Night with the sickle-moon engarners wheat,
And binds the sheaves of stars beneath her feet.

Rest, weary heart, and every flight-worn bird!
The brooklet of the meadow lies unstirred.
Sleep every soul against a comrade breast!
God grant you peace, and guard you in your rest.

Perhaps all that need be said of this poem is that it is clearly of the old dispensation. Already, before it was written the reader had the clue of its significance, as all men have it, in the common affections with which he and they face life, and he judges it in its substance by the poignancy with which it gives realization to sentiments latent but inarticulate in his own mind. It is as though it were not so much a creation as an evocation, so quickly does his response leap to the appeal. He has already the criterion by which to estimate the quality of its magic. His pleasure in it is a measure of the perfection with which it matches the very truth that it had made him now first know that he already dumbly possessed.

It is some such response as this, I think, that lies at the root of our value for what is universal in great poetry. How else, indeed, is the universal to be recognized? Specifically the thought may be new — all the better for that. But already in the common foundations of our common culture we find that it has a place which it fits inevitably. And in the measure of that fitness it finds its welcome home.

If the reader should pass on to the next poem in the same volume, however, he would find beneath his amusement or shock at the substance of its statements a sharp contrast in what may be called its rational structure:

This is the song of youth,
This is the song of myself;
I knew my father well and he was a fool,
Therefore I will have my own feet on the path before
I take a step. . . .

. . . .

Behold how people stand around!
(There are always crowds of people standing around
Whose legs have no knees) —
While the engineers put up steel work. . . .

. . . .

I can no more walk in the stride of other men
Than be father of their children.

. . . .

There is not anything in me save mutation and laughter;
My laughter is like a sword,
Like a piston-rod that defies oceans and grades.

. . . .

I have eaten locusts with Jeremiah;
I invite all hatreds and the stings of little creatures —
They enrich me, I glory in my parasites.

For my own part, after reading the poem of which these lines may give the flavor, I find myself at a loss. It has knocked at my door and I have let it in over the threshold, but I do not know what it means. It does not speak with the known voice of adolescence, as it purports to do, and so has no value to me as truth. Its substance is moral, but I can fit it into no moral sense. It is unlovely, and I cannot cherish it for its beauty. I seem to myself inhospitable, but it has not struck from me the spark of spontaneous recognition. I can find no place for it in the inner rooms of my consciousness. I have nothing by which to judge its identity, or its sincerity, or its appropriateness, or its perfection. I cannot make it at home. I can neither fit it in nor measure its unfitness. It has escaped the patterns of my mind.

Now what is left when the patterns of the mind are abandoned are first a direct sensuous image, and second an emotional color to the image. Both may be very vivid. It is probable that they are the more intense the more free they are from other prepossessions, as we commonly believe to be the case with primitives and children. At all events it is something of this primitive directness of vision and naïve idiosyncracy of feeling that the new poets seem to have set up as their object — an Adamic sense of the world as made up of bright particulars on the one hand and quick, surprising, irresponsible emotions on the other.

We have been concerned with the pervasive temper that has enlisted free verse in the service of the new poetry. It is more than accident, it would seem, that has brought those who ignore the patterns of the mind to ignore the patterns of meter as well. A poet who is concerned only with the concrete object itself, and is not concerned to have his readers reconcile it to their understandings or their orderly feelings will wisely select a medium that confines itself as far as possible to telling him what is there and concerns itself as little as possible with what happens to it after it gets there. The appropriateness of free verse for this process may be sharply felt in a brief poem by the same hand that wrote in a different style the simple, significant stanzas on the death of the girl nun:

The sun falls
Like a drop of blood
From some hero.

We
Who love pain
Delight in this.

The unconcern here for the patterns of both mind and heart is obvious. No one loves pain on his own part. Few love to see it in others. Delight in blood dropping from the wounds of heroes is, in the large, an idiosyncrasy. The poem is a piece of startling personal information, and the more startling because it remains there detached and apart, finding no place for itself in the large harmony of the reader's understanding and feelings. On the other hand it deals frankly with the reader in making no appeal for a sympathetic response. And herein is the point. For if he will try to imagine it embodied in metrical verse, he will find it impossible to do so. The call upon an emotional assent would be an incongruity.

He will catch thus, from another angle, the peculiar effect of meter to petition for the sympathy of the rational feelings, and see, by contrast, the appropriate effect of *vers libre* simply to assert and then to abandon the fact. What estimate he puts upon such a feat is, in the end, his own concern.

Somewhere between prose with its responsibility to the patterns of the intellect, and metrical verse with its responsibility to the patterns of the heart, *vers libre* has the effect of escaping responsibility altogether. And with its irregular lengths disturbing the glide of the thought into the restful matrix of established form it offers an effective means to keep awake the lively freshness of apprehension and that alertness of immediate attention with which on our primitive level we meet the kaleidoscopic disorder of the outer world.

In how far the new poets will prove satisfying interpreters of life to us will depend, in the nature of things, upon how we take that life. But if in those moods of leisure and sincerity in which we go to poetry to catch the inner echoes of the spirit, the new poetry should prove to be the reflection of what is most genuine in us, it will throw a curious and ironic light upon the new social morality that has come to be the professed, almost the official, note of our modernism. For the quality of the new poetry is its intense anarchy. In rejecting the metrical pattern it foregoes the power to bring men together into the atmosphere of a common mood, and in rejecting the patterns of the mind it foregoes the power to build its thoughts into common, passionate judgments. Common feelings and common judgments in the region of our deepest spiritual convictions are, however, the *conditio sine qua non* of that socialized life that occupies so much of our current attention. Whether the cult of the new poetry or the cult of the new democracy is the more sincere, it is not the place of the present discussion to inquire. But it is interesting to notice that both have arisen at the same time, are sponsored by much the same protagonists, and throw much light upon each other by their reciprocal antagonism.

IX

THE CRIERS OF THE MUSICAL SHOP

IX

THE CRIERS OF THE MUSICAL SHOP

YESTERDAY I culled this passage from an appreciation of Matisse:

" His glory is to have thrown over everything that could be taught, to have rid himself of experience, of tradition, of learning, of all the distorting veils of cultivation, and to have seen with his pure spirit, without a preconception, as a child might see, or a primitive savage, or, better, the first man without an ancestor to catch an atavistic predilection from."

And to-day an eulogy of Richard Strauss:

" Cacophony rules . . . this episode is repulsive in its aural cruelty. . . . Often we cannot hear the music because of the score. . . . Richard Strauss is the musical enchanter of our day. . . . What a gorgeous, horrible color scheme is his! He has a taste for sour progressions, and every voice in his orchestral family is forced to sing impossible and wicked things."

There should be a tacit wink in such language to belie the sober implication that painting is great for its barbarous crudity, its brainlessness, and music great for its cacophony, its aural cruelty, its sour progressions. But the wink is clearly not there. These readings were done in learned libraries, in books dog-eared with sedulous perusal. They meet with a sober response. And wild as they are they seem to be of a piece with the current sense of the arts, and this, curiously enough — and alas! — at a time when the arts are cried up as the stuff of culture. The case has its humors.

Not to bend too solemn a brow upon it, lest the comic spirit find its perch there instead of on the situation, I yet suggest that it is time for common sense to step in and take the word from the appointed appreciators and eulogists. We commonly say that the state is lost when authority slips from the civil to the military; and life no less goes to pieces when the specialists drown the voice of the general intelligence.

What we like to call the life of the spirit has of late been curiously parceled out and hedged in by the technicians. The large coördination of it has suffered accordingly — if it is not dead and beyond suffering. The play of the discursive reason, with its broad perspective and sense of proportion, seems latterly to have gone out and to have left, as our eulogist says of Strauss's music, "an entirely new scheme of orchestration, the basic principle of which is individualism of instruments, the pure anarchy of the entire orchestral apparatus." Whatever this may mean for music, for the general intelligence it is a case clearly enough in point. There are moments when we seem to be going a little mad, from too much centrifugal advice cried at us from a hundred shops like bewildered travelers in an Eastern bazaar.

Learning itself is guilty enough: witness in passing the swelling strut and mouthing in front of the psychological shop. Learning, however, has the eternal check of reality to keep it sane in the end. Reason is there to protest. But art is the perennial prey of the mountebanks. The arts spring at their best from the mystery of genius, and appeal to the eager senses and willing emotions. They live to please, and a dash of extravagance is spice to the palate. They escape the natural drag of obvious reality, and the natural ridicule of obvious common sense. They are the privileged, the concessionaires of the bazaar. And catching us at a moment when the general intelligence is in disrepute, they have launched their licensed criers at us with a gay confidence in our credulity. We are beset with their seductive antics. And they are taken at their word, greeted with sober faces, quoted, retailed.

"We catch glimpses," calls our musical crier, in hushed tones, thumb over shoulder toward the musical shop where the wizard is about to begin, "of vast vistas where dissonance is king; slow iron twilights in which trail the enigmatic figures of another world; there are often more moons than one in the blood-red skies of his icy landscapes."

Surely this is parody. As Bickerstaff's thousand gentlemen said of Partridge's almanack, no man alive ever writ such damned stuff as this. It is indeed parody. But there it is on the page before me, done by the crier and not by the satirist — done to be swallowed by the gullible, not to be enjoyed in the laughter of irony. And there have been enough of the gullible to give a kind of currency or repute to this kind of " stuff."

It is little wonder that the crier has begun to take himself as he sees himself in the eager, solemn eyes of the crowd. He doffs cap and bells, dons the frock coat and the professorial eye-glass, climbs down from the gilded box, and walks up and down in the earth like his prototype. Or he appears with the gilt license tag of a reputable publisher, to catch the ear of those who have not wandered to the bazaar for the frank, abandoned pleasure of being duped. He has caught the general ear. His talk has got currency. Really it is time for the general intelligence to step in and nail to the shop door of the arts its ninety-five theses against further indulgences.

And especially to the door of the musical shop. For music has out-topped the other arts in a certain kind of insidious extravagance. Architecture, when it strays too far, is brought back to sanity by its alliance to vulgar usefulness. Sculpture may go a little mad, but it is still responsible to something outside itself. Painting may have its periods when it out-Hamlets Hamlet — is indeed passing through a period when the wind is far from south. But it too has an external check, an anchor in reality, and is safe to come back eternally in its lucid intervals. Music, however, is free, is responsible to nothing.

It is trite to allude to Chinese music, but Chinese music holds a Chinese audience spellbound, and carries to Western ears the blunt, disillusionizing message that music is, after all, a matter of taste in noises, and that one may come to like almost any kind of noise. And to those who would like to feel that in melody and rhythm and harmony there lies something in the "nature of things," some correspondence with the human spirit whereby developing music might open up new recesses of the soul, probe to new depths, the disillusionment is great. The criers make much, indeed, of such mystic promises, and hail each new school, and each new meteor in the musical sky, as a discoverer of new revelations of the spirit, as a scientist uncovers new truths and enlarges the scope of knowledge.

But those magic promises are illusory — mystic bait for the credulous. We need no allusion to Chinese music. Our own, eschewing rhythm, disdaining melody, enthroning dissonance, is moving in the same direction, and assuring us that we can come to like any noise, genuinely like it, and respond to it with our emotions. But the emotions are the old emotions, the spirit the old spirit, dulled perhaps to old noises and eager for new, but with no new power and no new scope. There is nothing outside the voices of the criers themselves to make us believe that we have ampler spirits than were had in Athens of old, for all its simple music, or that Beethoven was of poorer spirit than Humperdinck.

Change and decay! We like the new sounds or we do not; and our emotions respond to what we like. Music is a pleasure in sounds. But music has the strongest hold on our mystic credulity, for it lays the surest hands on our intangible feelings. And it is at the door of the musical shop that I should like to make a few protests, not against music itself — rather in its defense — against its criers in the market place.

It is on the word of the criers that music has been taken with solemnity into the body of that curious thing called culture. And the particular note that recurs in cultural circles is that music has something to impart, some content — " message " is the word that will be recognized both by those who talk of culture and by those who shudder at it. At all events this content is a part of the serious regard in which music is held. It is reasonable, therefore, to inquire into the nature of those impartations — to search for " messages " among the musical, in programmes, and in those thumbed octavos that attest the seriousness of the cult. But a wide perusal ends in mystification.

" The quaking swamps echo with the shriek of flaming death," interprets one crier.

If this is the type — and it is the type reported — one is tempted to ask, Why say it? Or what is the good of being told so, or led to fancy it so?

" Wagner first set the fevers of the flesh to music. . . . In the music of Strauss the Germans have discovered the fevers of the soul. And that is indeed what Strauss has tried to interpret."

So writes another crier in the market place. Whether music *can* do such a thing is another question. But if it does — I speak the blunt language of common sense — is there not some room for doubt as to its health, even its sanity?

There are, indeed, other " messages " more sane revealed by the interpreters — sunny meadows that comport themselves more seemly, moods that are unmorbid, active impulse that moves with the stride of untainted purpose. But a search among the appreciators and programmes fails to give up anything that in speech would seem more than elementary. Compared with the subtleties from the pen of the simplest writer, the reported " messages " of music are something barren. Oftener they are gross.

" And such an exposition," comments one crier on the composer's orchestration of his " snarling, sorry crew of critics," " it is safe to say has never been heard since saurians roared in the streaming marshes of the young planet, or when prehistoric man met in multitudinous and shrieking combat."

And yet we are asked to associate such matter with the gentler amenities of culture! It is one of the curiosities of the current vogue of the criers that they report no messages which bear in themselves the high seriousness or the deep penetration that are the mark of that nobler expression which has given to genuine culture its place in human regard.

I am comforted on behalf of the more genuine culture, however, by one reflection. Music cannot say those things. There is danger, I know, of over-solemnity in chipping at this crystallized metaphor — metaphor it is — of a content in music. It will have a tendency to run fluid again. But that music can speak, that it can convey a thought, that it has a content, is, in the moving eloquence of the criers, the lamp that lights its entry into the preserves of culture. And the lamp is not left dull for want of rubbing.

" The conception is breath-catching," writes a crier of his hero, " for it is the chant of the Ego, the tableau of Strauss's soul exposed as objectively as Walt Whitman's when he sang of his Me."

Our light-hearted crier admits the next moment, indeed, that this objective exposure cannot be understood by listening to the score. Where then, one may surely ask, is the exposure?

" This kind of music," writes another, " adds to our knowledge of men and of the world as much as does a play of Ibsen or a novel of Tolstoi."

" Why cannot music express philosophy? " Strauss himself asks. " If one wishes to approach the world-riddle perhaps it can be done with the aid of music."

What is most in evidence here is a deliquescence of thought that meets more than half way the proclaimed potency of music. And part, no doubt, of the musical illusion is due to the kind of iridescent haze that goes, to the crier mind, by the name of thought. It is said, indeed, — and here is an illustration happily to hand — that " music is another language, addressed to the soul, a thing so subtle that speech can never more than dimly render it, its very essence lost in translation." Such words may have a meaning dimly illuminating their dulcet cadence, but I think that it is only such meaning as is explicit in the parallel statement that the smell of the rose is addressed to the soul. No language can dimly render the smell of the rose. The senses are beyond translation into speech. And yet even in the common vernacular there persists a distinction between sense and soul.

The great tactical mistake of the critics is that they are not content with their radiant nebulae; they insist on literal translation. And their translations are not far from soul-curdling melodrama, disordered dream-stuff, chaos, and old night. As for the explicit content of music, its thought, it is humorously significant that no composer has orchestrated a definite statement of the potency of music in this direction, to lay the natural doubts of the common sense. The criers themselves are forced to use speech to put its claims, to say what music means — to say that it means anything. And M. Rolland writes the ten volumes of his *Jean-Christophe* — that noble work marred by the musical illusion — and writes them in words.

After all, it is only language that can convey ideas. For conveyance implies not only utterance on the one side, but comprehension on the other. When Jean-Christophe in his old age came back to Paris, he found a new generation growing up around him, and a new school of music. It was a little naïve to have pictured him, as M. Rolland has done, going on uttering tremendous things which no one but he himself could ever understand. In uttering particular sounds one is likely to be meaningless unless the hearer is let into the secret of them beforehand. It is just because in language one *is* let into the secret of every articulate element — every word — beforehand that the meaning " gets across " — to use the expressive language of Broadway. Anyone who knows the pains of search for the right word, and the trembling lest its secret be not understood with nice precision beforehand, will know the hard truth of this particular assertion. It is not made clear how music, selecting its sounds solely for their tone-value, can arrive with a meaning. And there comes to mind the picture of Flaubert:

" Possessed of the absolute faith that there exists but one way of saying one thing, one word to express it, one adjective to qualify it, one verb to animate it, he gave himself over to the superhuman labor of discovering for each phrase just that word, just that epithet, just that verb. . . . To write was therefore, for him, a redoubtable thing, full of torments, of perils, of fatigues. He would set himself at his table with the fear and the desire of that beloved and torturing quest, and remain there hour after hour, immovable, desperate, over his frightful task, the task of a colossus, patient and minute, building a pyramid of the marbles of childhood."

When one compares with the significance of this picture the vague approximations of music — its utter uncertainty that any two auditors should conceive from its expression the simplest objective image:

A violet by a mossy stone,
Half hidden from the eye:

its utter inability to mention names or give utterance to a fact:

Even copious Dryden wanted, or forgot,
The last and greatest art, the art to blot:

its impotence to reason or to state a truth:

Great wits are sure to madness near allied,
And thin partitions do their bounds divide;

— when one compares the thinker searching for sounds of arbitrary but definite sense-value, with the musician searching out sounds for their sensuous tone-value, he may well despair of finding here the clue to the illusion of musical content. We may ourselves blush to have haunted the poor game in so empty a field.

I know that I am wholly beside the point in these animadversions of common sense, for thought and music are incommensurate. The point lies, after all, not in the province of thought, but in the province of emotion and fancy. It is the gift of the senses that they touch the emotions with no uncertain hand — beautiful faces loosing the pent yearnings of years, faint odors calling back for magic moments the lucid purity of childhood wonder and content, and sounds potent in their infinite variety of pitch and timbre, rhythm and succession and harmony, to stir the subtlest motions of the heart. And the quickened feelings teem with imagery to match the blended colors of the mood.

Fine Gallic distinctions among the mental faculties are not at present fashionable, but it is hardly Gallic, or a fine distinction to declare that imagery and emotion are not thought. They may accompany thought — indeed in the noblest expressions of it they do.

One recalls — extreme example — Arnold's apostrophe to Oxford:

" Beautiful city! so venerable, so lovely, so unravaged by the fierce intellectual life of our century, so serene!

" There are our young barbarians all at play! And yet, steeped in sentiment as she lies, spreading her gardens to the moonlight, and whispering from her towers the last enchantments of the Middle Age, who will deny that Oxford, by her ineffable charm, keeps ever calling us nearer to the true goal of all of us, to the ideal, to perfection, — to beauty, in a word, which is only truth seen from another side? "

There is emotion here, and imagery. But music would try in vain to convey just those images, just that emotion. For the musical mode reverses the literary, and in just the element that conveys the thought and adjusts the feeling to it. The user of speech puts his thought first, and the feeling flows from the *idea;* the user of tones rouses the feelings first, and the thought that follows — if it does follow — is the irresponsible stuff of dreams.

One may guess, then, in this region of fluid values, the submerged and slippery road over which has come the saying that music, if not parallel with prose, is parallel with poetry. It is, indeed, possible to find poetry without thought; there is a school of futurist poets. But poetry, like prose, presents its idea or its imagery first; they are its only sure substance of conveyance. And if emotions do arise they flow from the idea, secondary and incidental. To find music in poetry along with its thought is hardly basis for the belief that music alone is potent to convey ideas.

All this, however, is still beside the point. There lingers yet the mystic faith that in those subtle leapings of the heart that respond to the discourse of sweet sounds something momentous must be meant, "something that slips by language and escapes." We are in a region of susceptibilities. To feel deep emotion — emotion that in normal life springs from touching and deep meanings in experience or thought — to feel such emotion *is* the illusion that something is meant. In the market place are persuasive voices crying that something *is* meant. And the culture of the polite world, with its chagrins for those who give signs that they do not belong, has added the sanction of its social tyranny.

"Certain poets," remarks the charming humanist, La Bruyère, "are given in their dramas to long passages of pompous verse, which seem powerful, elevated, and full of grand sentiments; the people listen eagerly, eyes uplifted, mouths open, and they believe themselves pleased, and in the measure of their incomprehension admire the more. . . . I believed at one time, and in my early youth, that those passages were intelligible to the actors, to the pit, and to the balcony; that their authors understood them themselves, and that with all the attention that I could give to them I was in the wrong not to understand them. I have been undeceived."

We were questioning the source of the musical illusion. I am not sure but that here, under the tutelage of fashion, and under the sanction of that curious melange of preciosities called culture, the credulity of the emotions has been carried away to believe that music does mean something to the performers, to the pit, and to the balcony, and that the composers understand what they mean themselves. And they have not yet been undeceived.

X

A MUSE'S QUANDARY

X

A MUSE'S QUANDARY

THERE is no doubt that that rather hoydenish muse, Academica Americana, for all her noble lineage, her wealth, and her often brilliant entourage, is desperately uncomfortable. As a muse she derives her dignity and authority from her title to some defined province. And now a vagueness has come upon the bounds of that province; even its capital is uncertain. And with her territory in doubt she is left, for all her lineage and wealth and entourage, uncomfortably doubtful of both her dignity and her authority. It is very well being a muse, but not to know what one is a muse of is a little disconcerting.

Her predicament is so relatively recent, and her relations are so intimately social in their bearings, that it is not impertinent to inquire whether her plight does not tie itself up with democracy, now that democracy is coming into its own. The less impertinent that something of the same vagueness is creeping into the faces of her sisters abroad. A dozen years ago "Agathon" stirred a ripple in France with his *Esprit de la Nouvelle Sorbonne,* in which he traced a development in the liberal culture of that country in harmony with the spirit of those changes which are going on wherever democracy is growing democratic. Cambridge is already " liberalized "— so hospitable is our tongue. Even Oxford, " home of lost causes and impossible enthusiasms," is rejoiced over — or wept over — for modifications of what at one time at least was held to be the model for all liberal culture in the English-speaking world.

It is not that the muse herself is impossibly squeamish, or set intransigently on maintaining old frontiers. It is her own she is all for, old or new. And subtly discernible in the subliminal impulses of the democratic spirit there appear certain impasses, not hostile to her herself — far from it, I think, in any fair view — but troublesomely in the way of any definite survey and definition.

I

A faint odor of tradition, vague and elusive, still clings about the idea of a liberal culture — an odor of leisure, of good manners, of taste, of literature, of philosophic curiosity and reflection. It has apparently lost, to the general sense, the salt tang and edge of intellectual seriousness, but it is still an odor of things intimately human, and one likely, as a consequence, to linger hauntingly in the neighborhood of the muse's garden.

All this is dim and evasive. Yet one sharp distinction emerges, heightened if one looks for it — and obscured if one doesn't — by the lively activities of those technical cultures that have sprung up around it in most of the centers where a liberal culture used to thrive and propagate. It is — it is a commonplace to say it — that while every technical discipline conceives a man as a means and bends its efforts to giving him the knowledge and judgment to do some one kind of thing and do it well, a liberal discipline conceives him as an end, and bends its efforts to making him a good kind of thing in himself.

This, however, is not a distinction without a difficulty. It demands a definition, and the most difficult one of all — the definition of a man who *is* a good thing in himself. But who, in the end, is to frame it? That nice balance, and symmetry, and temper of parts that must go to his making are conceptions that shift and vary from person to person. They involve elements too elusive to be isolated and compared, and too subtle to be palpably felt and weighed. Moreover the judgments that must weigh them are themselves tangled with instincts too autonomous to be accountable and tastes too spontaneous to be analyzed — judgments that spring from men's individual and unalterable sincerities. Concensus diffuses. And the difficulty is that a working definition demands among just such sincerities a concensus that consents.

On this rock the old college struck, now some fifty years ago, when new ways of looking at life and new estimates of man and his place in the sun came in with the inflow of new knowledge. An encouraging recollection — or perhaps a discouraging recollection — is that there have been periods with such a concensus. The Sixteenth Century stands out as one, and the Eighteenth as another in our own lineal tradition, with no disconcerting break between or since, until the present. But one thing will be noticed of them: they cover a time when a dominant class, homogeneous in manners and culture, with a binding sense of solidarity and an assured prestige, set the pattern.

A democracy, however, is another thing. By definition, and by the deepest impulses that produce it, a democracy releases and cultivates the widest range of evaluations and ultimate judgments in just this personal department. In such a society values that hang upon a community of sentiment, or of motive, or of experience, or of culture, tend to lose solidity. By breaking up classes democracy breaks down the prestige of any single pattern. It is the prestige of the single pattern, indeed, that makes an aristocracy so invidious. For any assertion or assumption of superiority in the sensitive field of personal worth is an arbitrary affront to those whose ultimate sincerities find other patterns fairer.

But the point of a liberal culture is to invade just this final region of personal consciousness, the seat of men's dignity as men, to set up standards there, and publicly to proclaim final superiorities and inferiorities behind which there is no retreat. Without such standards, as the comedy of experience has shown, a liberal education is naught. To set them up, none the less, is an affront.

No one, I suppose, reasons explicitly in such

terms. They are thrown out at what seems to be a tacit perception on the part of democracy. The mystic undercurrent of the democratic impulse finds crude expression in the saying that all men are equal. The expression sticks, though every man knows that men are not equal. They differ cruelly in body. They present no equality in the gifts of heredity or of later fortune. In their minds they run a long gamut of differences. Still, the assertion is not meaningless. Behind the blatant inequalities that lie on the surface there remains to each man his inalienable identity, his ultimate self-consciousness, immeasurably closer home to him than the outside he presents to the world. If this too is to be subject to invidious comparison, democracy has no meaning. And a liberal education does frankly say that there is a better and a worse in these sacred places. It sets up a standard and tries to cultivate superiorities — and, retroactively, inferiorities.

Is this fantastic? Certainly as democracy has come into its own every other discipline has flourished and only this has lapsed. The circumstance is at least suggestive.

By other calculations a liberal culture would seem to be the only discipline a democracy could tolerate. It rebelled at first against aristocracy for depriving the mass of the people of their equal chance at spiritual enlargement. Aristocracy had condemned "common" men to useful functions; it had treated them as means. In idea, at least, only the aristocrat was thought of as an end in himself. And a liberal education was the chief agency by which his spiritual enlargement was secured to him. Democracy, on the other hand, was the assertion of the supreme dignity and worth of just that essential humanity in every man that a liberal education was calculated to enhance. Liberal, therefore, and not vocational or technical training would seem to be the democratic education *par excellence.*

But the fact remains that after flourishing through nearly four centuries of our tradition under aristocratic impulse, liberal education has nearly perished under democratic impulse, and the training of men as means has prospered. Even a technical discipline will create classes, indeed — engineers, doctors, lawyers — and stamp its failures with unmistakable tokens. But entry into these classes is voluntary. Complete withdrawal is always possible. And the chagrins even of failure are relatively mild. Self-esteem will still find an inner retreat into a region more intimately home than any outer function can be — into the personal consciousness and individual identity in relation to which the outer function is a mere gesture, a garment to be put on or off at will.

And here is the difference. From the field of a liberal discipline there is no escape. Cultivated or uncultivated it is still there, and subject to invidious comparison. The sharpening of that comparison is the affront. And soberly, by what warrant is any description of man to be set up as intrinsically better than another? The sensitiveness of the rest, in just this region where freedom is absolute, is affronted by an assertion of superiority for a type that has not their sympathy. I am not referring invidiously to the "common" man. The impasse sweeps through the whole democracy, and is perhaps most astringent at the top where in the nature of the case it is most articulate.

II

This democratic sensitiveness is edged by a further touch of nature. Those who assume to sketch in a standard for a liberal education do so in contours conspicuously like their own. How indeed can they do otherwise if they have followed the gleam with a decent sincerity? But this touch of nature is scarcely one to make the whole world kin. And in the little world of the college itself, where the clash is always hand to hand and the likeness immediately observable, it serves to stiffen the natural antagonism.

Atticus, for instance, who wears out the Plato on his shelves, carries a Sophocles in his pocket, chuckles over Matthew Arnold, and dissipates on Boswell and Thackeray, puts at the top of his pinnacle the humane philosopher saturated in the traditions of civilization and its long catholic experiment in actions and thoughts handed down in the records of its broad literatures — the philosopher so at home in the stores of his own enlarged spirit that he can give an intelligible account of himself and so render the legacy of the past a contemporary and living thing. Atticus it is true has the vice of his virtues. If the humane philosopher seems to him the finest figure of a man other types seem to him inferior. He has his scorns. And he is undisturbed that but few have the native taste for such a rôle, or the fortune to be born where such a taste is bred, or the intelligence to lift their passive absorptions — granted the bowels even for passive absorption — into creative independence. But then, not many come to that in any rôle. He believes that behind all the ways men take, and behind all the things they do, the judgments they make, the pursuits they follow, and behind all the products of hand or brain that they encourage, the final springs of them all are the *values,* hotly, or lukewarmly, or apingly felt, but genuinely felt, that lie potentially in their spirits. He thinks, therefore, that if the final source of what is humanely made of life lies here, the finest type of man is one whose values have been formed from the widest contact with human experience and thought, and from an intimate acquaintance with the human mind and heart. And thus he would set up his standard and order his discipline.

Scientius, who reveres the names of Bacon and Descartes, to whom Darwin and Spencer are archangels if a little tarnished, who spends his days in patient research, and whose nights are made spacious by visions of an organic cosmos in which man and his values are casual incidents, curious eddies in the passionless flow of necessity — Scientius mounts on the top of his pinnacle the natural philosopher steeped in the spirit of empirical science and in the lore of the new worlds experimental methods have revealed. If the man of science seems to him the finest human type, other types must seem inferior. He too has his scorns. What is man to impose his *values* upon life, or think his little desires important to the universe! And how is man's spirit to be enlarged by confinement to the little circle of his own nature and the ambiguous tale of human experience, as though he and his race were the conscious end and aim of nature's experiment? How can men's thoughts be freed from fallacy if they are grounded on the loose sands of emotion and desire, or bred on the petty fancies of poets and tellers of tales, or the dreams of dreamers? To Scientius the drama of human life is lost in the wide sweep of impersonal law. And to him the enlarged spirit is one which, catching in the crystalline motions of the intellect the faint intimations of something within itself in harmony with that law, perfects that correspondence — in part by increasing the points of conscious contact through knowledge of the facts of nature, and in part by truing and fining the process of the intellect itself through a grasp of the relentless logic of the universe. And thus he too would set up his standard and establish his discipline.

Corinthius, to whom Greece means beauty, who

dreams with Rousseau, treads the mountains with Wordsworth, and with Bergson thrills at the abdication of the intellect, caps his pinnacle with the creative artist — the daemonic, the spontaneous, the only projector of the new into a progressively dying universe. To him life is inherently incalculable, a pure adventure, moment by moment dropping into the dead and immutable past, but going on and on, and taking its noblest form in him who can best dip into the stream of it as it flows through his eternal present, and fix the fleeting instant of realization, externalize it, and add it to the growing sum of what life has triumphantly created. He who fails in part or in whole, so to fetch up the unique thing that life has been to his consciousness has wasted his one chance. He does not count. The man of science, who catalogues with infinite childish patience the immutable relations of the brute detritus of the world is but delving into what is dead and done for, past and gone. And those others, the humane philosophers, who think to understand life by poring over the broken array of its past, hoping to trace a clue to the drift of it and so order it more happily for the future — well, they pore in vain. For all its past manifestations were unique, and serve only — each remaining relic by itself — for what it is worth in itself to appreciative contemplation. Beyond that, perhaps, old creations may stir men's emulation — not to do what has already been done, but rather to dip anew into the endless stream. And so Corinthius would set up his standard and order his discipline.

Politicus and Civilius reflect the shock of current life, and represent the cleavages that agitate it collectively. What one of them reveres, indeed, the other reviles — Adam Smith, Burke, Mill, Marx, Wells. But they are alike in this, that they think of men chiefly in relation to organized society, and find them at their best when the give and take of that relationship is at equilibrium. They differ as to what constitutes this equilibrium, but they agree in thinking it the axis on which civilized life turns. They are in touch with the long story of the human struggle — the rise and fall of civilizations — and they see in it an endless spectacle of this swaying balance. At the tops of their respective pinnacles, therefore, they put the perfect citizen and the perfect state. They differ, indeed, as to which is cause and which is effect; they have their scorns for each other. But together they scorn ideals of individual and personal perfection to which the formal organization of society is secondary. And so they too would set up their several standards and order their several disciplines.

All these in their various ways ignore Demus, who feels himself, by the theory of the civilization of which he is a part, the equal of them all, but who, when he tries to look down the vistas thus pointed out to him, finds himself gazing through barred gates. He has come from a home where labor and virtue have found the primitive struggle too hard to admit a third mouth to be fed at their board. And he finds something alien and hostile in these claims of superiority in regions where his imagination can only dimly follow, and where his tastes falter or revolt, and whither if he would it is too late for him to go. Vaguely he resents an imposition from without voiced by others better than he only by their own suffrage. With no counter ideal of his own, but with a yearning desire to share somehow in an equality which he none the less feels is already his, he resists the definition of any standard and the ordering of any discipline.

Such in brief are the outstanding terms of the present conflict inside the college itself, where from time to time it comes to words, bitter, or tolerant, or despairing, or amused, according to individual temper. It is flavored to taste. It is recognized, however, as an impasse. Neither Atticus, nor Scientius, nor any of the rest can give in. In his dreams each one has set up a standard and ordered a discipline out of his deepest sincerities. Behind them it is impossible for them to go. And there, at the present moment, the college stands — or falls.

III

One practical solution is obvious — has even been tried here and there — that Atticus, Scientius, and the rest each set up his own discipline and fight it out side by side in the natural competition of results. This for a time at least would do away with that vagueness of definition that is at present so distressing to the poor muse. The conception itself is a liberal one. But even as a practical solution it is crammed with the promise of failure, for there is no limit to the amoebaean process once it has its charter. Or more accurately there is a limit — in the number of individuals to revolt and set up on their own. And this in effect is the muse's malady to-day.

Such a practical solution, however, evades the real problem. So long as the intelligence of men is healthy and vigorous, voyaging fearlessly on every sea, venturing outward toward all the points of the compass, so long will there be a problem of the center. The task of a liberal culture is to find that center and to set up its outlook there. And that center, when all is said, lies, for the human intelligence, in humanity itself, in human nature, body, heart and mind, of which the ideal definition still to seek is the working standard. If democracy, as democracy, is hostile to any definition, feeling instinctively that in this region, where there is no final authority but men's opinions, the opinions of one group have no more authority than those of another, the muse is at a sorry pass. For *without* a standard her inspiration is dissipated, and *any* standard will be the conception of a few and not of all.

The comment upon democracy itself is curious. Is a liberal education, as an effective force in leavening and harmonizing and unifying a people, broadly unattainable in a democratic society? Is solution possible only where there is some group or class of common station, common manners, tastes, and way of looking at life, conscious even to jealousy of its distinctive character, and so with *prestige* to take the place of that intellectual authority that seems impossible in the free play of ideas themselves? I put the question in good faith.

XI

THE INTOLERABLE SUBJECT OF EDUCATION

XI

THE INTOLERABLE SUBJECT OF EDUCATION

Wine, cigars, anecdotes; and suddenly, like a jack-in-the-box absurdly crowned with ivy, the intolerable subject of education.
Appearances: G. Lowes Dickinson

IT is an intolerable subject. And not from any general indifference. On the contrary there is something almost egregious in our active faith in it. Glance at the generosity of modern endowments, the free-hand voting of taxes, the cheerful pinchings at home, the amazing submission of high-mettled youth. Certainly the like has never been seen before. The acclaim is universal. Our trusty weathercocks, the platitudinists, cry up education as a panacea. On a lower level the quacks reap fortunes in exploiting the simple trust of the credulous. And on a higher level, if we have overpassed our cerebral minority and escaped from the tyranny of appearances, we have occasion, above the reach of the platitudinists, to realize how hazardous a life most things of the mind lead, and how precariously they hang on the quality of their renascence.

Oh, we are lively enough in our sense of the importance of education. Our reluctance does not come either from indifference or obtuseness. It is simply that the subject itself, spite of its momentous issues, is intolerable to just those minds that, with no axe to grind and no bias of fanaticism, are best able to think sanely about it. It is simply dull thinking. An axe to grind or a bias of fanaticism makes any body of reflection interesting to the reflector. And there is, of course, plenty of both over education now that the vogue is at its height. But as most men of balanced and disinterested minds do find the subject at once important and intolerable, the paradox has an interest in itself. The subject suffers neglect. Neglect? There is, in truth, an unprecedented bulk of writing about it. But there we are; it is all intolerably dull and remains unread.

I

By way of experiment let anyone who has a balanced and disinterested mind sit down some idle afternoon to think the subject over. He won't think it through, but he will emerge from his reflections both sadder and wiser; and he will see why men of clear intellects tend to go about their immediate or their remotest business and give it a wide berth.

At once, as he sits down to the subject, our doughty inquirer will be attacked by a sudden sense of its impertinence. For him the moment is untoward for such reflections. By hypothesis a cultivated being, he has got himself arduously to the point where he has mastered the commonplaces of knowledge and realized how commonplace they are. He feels his own mind beginning to emerge from the suffocating muddle of immaturity. He feels younger and simpler than when he *was* younger and simpler. He is ready for his reward. And the one reward for a mind that has found itself is the liberty to go ahead. But he has no sooner arrived at that point, conscious that for him it is a sheer beginning, than on comes a new generation that knows nothing, literally nothing, not even how to know, but equipped with all the impertinence and assurance and wrong-headedness of the ignorant and undisciplined — not even themselves, bless them, asking to be brought on — resisting rather — but there, none the less, creating a gratuitous problem that ends at just the stage where they begin to engage an intellectual interest. It is all back work.

Meanwhile other men of intelligence, neglecting these responsibilities, are going ahead into new fields or over the borders of old ones, trying their mettle where even failure has its consolations in the adventure. But for him, setting about this problem — he is lingering behind. Even old knowledge and ideas, above the reach of his nonage, are of inexhaustible interest; he will read and hear about them with a lively attention — new grist for his own mill. But let the eternal schoolmaster in him drop into shop, and a pall descends upon him. It is all arrears, a going back, a beginning over. For the born pedagogue it may be interesting; it must be; he is forever talking shop. But for himself —

Even so soon our friend is tempted to leave the

whole problem to the pedagogues. They have taken on the responsibility. Presumably, they have found it tolerable. And they have made an unprecedented go of it. School, college, university — never such a multiplicity of them till now, never such elaborate foundations till now, such intricate systems, such teaching of everything teachable, teaching of teachers, teaching of teachers of teachers. And never before have the generality so eagerly submitted, trusting the teacher to teach them whatever it is of importance to know.

But it is just this egregious success of the institution that stirs his skepticism. He knows that institutions of all kinds drift toward a certain point, and that beyond this point they become no longer means but ends. And he knows that it is beyond this point that they blossom into their greatest outward splendor, and inward decay. The story is old and commonplace. And here in the daedal mazes of this institution, and in the minute division of labor among those who serve it, hierarchy above hierarchy, he finds the discernible evidence of its having rounded the point.

At one extreme are the pedagogues, who do the real work in intimate touch with the human elements of the problem. But they are so minutely subdivided, each one plays so limited a part, and each one prepares himself so specifically for the part he plays, that it is a sheer accident if some among them are what, to his own sense, our inquirer would have called educated at all. He has been among them from time to time. Who hasn't? And of all people he has found none so widely and so angrily divergent in their ideas as to what an education is. For them the forest is obscured by the trees.

At the other extreme are the administrators. And these are so arduous in coördinating and prospering the institution as an institution that they have lost touch with its humble purpose. The organization is so big, so much material substance and the fortunes of so many persons are at stake, and success is so dependent upon the favor of the public or some part of it, that their maneuvers have to be adjusted to winning and keeping that favor, rather than to working out ideas of their own — if they have time or temperament to have ideas. Inevitably they favor the drift. If now and then one does resist the drift, he is soon done for.

After all, as the inquirer comes to see at this point, it is the outsider and not they — neither they at the bottom nor they at the top — who determines the matter in the end. They may theorize as they will, and offer to teach what they please, but they can not teach if no one comes to them to learn. The learners will go where they can learn what seems important for them to know; and that semblance they pluck out of the intangible atmosphere they have grown up in — out of the bent and temper of the times. But the problem remains. And if it does remain for the outside world to settle, our inquirer is curious to see still further why men of intelligence there find it intolerable.

II

He begins, therefore, by clearing a space in his imagination for the picture of an educated mind. The problem is a practical one of means and end, and the first step is to conceive the desired end. So much is elementary. But complexity soon crowds upon him; this first step is not simple. He could compass it of course, offhand, but being intelligent, and having a grain of salt in his humor, he sees how desperately he must guard against a foible that he has detected in everyone he has chanced to overhear on the subject — perhaps in everyone who has ever discussed it. . . .

"You see me, young man," said the Principal of Louvain to Goldsmith, "I never learned Greek, and I don't find that I have ever missed it. I have had a Doctor's cap and gown without Greek; I have ten thousand florins a year without Greek; I eat heartily without Greek; and in short, as I don't know Greek I do not believe there is any good in it."

Greek, natural science, mathematics, humane letters — the keynote varies but the tune is recognizably the same.

Our friend himself has been brought up on natural science, say, and has entertained his leisure with the literature of philosophy; or perhaps he has been nurtured on Greek and hardened his mind on mathematics. The point is immaterial; he sees his own liability to the foible — not so much the gross one of the Principal of Louvain as the deeper one lest other men of a like mental experience to his own, like intellectual furniture, like sources of allusion, like counters of thought, shall seem to him in all honesty to have richer minds than those as amply furnished in another style. He knows the danger of mistaking the special harmony of understanding among men of a like discipline for understanding of a truer kind. The recollections of youth, too, and the perspective of time, and the special color they have lent to his own peculiar vision have their deceptive endearments. He must guard against them.

And then, when he turns again, wary of all these dangers, to build up his picture of an educated mind, he discovers that he has stripped it of reality. He has on his hands an abstraction — a fine balance of faculties, to be sure, but a balance of mere algebraic values — quick perceptions, strong feelings, rich and orderly knowledge, lively imagination, taste, clear and sure reason, all in just proportion and symmetry, but still an abstraction. These things are not realities. They emerge into reality only in conjunction with the specific data of thought.

But what data? And for the matter of that, what balance? He has reflected enough about the history of human experience to realize that as period outwardly alters into period the inner change that has taken place is a change in the tacit conception of this balance — that each age conceives a new one and reacts against the old. Now reason bulks large for a century, now emotion for a stormy period, now taste, now imagination, each age crying up its own vision of the perfect thing, and denouncing its predecessor. And which is just? His humor has robbed him of his only premises. All he has to go on is his own inner sense of the perfect balance, and that is based — how else? — on his own ultimate admirations — not on himself, to be sure, but on a vision colored inevitably by what his own mind has been nourished on.

This is a blind alley, and the mind that follows down it ends in a circle. He has scored one for dullness. His very premises are indefinable.

III

At all events, as he points out to himself while he looks about for an escape, he has not yet fallen into the vulgar error of supposing that education is the mere inculcation of knowledge. He pauses over the recollection of learned fools he has known. The learned fool knows much, and so he is learned; but he lacks something and so he is a fool. To be educated is to have a quality of mind and not a quantity of knowledge, and that quality is antipodal to the quality of the fool. Still knowledge is not irrelevant. At least it is the vehicle by which the thing is to be accomplished. But then, what knowledge? The question opens a new vein of inquiry. Any knowledge? Or is there some that on the face of it tends to carry with it the quality and character of mind that he is in pursuit of?

The indicated procedure from this point is pellucidly clear to his perceptions, but it is grotesque — the critical examination of the universe of human knowledge, which is, of course, for men, *the* universe. No one, though he gave his life to it, could for the life of him exhaust a single province of it. And our friend, who has his own life to lead, recoils — not from the brink of this pit, for he has no impulse to plunge into it, but from the only alternative he can see — the substitution of suffrage for an essential term of his reasoning.

Short of examining and comparing all knowledge what is there for it but to take different men's opinions? Even ignoring the diverse suffrage of others, he sees how helpless he is to have anything better to go on than his own. What actually does happen in the practical world of the institution is, as he sees, just this response to suffrage, a suffrage influenced partly by the inertia of tradition, partly by the rebellion against tradition, and partly by immediate particular desires conceived not in perspective but piecemeal. He has set himself, however, to thinking out his problem, and what actually happens in the amorphous institutions has no relevance — except, perhaps, to make him see more clearly why men of intelligence do let the problem alone.

IV

He has been a little hasty, however, in his impatience — as hasty, in fact, as the practitioners who have given up at this point, and at whom he has been smiling. Suffrage is not the only alternative. Two lines of inquiry, indeed, offer themselves to his now thoroughly roused skepticism. If instead of a hopeless examination of all knowledge he can come upon a touchstone or talisman which will of its own nature, like a magnet, select out of the welter such knowledge as will, better than other knowledge, tend to produce that quality of mind he is aiming at, he will have simplified his quest immeasurably. And two such touchstones entertain his reflections for a while.

To the first of these he hesitates to apply a definition; he approaches it on the flank. He is in the province of cause and effect. Knowledge of infinite variety stands on one side in the putative rôle of causes. A quality of mind stands on the other in the rôle of desired effect. Ignoring for the moment the complexity of the causes and the vagueness of the desired effect, he asks himself how much is known, as a matter of positive science, at just this causal node. How much is known, as a matter of positive science, of the effect of any knowledge upon the mind that grasps it?

If anyone can help him it should be the psychologists, and they have dealt copiously with his problem. But he has in his time pursued the psychologists, and, like Socrates among the Athenians, perceives that they know nothing — nothing at least to the purpose. So long as they have remained in the positive field of mental physiology, where one set of their terms is made up of tangible, measurable data, they have done something, even much, being able to say that a lesion in this brain area will produce this mental or physical result, and a lesion in that area will produce that result. But when the causal data are not tangible and sensuously measurable, as knowledge is not tangible and sensuously measurable, their own knowledge ceases to be positive and they are on a level with other men — with our inquirer himself — reduced, that is, to watching the wide variety of human kind, and the wide variety of effects from apparently the same causes. Plato, it is said, makes some men sober and some men drunk. The whole positive foundation of their science has no least help for them or for our friend in the present quest. They can, and do, look on at the spectacle of life as the poets have done before them. And the poets have as yet the better of them.

In this last reflection our friend is aware that he has been a little unjust. The psychologists have done something in this field of human nature that the poets have not done. The poets have put down their observations sporadically; the psychologists theirs in categories. Examination, however, reveals one disconcerting thing about these categories; they are most categorical where the aspects of the mind examined are most primitive, nearest to physiology — instincts but a stage above the instincts that keep the heart beating and the lungs breathing, and habits that tend to repeat themselves without calling the attention of the consciousness and the interference of it. Above this level, where the consciousness enters more and more to play hob with the predictable regularity of conduct, the psychologists grow more and more helpless. The consciousness is just what remains for them, as for the poets and for our inquirer himself, a mystery.

He comes back to his problem with the recollection that when he is thinking about education he is thinking about just that mystery. For education as he understands it is the enrichment of the consciousness itself, and its encouragement to take over more and more of the government. So that just here where his whole concern is centered he finds that he has left the psychologists behind.

He abandons, therefore, his pursuit of a positive nexus between particular knowledge and the particular consequences of it. Even if he could define with all precision the desired consequences, there would be no hope of settling upon the specific causes. He has been following a second blind lead.

V

Some time since, however, he foresaw the possibility of another talisman of a different kind, and he turns toward it now with a premonitory hope. May it not be, he asks himself, that those qualities or powers of mind, in the abstract condition in which he was forced to conceive and leave them, are congenital, like the color of the eyes or the shape of the skull, and not in themselves susceptible of alteration or development? The sporadic and incalculable appearance of talent and genius and exceptional intelligence suggest the probability.

If this is the case his problem is wholly changed. If those mental powers are sheer congenital constants, unalterable by education, they cease to figure in his problem. His problem is no longer, say, to find something to enhance the powers of imagination, but rather to find such knowledge as, used by the imagination, may be built into significant conceptions — no longer to find something to strengthen the faculty of reason, but rather to find such knowledge as the reason finds significant for the reasoning process. If he is justified in this alternative — and it is the only escape he can discover — he has gained something; he has got rid of his indefinables. His problem is now wholly one of knowledge, and knowledge, if infinite in variety, is at least definable.

This turn of his reflections would leave him again exposed to the whole universe of knowledge if his second talisman did not now come to his rescue. Again he is at a loss for a simple definition of his touchstone, and again he approaches it from the flank. He calls to mind his lawyer, his doctor, his plumber, his shoemaker, the philologist who explained Grimm's law to him, and the astronomer who taught him to calculate the syzygy of the planets. An educated man may know the law, or he may know medicine, or the processes of plumbing or shoemaking, or the application of Grimm's law, or the syzygy of sun and moon. But surely no man would be called uneducated because he was not learned in the law, or in medicine, or could not plumb or make shoes, or was unfound in philology, or had never heard of a syzygy. And equally it must follow that no man could be called educated simply because he knew any or all of these things. He might go on with his list till his list was complete, but his additions, as he sees at once, would be of a certain kind — of those functions and their associated knowledge which are distributive, some men responsible by voluntary choice for one, some for another, and so on and on. Ignorance of this kind of knowledge does not leave a man uneducated. What is left for him to associate with the idea of education is such knowledge as falls outside this kind — and that is such knowledge as is involved in those problems that all men are responsible for in common. If he can designate that knowledge he will have reached his goal.

That all men are not responsible for all knowledge may be a happy circumstance, but it leaves the remaining question far from simple, so minutely has the labor of modern life come to be divided, and so little apparently is the space where common responsibilities overlap. He recoils from this platitude, and then it begins to interest him. He scents a paradox. At just the time when life has grown infinitely complex through a minute division of labor, we have overthrown the division of labor in the management of it. We have made all men suddenly responsible for the conception of our common aim and purpose, and for the correlation of the details of life to accomplish that purpose. We have become a democracy.

He enjoys for a moment the smile he imagines on the face of Clio as she looks down on this situation, taking notes. But his feelings are mixed when he sees the smile broaden at a further development of the paradox. For at just the time when all this is happening — while everyone is in training for his special part and no one in particular is in training for the management of the whole — that training has become a lost art. Everybody's business has become nobody's business. The very idea has evaporated. It has so thoroughly escaped that our friend finds himself here, baffled and alone, trying in desperation to recapture it.

By grace of the paradox he has just been equivocally enjoying, he does, a little vaguely, capture a glimpse of it. He sees that what he thinks of as an educated man is one whose mind is competent to take on something of this common responsibility, who has some vision of the whole and sees the parts in some perspective, whose intelligence is of a kind by which here and there life is endowed with orderliness and measure and harmony, and some steadfastness of aim and purpose. That, in an aristocratic age is the responsibility of the few; in a democratic age it is the responsibility of everybody. In either case his task would be to discover, if he could, what kinds of data are chiefly involved, and what kinds of knowledge must be mastered to meet this responsibility.

Knowledge of one kind he can point to at once — such a knowledge of the thinker's own mind as will get him into touch with the mind itself. His mind is his instrument; it is the matrix in which he moulds his solution of every problem. And it is a very complex, elusive, tricky affair. He must know what goes to right thinking. And to know this he must know what goes to wrong. He must know the pitfalls of his own mind — the suave fallacies of egotism and vanity, the persuasive subtlety of self-interest, the stubbornness of old prejudice, the deceit of appearances, the falsifying endearments of feeling and passion. Whatever else enters into any problem he confronts, his own mind is always involved. And here, at least, he must be on intensely intimate terms with his data. He cannot escape himself.

This is not quite so clarifying as it appears, as our inquirer realizes after a moment's examination. How, after all, is one to know his own mind — know it critically, that is, and distinguish its right from its wrong? Either right thinking is anything that comes into the mind next, in which case one thing is as good as another; or there is some test by which to distinguish the good from the bad. Any sequence of thought may seem reasonable to one's self alone. Men's powers of self-deception are notable. What then, is a reasonable sequence?

In the end it proves to be such as meets the assent, not of particular individuals — individuals are as gullible as one's self — the assent rather of what, for want of a better term he calls the generic human mind. It is that common mind of which the universal convincingness of mathematics is perhaps the purest evidence, but which spreads beyond the abstractions of mathematics over the whole range of thought. It is the mind we reveal when we try to clear our own thoughts from the elements that are personal to ourselves alone, and the mind we reach out for when we push past what is personal to others and address what is disinterested in their attention. And to know this mind he must know his mankind. With that knowledge he can check his own sequences of thought, truing his own acquaintance with himself by seeing what the elements within him look like when viewed from without, and how they match with the common mind of the race. A knowledge of mankind, then, of human nature, is inseparable from a knowledge of his own mind, because only by such knowledge can he have a critical check upon himself. Here, then, is a second field of data for an education.

Incidentally now, as our friend looks back, he sees that the *quality* of mind, which at the outset he sharply distinguished from knowledge, and which, instead of knowledge, he took for the mark of an educated man, may be simply the character of the mind's workings when it has self-knowledge to work with. If the mental powers are congenital and unalterable, self-knowledge at least can be acquired and can alter the quality of thought. And he sees in this knowledge the promise of that sweet reasonableness that is at the other extreme from the character of the ignorant—the clarity and certainty with which a man may detect and disengage the essential idea from out the tangle of irrelevancies which tend to distort and prejudice it in his own mind, and the penetration with which he can find his way past the irrelevancies which tend to distort and prejudice it in the minds of others—to the end that he may discover that common mind where a mutual understanding may conform to the verities involved in the idea itself. He sees here the secret of that quiet self-control which comes to the cultivated mind from an intimate knowledge of its own works. He sees here the secret of what is called clarity of thought—and that what is called clarity of thought is called so because it reveals the idea in a light in which men may see it in common.

All this, however, is but one aspect of the matter—the instrument. He has still to find the special data for the instrument to work on. What problems fall to the common lot and within the common responsibility? Or better, if it can be conceived whole—what is the central problem about which men's common responsibilities revolve? The distributive responsibilities take care of themselves; but the common ones?

Our inquirer finds the answer not so remote as he feared. As he looks out on the material universe and men's animal existence in it, he sees that so much is *given,* as the geometers say. For that, certainly, men are not responsible. The universe takes care of itself. Its immutable laws go on immutably no matter what we know about them and no matter what we do about them. And so do we go on, like the other animals, so far as our animal existence is concerned. It is only in so far as we are not content with bare animal existence that we have assumed any responsibility at all. The whole human problem is a problem over and above sheer existence. It is a problem of the *quality* of that existence. It is this problem of *quality* that men are responsible for in common. And it is to meet this problem of *quality* that such a thing as education is conceived at all.

This conception of the *quality* of human existence, as our friend sees with trepidation, is a ticklish one. What is the criterion of this thing which he has called *quality,* and within the bounds of which the whole question of education lies? Clearly it is a thing created by and altogether based on what men think and want. Out of their own minds — perceptions, desires, imaginations, judgments — they conceive an idea of what might be made of life, and what might best be made of it, out of its possibilities and within its ordained limitations.

The ticklish aspect of the matter is that, seen thus, the central human problem proves to be wholly anthropocentric; and our friend knows that since the middle of the last century the term *anthropocentric* — barbarous word! — has been an epithet of scorn and derision. Indeed he can understand how in the enthusiasm of a new point of view men like Huxley and Spencer and Haeckel should look upon the little desires of men as petty and negligible, laughable impertinences in the mighty sweep of an indifferent universe. But for the life of him he cannot see how to such men the desire for scientific knowledge should have seemed of any importance either. It was as human a desire as any other. Here was a touch of high comedy, that the world has not even yet come to smile at.

For himself our friend can sympathize with that desire for knowledge of the material universe. But then, he can only see it as one, perhaps one of the finest, still only one of many human aspirations. And he sees also that men go on responding to it because mankind, in trying to solve the problem of quality, have agreed that this aspiration is a good thing — that the pursuit of reality and truth is itself one of the finest possibilities of human nature. Certainly if men had agreed that the pursuit of natural science was an evil, as they have agreed about astrology and demonology, it would have languished.

In other words, the problem of natural science is one aspect of the human problem, and, important as it may be, it is subordinate and incidental. Whether to indulge the desire for a knowledge of physical nature, and how far to indulge it, are questions which nature does not answer, study it as men will. They are questions answered only by our sense of relative human values, and answered wisely only by those who can weigh the proportionate value of this knowledge among all the values which make for the finest quality of human life.

He has lingered over this aspect of his question because it is patent that the natural sciences bulk large in the current processes of the schools. And he is forced to wonder whether the confusion and uncertainty that is prevalent in education may not be explained by the fact that a generation largely trained in scientific data has necessarily missed, in so far, many of the other data that enter equally into the human problem. For the problem of natural science, wholly concerned with what tangibly and materially *is,* stops just where the human problem takes up. And the human problem, created wholly by men's desires for such and such a quality of life, involves imperatively a range of data for the thinker to master which natural science rigidly excludes.

Our friend is no enemy to natural science. On the contrary. But he sees that men will best realize the significance and the value of it, and give it its justest proportions in the whole, if they come upon it from a sense of its relations to the central problem of quality. And he doubts whether that problem is likely to be the better perceived and understood by virtue of a discipline that carefully excludes its essential data.

This data is, as he sees at once, humanity itself — in its background, it is true, of the material scene — but chiefly and centrally the human mind, its thoughts, its impulses, its aspirations, its judgments, by which the ideal of the quality of life is created, and by which the values that go to make and mar this quality are weighed.

Oh, as he well knows, this ideal is not a single thing, not a formulable thing, not a thing that men agree upon, not a thing that may be taught and learned. To conceive it so is to commit the *bêtise* of supposing that education is a process not of teaching men to think, but of teaching them *what* to think. If it is true even in a democracy that some men do need to be told what to think, that implies that there are others to tell them. And if that is true it is these others alone that are involved in any problem of education.

Not to foist a given ideal upon them, but to bring them into understanding intimacy with the data out of which, as free men, they may form, each one, his own ideal. That, as he comes to see it, is the aim of education. And the means to that end, in each one, is a knowledge of his own mind, its processes and its pitfalls; a knowledge of the human mind by which he may true his own; and a knowledge of humanity in wide perspective by which he may build, with a mind thus equipped, his own ideal of the quality of life and judge of the values that go to the making or the marring of it.

That instruction in other matters may be a valuable thing he is eager to acknowledge. But he would not call this instruction education. Or if that word has lost its distinctive meaning and has come to cover all processes of learning, he sees in the kind of knowledge he has so carefully segregated the means by which the common responsibility for the quality of life is to be met. And that, as distinguished from the particular means by which individual men seek their individual ends, is the thing he has been concerned for. Men may choose their individual ends and prepare for them as they will; but whether and in how far those ends are valuable is the question. The knowledge and the mind to answer that question are the goal for which he has been seeking.

So far he proceeds, and so swimmingly to his own sense has he got on in these latter stretches that he has forgotten his initial repulsion. But now, suddenly, as he emerges and shakes the blurring drops from his eyes, he has a last glimpse of the reason why men of lively and sane intelligence refuse to take the plunge. Think the problem through as they might, the institutions would still go on by suffrage and not by thought. Think it through as he has just done to his own mitigated satisfaction, he can hardly suppose that even those who have followed with him to the end will see eye to eye with him now he is done. And even they, should they agree, would be but a negligible handful among the rest by whose suffrage, thoughtful or thoughtless, the great institutions drift on. And the quality of that suffrage is determined by the character of the education it establishes. The vicious circle is complete.

Perhaps, he reflects, only an age that has a common philosophy can have an education. And our own age, shivering in the winds of contrary doctrines or none, can look forward to an education only when the winds blow one way and all the weathercocks swing into the same quarter. Then the problem will solve itself. At all events our released inquirer now knows why the subject of education is intolerable. It is a surd, an irrational quest, an abtruse philosophy put to a popular vote.

XII

DESIPERE IN LOCO

XII

DESIPERE IN LOCO

IN the vivid future, as the grammarians say, when socialism shall have displaced sociability, and when even literature is dry, there will still, it is pleasant to hope, remain one vice for the lonely reveller, unless, indeed, education shall by then have superseded folly — and its complement wisdom. *In loco* — a deep chair under the lamp by midnight, a pipe filled and going, and a distant sense of work undone. *Desipere* — to take the most promising volume from a pile of three or four or five of that genre despised and scorned by the lower-middle highbrow — the detective story. Some word in the title to indicate the type — mystery, case, clue, an item of dress, a cab, a perfume — and within good print and forty chapters. *Dulce est,* I say, to poke the fire to a wasteful blaze, to give a pagan slip to duty, and to feel before you the stillness of the smaller hours for the last tense drawing in of the threads.

A pile of four or five, for the perfect detective story, like the perfect tobacco, does not exist; it is always to seek. And if the first of the pile yields no spell, or, more likely, is not the real thing, there is another and another chance. To be stranded with but one is a frail hazard; to find one in the pile to meet an exacting taste is to reap an oblivion that is neither mured in an ivory tower, nor quite exposed to the raw edges of reality. It may be philosophic to do the work that lies to one's hand, but to be exigent in the moments of escape is the last joy of the discriminating. And like humor it is best taken a little sadly.

The special discrimination that is required of the initiate is that the genre *is* an escape. That scorn alluded to at the outset is quite misplaced; it belongs to bad literature. And the detective story is not bad literature; it is not literature at all; it is a game. And as a game its rules demand that respectfulness of consideration, almost the solemnity, that belongs to play — to golf, say, or to whist.

The underlying convention of the game, then, is this — that first and last the detective must bring to bear an intellect. Here at once he violates the literary tradition and establishes his distinction from the real heroes of romance. Your Romeos, and Tom Joneses, and Copperfields are not quite notable for brain. Even your Mr. Britlings of the sociological school, who pique themselves upon it, are rather given to seeing things through than to seeing through things. But whatever may be true of your heroes of romance, your hero of the game enjoys no such immunity. He must have the real thing.

For all this impediment, however, he attains to some degree of dramatic effectiveness by virtue of his peculiar relation to the story. The other personages belong to the plot. And as for the plot itself, the deeper the moral complication and the more interestingly human and significant the characters the better. But properly speaking the detective does not belong to the plot at all. He belongs to you as you sit in your chair under the lamp by the blazing hearth. He is your projection on the spot, your observing eye, your knowledge of men, sympathetic and nicely skeptical, especially your knowledge of women, and finally your court of review. He is the retina and the brain through which the whole tale unfolds without digression. None the less he stalks through the scene the most impressive figure of all.

If it were to the point in this connection, to insist on the unliterary character of the genre, other traversals of the literary canon might be revealed. Your reader of literature has his pleasure in his superior aloofness; he is the spectator, full of nice perceptions of things which the characters are blind to, and of those understandings which lurk behind the sympathy, and which create the irony that is the zest of all dramatic enjoyment. In the detective story, however, this relationship is inverted. Here at least one of the characters knows more than the reader. And it is just the challenge of this circumstance, and the further uncertainty as to who of all the characters do know more, that make the appeal unliterary — and make, it may be added, the unliterary appeal that is the defiant joy of the initiated.

In all this the detective and you are one. He plays on your side. If he is allowed to know more than you, you are his dupe. You and he, indeed, are often deceived. If you were never frustrated the ardor of the chase would never kindle. But you must be duped together, and always by dramatic circumstance, never by the direct contrivance of the author. And there you come to the first rule of the game — that you are to share at once and on the spot in whatever the detective knows.

You, on the other hand, must know no more than he. For the author to change the point of view, for example, and recount happenings that the detective is not privy to is to cloud the fine rapport that is the very heart of your relationship. The detective then becomes a pawn, blind to data that you are in possession of, stumbling through darkness through which you can see. He becomes a mere minor character in the story. The trick is unforgivable. The omniscient author has intruded his unskillful hand. Of course *he* knows what has happened; that goes without saying. He has already written the last chapter; there it all lies between you and the end. But it is the honorable convention of the game that you are to ignore the author's omniscience, and to hang upon the unfolding of the riddle through the medium of a human agent that has been thrust into the affair for no other purpose.

For all that, the detective must be flesh and blood, no abstraction and no puppet, for he has to appear as a convincing reality among the people and events of the actual plot. He may have a wife and four children in a neat cottage in Brooklyn, take cold, and be altogether human. He may even be allowed eccentricities if they help to heighten the dramatic moments of the development. He may, however, bring with him into the tale no qualities which conflict with the exigent demands of his rôle. And those frail writers who fret lest they miss the point of an appeal that is conventional, and thrust upon him the fatuity to fall in love, or the pathos of personal discouragement, by so much miss the keener point of a convention that is vital.

The need is that his accumulation of evidence should proceed within the bounds of human probability. Your superhuman detective, or your scientific detective equipped with fabulous instruments for the discovery of data not open to human apprehension, spoils the game. For the real game is the finding, the sifting, the piecing together of clues. And that must be done normally, humanly. To go beyond human powers is to destroy the fairness of the play; it is to have a card up the sleeve. You don't want more than can be humanly got. Therein lies the honor of your sportsmanship.

For yet another reason he must be no intellectual abstraction, but sensibly human, like you yourself. For if he were only an intelligence, and brought in the evidence sifted and sorted, as the intelligence does in the end, there would be no occasion to write more than the first and last chapters. The zest of the whole affair lies in the sifting and sorting, at a hot pace, perhaps, but at a possible pace, and credibly after the manner of life. The process of sifting, however, implies the accumulation of superfluous baggage, and hence human fallibility. There is the hat on the chair, the upturned ink-stand, the scuff on the carpet, the broken pen-point, the glove burst at the thumb, the blotter scrawled with illegible characters. That is the casual dumb array. In the end only the scuff on the carpet counts, but meantime it is the plight of the human observer, and has no business to be anything but the plight of the human detective, not to know which one does count. For this is the next skill of the writer after the creation of his plot, to bring the clues under the eyes of the detective dramatically, after the undramatic manner of life, casually, unlabelled, mixed with the varied array of the insignificant. And it is the exigent rule of the game to make the detective no more canny — or uncanny — to seize on the significant scuff than you can feel that you yourself ought to have been if you had had your wits about you.

Therein is the point of the detective yarn. It is a trial of wits. The detective must be clever. He must be even cleverer than you. It is his to find the right combination, tease out and put together the right clues, reconstruct the crime, before you have come to the end of your speculations. But if the tale has been bravely told, he will do it out of data that you have shared as well. He will be given no advantage that you have not had. Up to the moment when the facts are all in, you and he are one. Neither has had the start of the other. From then on, however, it is a contest, your wits against his. And the final joy and consummation is in the race to the goal. If the detective is ahead he must never have got there through a *deux ex machina,* but by pure superiority of comprehensible wit.

If you are ahead, on the other hand, you have an uncomfortable sensation. The thing has been stupidly done, the situation is obvious, the detective a sorry figure, the whole complication not worth the pother of the slow accumulation. With his last card face up on the table, the detective must take the last trick; he must have one more marvel at the bottom of his bag — but still a marvel that you might have laid your hands on if you had been the cleverer of the two. In this, indeed, the detective shares with the characters of literature the need ever to surprise, and yet ever in the next moment to have seemed inevitable. If you have anticipated him you have lost the last fine flavor of the whole draught.

Personal tastes every reader will have. I admit a preference for an opening murder. Other crimes have been used successfully. Inestimable jewels have disappeared; happy brides have vanished before the last guest has left the church; secret treaties have been filched from prime ministers. But murder is still the flower of crimes. It lies nearest the heart. The disappearance of life is the last and extremest of shocks; the taking of life the last and extremest of adventures. And if, as at its most effective, it is the murder of one who has least deserved extinction, someone who has been loved and is poignantly regretted, there is not only an added eagerness to get about the business, but a heightening of the mystery as well. Your patent villain may be killed and no one is either concerned or surprised. But your eager, hopeful youth, or your benevolent elder, cut off in flower or prime, gives the just pitch of shocked momentousness to the outset, and the right touch of mystery to the pursuit.

A second murder, while the data are gathering, is a tingling fillip to the complexity of the problem. Rightly timed — when the accumulation of the evidence has seemed to flow smoothly toward a ready and growingly obvious conclusion — it may suddenly dam the whole current, point to new and unsuspected data, implicate persons who had hitherto shared the confidences of the innocent, and throw a new and startling color upon all the revelations of the past. But more than all else it thrills with the news that the forces of the original crime still lurk in the offing. A new light, but also a new mystery and a new and stalking terror are present in the developing situation. From then on anything may happen.

But if something is gained by such a dramatic heightening of the action, something is lost, too. For if danger still hides behind the arras, the detective becomes a dramatic person among the other personages, and what he gains as a hero of adventure, he is likely to lose as a node of pure intellection. And though adventure is a high and serene delight, it is not the peculiar stuff of the detective genre.

The initial crime will occur, by preference — I still speak of personal tastes — in a milieu rich in background and associations. A hotel is too heterogeneous; an office is too casual. The sleeper of a moving train, or a boat in mid-ocean, has the advantage of narrowing the problem within precise limits. But best of all will be the rich and peaceful library of a large house. The house will contain a butler and many servants, a family rich in uncles and aunts, a few guests, and young people, but no children. The innocence of children mars the sophistical joys of crime.

The butler has infinite possibilities. He is last to bed at night and first up in the morning. Behind his trained manner anything may be hid. His freedom of the house, his touch with the servants, guests, and family, his silent tread, his imperturbable deference, make him a vehicle of infinite potentialities. Servants bring in the incalculable. They may be anybody — anybody in themselves, and anybody in disguise. Uncles and aunts not only enrich the human scene with variety of character and temper, but they belong to the intimate complex of the home, and there they not only touch the present, but spread out into the remoter reaches of the past. Guests, too, add to the human variety. But their peculiar addition — though a danger to the plot — is their introduction of the outside world. They are there as acquaintances, but they have facets that are unknown, and connections that ramify beyond the intimacies of the immediate circle. Finally young people are indispensable. Their imprudences, their high spirits, their spontaneity, their unmasked psychology bring out into the open the keener surprises of the situation.

Whatever the pleasure of the last moments of the game, there is no moment of its duration more edged with the reader's peculiar zest than these first scenes in which the human materials of the tale are mustered in. There is a keenness of expectancy in the early leisure of these introductions, and a luxury of point — while yet the possibilities of the problem are fluid and infinite, and before partisanship has marred the aloof serenity of the reader — that never returns after the lines of the development have stiffened into convergence. One by one the dramatic current throws up the candidates for suspicion, not in formal array but in the casual order of life, each one casting light or shadow on the event, and each one momentous in his revelations, conscious or unconscious, and his concealments explicit and implicit.

In this early period of the muster no weakness of solution has yet come to spoil the fine promise of the implication; perhaps it may never come. Meanwhile nothing is unimportant; at any moment the casual cravat, the crooked smile, the passion for flowers, the half-cousinship once removed, may leap into first importance.

Here in this chess or patience of letters, intrinsic values give place to the players' values within the circle of the game. The larger responsibilities of life that weigh upon the reader of literature slough off. Not that the values of life are perverted; an implicit acceptance of the *mores* is the very premiss of the genre. But they ride light; the moral cargo has been distilled into an intellectual one. A rigid orientation about the crime simplifies the point of every detail. And the joy of discovery is heightened by the definiteness of the touchstone by which each point is to be seized upon and judged — the pure values of the game without the pure game's departure from life.

For my own part, among the conventional moves, I have a weakness for the crowner's gambit. Following the first orderly array of the pieces upon the board it discloses at once certain characteristic resources of the antagonist's style of play, and rids the field of certain pawns with a neat economy of dramatic devices. By its publicity an inquest puts each character in rapport with the rest and with the progress of the investigation. It crystallizes fluid relations. Variations thereafter have a standard to be judged by.

Above all else, however, it reveals, not the real solution of the crime, but the obvious solution. Coroner and coroner's jury are the symbols of the obvious. Their verdict is the obvious verdict. What has made the crime worth recounting, however, and the mystery worth pursuit, is just the fact that the real solution is not the obvious one. And the inquest marks the divergence between the superficial and the recondite. The pompous, capable, bustling coroner, and his stolid jurors from the shop and the street emphasize the insufficiency of the workaday mind and the piquancy of the problem.

Comparable to one value of the inquest is the value of the frequent summary. The detective will have what is known on the stage as a feeder — someone to reflect aloud to when the accumulation of data threatens to grow confûsed. Happy are those moments in the company of your detective and his piccolo in some snug den beyond the harking of walls and little pitchers — relaxed moments of perfect leisure, when time and events have brought a lull, and you sit down with a pipe and glass and easy chair to summarize and digest the situation to date. Then you ravel out knotty tangles, compare impressions, check up interpretations, discard the insignificant, gossip significantly and with clear conscience about the people good and bad of the day's work, delve into motives, and speculate about human nature. You go from such a siesta with the ground solidified under your feet, to meet new complications and new data in the maelstrom of the plot itself, awaiting with eagerness the moment when new light and a new stage in the progress of events give occasion for a new hour of confidences and a new analysis.

It may be added by way of divagation that crimes are committed not only by middle-aged gentlemen of otherwise immaculate and lovable lives, but by the recorders of their deeds as well. There are writers of the genre who commit atrocities as heinous as those they chronicle. I have mentioned the superhuman detective, and the dull mechanic operative of detective apparatus. One may also pray to be spared the introduction of the Hindoo. In the Hindoo mind — such is the convention — anything may happen. The Hindoo criminal is supernatural in his psychology. None of your knowledge of human nature serves you with him. Your calculations are beside the point, and the pleasure of your intellection is dashed by the sense that your wisdom is useless.

Little less offensive than the Hindoo is the affront of those tales in which the threads are tangled in a hopeless knot, only for the detective to come in at last and show his cleverness by finding clues that have been concealed prepense from the reader — concealed not after the sardonic manner of life, which conceals by revealing too frankly, but after the pert manner of the trickster, who withholds them altogether. These are the illegitimate shifts of the charlatan.

Another perversion, not illegitimate, but none the less a perversion to the sense of the judicious, is the explanation that harks back for solution into the remoter past beyond the province of the immediate complication. Some elements of the past will enter into every crime. But there is a point, delicately to be perceived, beyond which this method spoils the typical interest of the detective yarn, and makes it a novel of foregone events rather than a solution of current entanglements. In such tales, the confusion of times and scenes not only wrenches the interest from the dramatic present, but turns its solution out of another situation altogether. It makes the detective story but the vehicle for the telling of another tale.

I have a pleasantly irresponsible belief that the detective story has its classics. Since our doctoral theses have not yet exhausted the store of what the Middle Ages gladly let die, and so have not pricklied o'er the genre with the roughcast of scholarship, the point is still vague. But there remains the impression that Gaborieau did the thing early, and suffers — with Shakespeare in another realm — the taunt of triteness in many of his pages. M. Lecoq is no mean ancestor to Rouletabille, to Sherlock Holmes, and to Mr. Gryce. Or was Poe before him? At all events, whether of the one or the other, the French genius is at the heart of the matter, and the *Mystery of the Yellow Room* tops the French tradition, refusing to yield to that grateful forgetfulness that lends to so many of the genre the susceptibility to reperusal. *The Big Bow Mystery,* the *Leavenworth Case,* the *Stillwater Tragedy,* and the *Memoirs* and *Adventures of Sherlock Holmes* have got bruited beyond the inner circle; they and their authors belong to the world at large and need no mention. The *Mystery of a Hansom Cab* has half escaped into the same region. The ones that yield the best reminiscent moments, however, are the ones that have come casually and without noise, third or fourth from the pile on the table — Austin Freeman's *Vanishing Man,* and his *Silent Witness,* Froest's *Maelstrom,* Walk's *Silver Blade.* Others slip from their authors and live in a detached immortality — a *Hampstead Mystery* and a *Man in the Car.* And there is one, striking and memorable, with the number of a cab in the title. The author and the story have escaped me, but it was an extraordinary affair altogether, bound in canary boards, I recall, and had good print. . . .

XIII

MIRRORS

XIII

MIRRORS

EVERYONE will know the place. It is in one of the side streets just off the Avenue and is devoted to the sale of everything in print — and out — from Caxton to Knopf, from heavy Tudor folios, foxed and wormy, to the lightest verse of the week immaculately bound for oblivion. Here are to be found all the *belles lettres,* all the *anas,* all the sleuth, and radio, and movie, and efficiency magazines, all scholarship and all journalism, all the *succes d'estimes, de scandals, de bêtises* — everything printable, in fact, and unprintable.

And here in the course of the day or the month comes everybody, or if not everybody then everybody's peer, representatives of every degree of cultivation, of taste, of intelligence, that makes up the pageantry of the period. So that for my own part, when I find myself browsing along the counters, lingering before the shelves, or craning among the stacks, I am filled with a quiet triumph. For here, so it seems to me, is not merely the flower of our civilization, but the peculiar aroma of that flower.

If everyone knows the place, not everyone, I dare say, will remember that just to the left of the stacks that shelve philosophy and spiritism is a little alcove, or rather cell — for it has a door and the door is usually shut. There is a glass panel in the door framed in rococo gilt, but it is too opaque to see more than a reflection in, and the eye is not tempted beyond. What lies beyond for those who know of it is a brown dusty cubicle smelling like a tannery, lighted — I had almost said blighted — by a grimy skylight, and lined from floor to ceiling with XVIII Century volumes in crumbling calf. There is an ancient table in the gloom beneath the skylight, with long benches on either side of it — a monastic touch, inviting to meditation rather than to reading, so dim is the light and so utter the isolation. I have rarely come upon anyone there, though I have gone there often to pore over some book from the shop — a neglect to be wondered at, for the place has a kind of spell at its command, or an atmosphere at least, of intensely social solitude, in restful harmony with the restless bustle of the shop itself.

On the special occasion which brings me to the mention of it I had come into this cell or cubicle after an hour's cropping among the new books. There was a drizzle on the streets, and the shop was crowded with even more than its usual custom — brisk, keen-jawed scholars seeking the last epoch-making book of the month, salesmen buying thick volumes of psychology, old-fashioned readers wandering restlessly from shelf to shelf, children eagerly thumbing the latest album of Mutt and Jeff, club women wavering between Browning and *Babbitt,* students dripping in for the last *American* or

Digest, fashionably clad ladies groping for the newer mysteries of Conan Doyle, shop-girls and school-teachers at an impasse before mammoth piles of Hutchinson, Wright, Grey, Curwood — the whole democracy come to meet literature at last, and literature come to meet the whole democracy. The thrill of the spectacle was therefore unusually strong for me. And having my hand at the moment on a new reprint of Godwin, the fancy struck me to carry him into the cubicle and enjoy my enthusiasm reflectively over his pages.

Whether it was the duskiness of the light or the fact that I had rarely met anyone there, at all events when I pushed the door to I felt myself pleasantly alone, and pulling out one of the benches I sat down in my accustomed place and posture, book flat on the table to catch what light there was, elbows flanking it, and head buttressed on hands.

I don't think that I read much. Reminiscences of Godwin came between me and the page. . . . Poor old Godwin — not a very pleasant fellow, perhaps. Who is, who is likely to borrow a guinea of you when you drop in of an evening? And who is, who translates ideas into conduct before they have mellowed into tradition and custom? Still he has his reward of fame, and perhaps his one chance at it lay in his walking the scene a century before his time. He would be inconspicuous enough now. None the less I couldn't help indulging a pleasant melancholy of regret that he could not be present to witness the fufillment of his dreams.

It was, I think, at this stage of my reflections that I was quietly accosted from across the table.

"I wonder now, what would he be thinking."

My own first thought, I confess, was that here was an apparition, and the features of Godwin himself crossed my mind. But the reality soon brought me to my senses. If I cannot give a very minute account of the man who sat there facing me, it is because of the initial gloom of the room, and because what dim light there was came from above, so that his hat, which was broad, came near to leaving him in total darkness. I made out a spare face, with long nose, and a mouth that turned the corners and lost itself in grim creases on the cheeks.

I missed the chance later on to see the mode of his departure. If it was an apparition it was an irascible one and in the end provoked me so that I was the first to withdraw. Meantime the conversation we had was formless and fragmentary, and like most conversations, without conclusion.

"You startled me," I said affably. "I thought I was alone, body and mind. But you came upon both just where they were. I, too, was wondering that."

I pushed the book an inch or two forward and nodded toward it.

"Well?" he asked.

"I was thinking how his hopes had been fulfilled —a real democracy at last, symbolized in this," and I waved my hand toward the door and the shop without.

"Mirrors?" he murmured, following my gesture.

"Books!" I returned a little sharply. "Books for everyone and everyone able to read them. And I wish poor Godwin were here just to triumph a little. Not a man or woman in the land at last but can read by his tenth year. It would have vindicated him — a real triumph!"

"Aye," he assented, and the creases of his cheeks deepened. "Aye, a real triumph, now everyone can do — what any child can do."

"Sir," I retorted, piqued again by his manner, "there is a way of putting anything in terms that belittle it. I ignore the mere feat of reading. I think of the ages when reading was the privilege of the few and jealously guarded, and for whom books were the open sesame to all the intellectual booty of the world — booty, I say, for the millions were robbed of it, not having the magic formula. And now I think of the millions for whom reading has become as easy as speaking — and of the press that has kept pace with the hunger of these readers."

"And the gain?"

"The gain!" I cried.

"Aye, the gain?"

"Why, sir," I said, "the press has responded, increase by increase, with the spread of the ability to read, till at last there is reading for everybody. From top to bottom everyone reads, and from top to bottom there is reading matter to meet every demand. Every interval in the gamut of humanity is reflected in print, and every human being not only reads but is met, sir, just where he lives."

" And the gain? "

I am, I hope, a tolerant man; but a gratuitous skepticism is a thing that no one need feel called upon to endure at the expense of his own faith.

" I am sorry," I said; " I have already, I see, said too much, and I have been met in a way that I had not anticipated. By your leave then — " and I turned pointedly to my book.

I was irritated. He had hardly spoken, indeed, but he had dropped his carping acidity on a tenderly cherished spot and it rankled. His skepticism left out of account the generous enthusiasm of a century which had never faltered in its resolve to open to everyone the wealth of its learning, and a century which had kept pace with this new appetite till at last to publish was all but as common as to read. I glanced at him again a little defiantly.

" I am a stranger," he said at once. " I have listened to you with profound interest, and I put my question in good faith."

I saw my error and bowed. If he were a stranger, with a yet stranger ignorance of the modern spectacle, here was a chance to savor afresh, through a virgin mind, those stirring accomplishments that at best custom tends to stale.

" I have been hasty," I returned, " and I beg your pardon. Still I find it hard to imagine anyone questioning the gain of our universal literacy."

" Literacy — universal literacy! " he ejaculated. He savored the phrase for a moment. Then flashing a glance at me from under his shadowy hat he asked, "You have no illiterates, then?"

"None," I answered; and though I may have exaggerated a little my negative was only negligibly short of the truth.

A quick breath issued from his lips, a gasp of amazement and admiration as I could not but take it. For a long time he sat staring before him. Then his high shoulders lifted for a perceptible moment.

"No illiterates," he murmured at last. "No illiterates! To live in a world," — his voice was musing, almost lyrical, yet with something else in it, something dry, something gritty — "to live in a world where every mind is gentled by the Muse, where servants draw solace from Epictetus, and labor soars on the wings of Homer; where the farmer beguiles the endless furrow with the majesty of Milton, and men of affairs, tired with the bustle of 'change, dignify their leisure with the reflections of Plato or recreate with Shakespeare on the boards; where shopkeepers bandy Horace with their patrons and butcher boys con sonnets on the streets — where a common knowledge of what the human mind has essayed, its triumphs and its futilities, makes communication rich, and where a common mastery of the subtleties of thought and speech make understanding sure; where a common acquaintance with the past follies of mankind prevents folly with laughter, and where a common — "

"Sir," I interrupted, for I could suffer this rhapsody no longer; there was more than a lyric exaggeration in his tone. "Sir," I interrupted, "you have misunderstood me. In saying 'universal literacy' I —"

"Literacy," he murmured, "literacy — a wide and intimate —"

"Literacy, sir," I cried, "as we mean it to-day! Literacy — the alphabet — A-B-C — the ability to construe them into words and words into sentences on the printed page."

We stared at each other across the table. Then he bent his head until his hat brim hid his face, and I heard him mutter but I did not catch his words.

I bent my own head over my book; I would play mouse to his cat no longer. But my tongue was tingling with retorts I might have made, and I could not read. When at last I looked up I half feared he would be gone, so incredible had he been from the first. But he was still there, sitting on the other bench and altogether substantial, as I at once perceived in the set creases that had deepened on his cheeks.

"Heaven knows what you are, sir," I said at last, "but I fear you know little of our society or the spirit of our times."

"Ah, ah," he murmured, "and if you would but enlighten me —"

"If I can," I interrupted, with I fear a touch of irony.

He settled forward, elbows on table and eyes questioningly on mine.

" We begin," I explained, and the words came fluently; I was on my own ground again — " we begin with a sense of the equal importance of everybody based on their common humanity, — "

" Instead," he interrupted falteringly, " of taking their common humanity for granted and starting from there."

" Precisely," I assented.

" Just grateful not to be beasts."

His voice was hardly more than a murmur and I ignored words apparently not meant for me.

" You will catch the spirit of it best in the large," I went on. " Starting from there we translate all opinion into force — that is, government — by consulting everyone's opinion and enforcing the greatest bulk of it, thus bringing the dominant power of numbers behind every decision and so perpetuating the system automatically."

" Neat, neat," he assented.

" Spiritually we do the same," I continued. " We translate everyone's opinion and taste into the total of our culture " — I waved my hand toward the shop without — " by unlimited publication and universal literacy, leaving every opinion and every taste its natural weight in affecting every other."

A look of baffled helplessness came into his face.

" Better and worse alike? "

" What else? " I echoed in quiet triumph. " For the quality of opinion or taste is itself an opinion. And there you are forever."

" You give up, then, the one human problem."

"Better and worse — who shall decide?" I continued. "And that" — waving my hand again toward the shop — "that is why I say that here is the very perfume of the flower of our civilization. Here is the expression of the human mind in all its infinite variety exposed in the ingenious outward guise of print — every conceivable subject, every conceivable opinion of every subject, every conceivable opinion of every opinion, every degree of intelligence and character, every variety of taste, every play of fancy, of imagination, of feeling. And here is everyone at last able to read — the perfect coincidence consummated. Every motion of the spirit of man reflected in print, and every man at last able to find there, at his own level, his own spiritual image."

I peered triumphantly through the gloom at the dim figure of my companion.

"And the gain?" he faltered.

A mocking retort came to my lips, but I thought better of it. There was no more to say. I rose therefore and bowed, and picking up the volume of Godwin from the table walked out of the gloomy cubicle into the bustle of the shop. The aisles were full of lingering, damp pedestrians. I pushed my way through them to the shelf and returned the volume to its place between Mill's famous essay and Hutchinson's latest triumph.